Realizing e-Business with Components

The Addison-Wesley Object Technology Series

Grady Booch, Ivar Jacobson, and James Rumbaugh, Series Editors
For more information check out the series web site [http://www.awl.com/cseng/otseries/]

Component Software Series

Clemens Szyperski, Series Editor
For more information check out the series web site [http://www.awl.com/cseng/cbdseries/].

Realizing e-Business with Components

PAUL ALLEN

 Addison-Wesley

An imprint of **Pearson Education**

Harlow, England · London · New York · Reading, Massachusetts · San Francisco
Toronto · Don Mills, Ontario · Sydney · Tokyo · Singapore · Hong Kong · Seoul
Taipei · Cape Town · Madrid · Mexico City · Amsterdam · Munich · Paris · Milan

PEARSON EDUCATION LIMITED

Head Office:
Edinburgh Gate
Harlow CM20 2JE
Tel: +44 (0)1279 623623
Fax: +44 (0)1279 431059

London Office:
128 Long Acre
London WC2E 9AN
Tel: +44 (0)20 7447 2000
Fax: +44 (0)20 7240 5771

Website: *www.aw.com/cseng*

First published in Great Britain in 2001

© Pearson Education Limited 2001

The right of Paul Allen to be identified as Author of this Work has been asserted by him in accordance with the Copright, Designs and Patents Act 1988.

ISBN 0 201 67520 X

British Library Cataloguing in Publication Data
A CIP catalogue record for this book can be obtained from the British Library

Library of Congress Cataloging in Publication Data
Applied for.

10 9 8 7 6 5 4 3 2 1

Designed by Claire Brodmann Book Designs, Burton-on-Trent
Typeset by Pantek Arts Ltd, Maidstone, Kent.
Printed and bound in the United States of America.

The Publishers' policy is to use paper manufactured from sustainable forests.

Acclaim for this book

'This is the first book that clearly and in detail describes how to do component-based development and design driven by business models. It does this with practical real-world e-business examples and describes not only the technology and the integration with the business requirements, but also a pragmatic process how to actually succeed. A book by one of the world's leading experts on components.'

Magnus Penker, CEO, and Hans-Erik Eriksson, CTO
Open Training

'Components and component-based solutions are driving the next generation of e-business solutions, yet very few people are able to design and build them effectively. This need is addressed by Paul Allen's book. It provides a wealth of material, guidelines, and examples for anyone wanting to build successful e-business solutions. It is an essential guide for the next generation of e-business solutions.'

Alan Brown, Technology Evangelist
Catapulse

'Paul Allen has written a valuable book that provides an excellent explanation, with worked examples, of a complex and important subject area. I strongly recommend the book to anyone wishing to keep up to date with using components for business advantage.'

Paul Turner F.B.C.S., Business Development Director
Parity Training

'Rarely does a product deliver more than is advertised for it, but this book is that rare product. Not only does *Realising e-Business with Components* provide important insights into its two advertised topics, but it also provides a valuable how-to guide for modeling and developing applications in *any* business. The book is packed with examples showing that the author has been there, done it and knows exactly how to explain the sophisticated concepts and techniques at the confluence of modern business and modern software technology. Well done, Paul!'

Meilir Page-Jones, Senior Methodologist
Wayland Systems Inc.

'For many practitioners who pioneered the concepts of component-based development, Paul Allen's *Perspective* was their guide. For them and new-comers, this new book provides up-to-date and practical guidance to the complexities of delivering e-Business systems using software components.'

David Sprott, CEO and Principal Analyst
The CBDI Forum

'The e-business arena is a huge minefield waiting to blast out the unpre-pared. Component-based development has never been more appropriate for solving the complex business and technology issues facing the e-business developer. This book is a timely reminder of the issues facing companies who dare to step forward. The author has created a pragmatic field guide for practitioners and managers alike.'

Alastair Gill, Process Improvement Specialist
EDS, UK Central Solution Centre

About the author

Paul Allen is Principal Component Strategist at Computer Associates, and is widely recognized as a thought leader in component-based development (CBD). He specializes in the areas of business-IT alignment, software process, component modeling and architecture, and e-business transition management. Paul's detailed knowledge is complemented by a uniquely practical understanding of the problems companies face as they begin to develop enterprise e-business systems. His pragmatism stems from 25 years' experience in the development of large-scale business systems. Among his many roles, Paul has worked as project manager on many large commercial systems; senior methods adviser to a major telecommunications company; and consultant manager with Yourdon, Inc. He was VP of Methods at Select Software Tools where he was a key player in shaping and implementing their CBD vision in the shape of the Perspective method, before joining Sterling Software (now part of Computer Associates) in April 1999 to lead their CBD practice.

Paul writes frequently on CBD and e-business and is a popular speaker at industry conferences worldwide. The co-authored book *Component Based Development for Enterprise Systems*, was one of the first and most practical descriptions of what was involved in building component-based applications. Additionally, Paul works regularly with industry bodies to help review software practices, ensure standardization and develop practical technology migration strategies. For example, Paul worked as chair of the DSDM task group that produced a white paper on DSDM and Component-Based Development in early 2000.

To Steven, Thomas and Charlotte

Contents

8 CBD funding strategies 144

9 e-Business team organization 161

Appendices

Foreword

The world of business is being profoundly transformed by the internet and the world wide web. I confidently predict that business historians will look back on this decade, the first decade of the twenty-first century, and rank it with a few other decades of extraordinary business change. It will be compared with the decades in which steam power was introduced into English factories in the late eighteenth century, or to the decades towards the end of the nineteenth century when railways completely changed the way materials and products were moved from one place to another.

The eagerness with which customers have embraced the web and have begun to buy products over the internet completely alters the economics involved in selling and distributing goods and services. The web provides the foundation on which the first worldwide retail and service companies are beginning to evolve. In a similar way, the use of the internet to integrate both internal legacy applications and the applications of multiple companies promises to introduce a new era of productivity that will reduce the cost of goods and services, and promote a worldwide surge in economic growth.

Others have already described the rise of the e-business economy and painted the same kind of glowing picture that I briefly sketched in the paragraphs above. This kind of overview is necessary to start people thinking of the possibilities. Those who are charged with actual creation of business strategies or the development of the software that will allow companies to realize the potential of this new approach, however, need a more detailed introduction. Planners need to know what kinds of business processes e-business applications can effectively support. Software developers need to consider how the e-business software systems will actually be designed and built.

It has recently become popular to discriminate between first generation web applications, and second generation e-business applications. First generation applications are sometimes called 'brochureware'. They are essentially websites that customers can visit. They may be supported with a database that makes it easy to update the information on the website and they may provide forms that customers can fill out to order products, but they do not do much more. Web applications are more or less independent software applications that are interposed between customers and the company. They are an important start, but they do not represent a serious effort to transform the manner in which a company's business processes function. They do not link the major, legacy accounting, manufacturing and inventory applications that the company uses internally in ways that will provide customers with a new type of buying experience. Nor do they link business partners into internet-based supply chains that can support a new order of business efficiency.

Second generation e-business applications require profound changes in the way companies are organized. They depend on major changes in core company business processes and they require a whole new approach to software development. Second generation e-business applications integrate legacy enterprise applications and make their resources available to customers and managers throughout the world. This type of integration requires the use of software components. The software components not only facilitate the necessary enterprise integration, they also guarantee that a company's resources can be made available to web browsers throughout the world. In effect, corporate IT departments are among the first company processes that will need to be re-engineered as large companies begin to create second generation e-business applications.

Dozens of books have described the value and inevitability of internet and web-based development. Many others have provided information about how to build websites or focussed on the other developmental problems facing first generation web application developers.

Realizing e-Business with Components is one of the first books to address the problems companies face as they begin to move on to second generation e-business development. It is the most complete, technically sophisticated introduction to the problems of second generation e-business development that I have read. It provides the kind of overview that managers need, and then proceeds to provide the kind of details that architects, designers and developers need. The book introduces a change model that moves systematically from creating the new e-business process, to architecting the application. It provides advice on designing component applications, on whether to buy or build components, on integrating component-based applications with legacy applications, and it includes a detailed discussion of the economics of component-based development. In other words, it provides a complete methodology for the creation of component-based e-business applications. And it illustrates each step in the process with examples and case studies documented with appropriate UML diagrams.

It does not surprise me that Paul Allen has written this important book. Allen has played a leading role in the development of many of the technologies described in this book. His 1998 book on component-based development, which he co-authored with Stuart Frost, was one of the first and most practical descriptions of what was involved in building component-based applications. Since then, Allen has worked with a number of companies that have undertaken serious enterprise application integration projects and with companies that have created large-scale e-business systems. His new book synthesizes his detailed knowledge of the best component development practices with a uniquely practical understanding of the problems companies face as they begin to develop enterprise e-business systems.

This is the next book to read, after you have read the introductory books on e-business and on website design. This book will provide everyone in your organization, from senior managers and business analysts to software developers, with a practical, step-by-step understanding of how one actually goes about designing and developing enterprise e-business systems.

Paul Harmon
Editor, *Component Development Strategies*
Senior Consultant, Cutter Consortium Faculty
San Francisco, 2000

Preface

In April 1999 I joined Sterling Software (now part of Computer Associates) from Select Software Tools. I was very excited because Sterling Software were doing great work with component-based development. Shortly after joining, however, I noticed I had a health problem, but was told it was nothing to worry about. During this period I settled into my new job, learning from my colleagues and enjoying working on different assignments. A few months later, after several misdiagnoses, I was diagnosed with testicular cancer. Before the end of the year, I had undergone a punishing course of chemotherapy. Right now I'm well again, but taking nothing for granted!

While the chemotherapy was unpleasant, it gave me plenty of time to think – if only to take my mind of its effects! I thought about the work I had done at Select, about the discussions I'd had with my new colleagues at Sterling Software, and the work we were doing with clients in applying component technology to the problems and opportunities of e-business. IT departments coping with the shift to e-business seemed like an aircraft that had to be re-engineered in flight. This book is the result of my reflections.

What this book is about

Unfortunately, there is a great deal of hype and over-expectation surrounding e-business. Many organizations are jumping on the e-business bandwagon without understanding what they are getting into. Lack of planning and analysis, resulting in inflexible solutions that are unable to integrate with existing systems, are all too common. At the same time, e-business calls for a closer relationship between those involved in business development and those required to support these initiatives within the company's information technology infrastructure.

This book is designed to provide practical advice for planning, analysis and design of e-business systems using component-based development (CBD). Just as e-business is more than a series of web pages, so CBD is not just an approach to problem solving using software building blocks. It includes architectures, processes, modeling techniques, economic models and organizational guidelines, all of which are well placed to ease migration of large organizations to e-business.

The book is long on practice and short on theory. Theory is included where relevant to practical problems. The core of the book is an extensive example that tracks the experiences of a typical company, with a traditional set of business processes and supporting software systems, through various stages along the road to e-business.

Who should read this book

This book is primarily intended for IT planners, architects, analysts and designers responsible for e-business solutions in large organizations. Equally it is aimed at business strategists, business process engineers and business architects. More significantly, this book is aimed at the new breeds of individual that are emerging, as the dividing lines between business and software grow increasingly blurred.

More broadly the book is intended for anyone interested in modeling business components. In particular, it is hoped that the increasing number of business component and framework vendors will benefit from the increased understanding that clear and precise component models provide of their products to their customers.

How to read this book

Naturally I would prefer it if you read the book cover to cover. However, with the exception of Chapter 6, which should be read after reading Chapter 5, each chapter of this book can be read individually and readers with specific interests can go straight to the subject of their choice. For those who are not familiar with component-based modeling techniques, it is important to refer to Appendix 2 for guidance. There are four parts to the book as follows.

First we set the scene and explain underlying principles

Chapter 1 introduces the need for a component-based approach to e-business systems, explains the basic principles of the approach and sets the emphasis on planning, analysis and business integration.

Chapter 2 looks at how to align e-business software development within the context of the organization's business goals and objectives.

Chapter 3 shows how to integrate business needs into a clearly defined component architecture.

Chapter 4 describes a truly component-based process framework and guidelines for dealing with these issues and to assist with planning and control of CBD for e-business.

Next we come to the core of the book: A continuous practical case study

Chapter 5 provides a practical case study of how to apply a component-based approach to e-business in an organization migrating to e-business, but wanting to protect and utilize its investments in existing systems.

Chapter 6 continues the case study and considers how to evolve the early solutions extending the scope to full business process integration and on to business transformation.

Third, we describe three key supporting strategies: Provisioning, funding and team organization

Chapter 7 looks at how components are provisioned and considers a range of different options including framework extension, wrapping, adapting, outsourcing, purchasing and bespoke design.

Chapter 8 describes tactical measures for funding component-based projects and provides metrics and costing criteria before considering how to identify benefits in the context of e-business.

Chapter 9 centres on team roles, providing guidance for projects at various stages along the road to e-business using components and considers how to use the roles to structure teams based on different organizational needs.

Finally, the appendices provide essential supporting information

Appendix 1 provides short descriptions of component and internet standards and typical accompanying physical architectures.

Appendix 2 provides a catalogue of component modeling techniques. The purpose is not to describe a complete definitive methodology, but to establish 'just enough' semantics and notation with hints and tips to guide the reader.

Acknowledgements

I have been fortunate to be working with a superb group of people at Sterling Software UK. First and foremost, I must thank the management team for their unwavering support during a most difficult time healthwise: Sue Dixon, an exceptional lady, for her great kindness and compassion, Dan French for providing executive support and an environment of wonderful team spirit and Lori Wormald, Steve Olding and Danny Glover for their encouragement and support.

The material in this book draws on previous work of others who have pioneered CBD in Sterling Software. Credit is due to Alan Brown, John Cheesman, John Daniels and John Dodd and for supplying much of the intellectual foundation.

Others in Sterling Software who deserve special mention are as follows: Danny Saro for providing comments on early draft material, Suzanne Martin and Steve Turner for helping out with the case study examples; and Desiree Brennan for her excellent marketing assistance.

Special credit is due to Alan Brown and Sebastian Nokes (NetB2B2), both of whom provided very significant feedback that caused some major revisions to earlier material.

I thank my team of reviewers for providing useful insights and help: Alistair Gill, Simon Johnson, Meilir Page-Jones, David Sprott and Paul Turner.

Thanks are also due to my editor Clemens Syperski for his insightful comments and to Alison Birtwell and Katherin Ekstrom of Addison-Wesley for their editorial and production management, and Candace Nichols for her copy-editing.

My most heart-felt thanks must go to Professor Horwich's team at the Royal Marsden Hospital, especially Dr Huddart, my consultant. Without them this book would not have been written.

Last but not least I thank my family for putting up with my distraction for the best part of six months!

Introduction   1

The internet age: An era of change

The brave new world of e-business is commonly associated with highly developed technical skills, ranging from web-wizardry, graphic design ability and Java programming to internet standards. The design talent to configure such systems in very short time periods also receives lots of attention. What is less well appreciated is that e-business systems also require the ability to tackle new kinds of business problems and raise the bar for today's Information Technology (IT) departments, in terms of architecture, planning, analysis and communication skills.

Though the technology grows more powerful, many of the methods, tools and techniques used in software development are no longer appropriate and consequently often not used. Witness the many commercial websites that have become labyrinths of common gateway interface (CGI) scripts, Java applets and ActiveX elements. Maintenance originally scheduled in hours runs into weeks. At a growth rate of 70% per annum (Daum and Scheller, 2000), e-business will dominate IT in a few years time. Software anarchy is not an option. It is vital to discuss effective approaches for the planning, analysis and design of e-business solutions.

1.1.1   The challenge of change

The reach of the internet extends far beyond the now traditional web page. An increasing array of internet-enabled digital devices, from wireless phones that include the ability to download and send e-mail to digital TV sets for accessing websites for e-commerce, are changing the very fabric not just of hardware but of business itself. These devices are being continually developed, introduced to market and revised every few months.

Change, once viewed as a short period of transition between two (much longer) periods of relative stability, is now a continuous process. Unlike the closed systems of the mainframe, client–server and early distributed eras, software is now increasingly never 'complete'. At the same time, the operational and tactical systems of earlier days – the legacy systems – still have a vital part to play and must be efficiently maintained. New legacy systems in technologies such as VB and C++ add to the groundswell.

1.1.2   Technology soup

A large range of technologies and standards position themselves as necessities for any internet-enabled business solution. Important as these technologies obviously are (see Appendix 1 for a discussion), their details are not the issue that this book is concerned with. The key point to note is that technologies will change and that new technologies will evolve into the mix. For example, the hardware platform market is becoming far more dynamic with rapid changes in internet-enabled wireless devices. These are leading to equally rapid changes in the infrastructure software that developers consider when they create new e-business solutions that use these devices. The distributing computing standards that have long been important for enterprise server environments are assuming an increasing significance for these new client environments.

1.1.3   The adaptive enterprise

Technological innovation and change is mirrored by unpredictable and discontinuous changes in the marketplace.

> It is a cliché to say that the Internet changes everything, the challenge now is to guess what, how and how quickly.   *New Economist*, 26 June 1999

Businesses are responding by becoming more adaptive. The only strategy that makes sense is to become adaptive, to sense early and respond quickly to abrupt changes in individual customer needs (Haeckel, 1999). Agility is needed both in rapid adoption of new technologies and in timely response to business change.

1.2   e-Business in brief

Before going further, we need to take a closer look at what is actually meant by e-business, at the different levels of sophistication on the road to e-business and at the software challenges that are posed by this shift.

1.2.1   e-Commerce versus e-business

Although there are no standard agreed definitions for the terms 'e-commerce' and 'e-business' there are common themes that emerge. e-Commerce focuses on enabling the buying and selling process through the use of electronic services, primarily based on the internet but not excluding the use of other technologies. The focus is on the customer. e-Business extends the use of electronic services to embrace all internal and external business relationships in an integrated real-time fashion. The focus covers customers, suppliers, partners, government organizations and employees. e-Business usually includes e-commerce as part of the overall business solution.

Additionally, the term 'e-business' carries strategic connotations that are absent in the more tactical 'e-commerce'. The idea of using the internet to transform relationships with employees, customers, suppliers and partners to create *value* and exploit market opportunities is integral to the term 'e-business'. Whereas 'e-commerce' is normally used to refer to the more tactical use of the internet to exploit marketing and selling opportunities.

It is worth mentioning a couple of other terms at this point. The term 'intranet' covers the use of internet technology within an organization, for example, to allow employees to access corporate information. The term 'extranet' refers to the use of internet technology by a group of organizations who wish to share electronic services or collaborate as partners, for example, to provide a group of companies with an integrated supply chain. Intranets and extranets are closed to 'outsiders'. In contrast, the internet is essentially universal; hence the term 'global village'.

The internet is already commonly used to exploit new business opportunities and to gain competitive advantage by dealing direct with the customer through e-commerce. Ultimately, e-business applies the technology at a strategic level by exploding traditional organizational boundaries to form new e-businesses based around ever more flexible partnerships and supply chains. Internal and external processes alike work in networked fashion to form new e-businesses.

1.2.2   The internet spectrum

The distinction between e-commerce and e-business is in fact something of a simplification. Many organizations had experimented with local web networks ('intranets' of a sort) long before the internet became mainstream. And early internet adopters often used the web for passive information display as a fore-runner of e-commerce. Similarly, the use of electronic data interchange (EDI) based on proprietary standards has been used to support the integration of closed supply chains ('extranets' of a sort) for a good decade. At the other end of the spectrum, companies are using internet-enabled wireless devices such as palmtops and digital TVs to change the customer's experience. Figure 1.1 depicts this spectrum of internet sophistication.

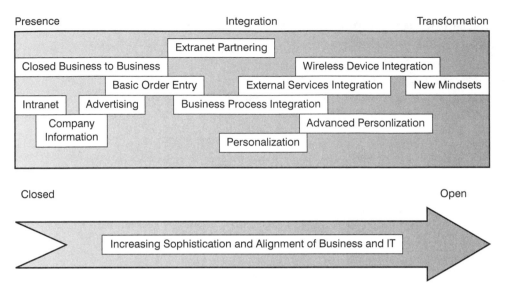

Figure 1.1 The internet spectrum

Moving to the right through the spectrum calls for closer and closer alignment of business and IT, a subject to which we devote Chapter 2. Information
itself ceases to be merely a support tool; it becomes a strategic asset for realizing
business opportunities. Increasingly through the spectrum, products themselves
are becoming virtual, for example, the customer purchases the right to read the
book online rather than being shipped a physical copy. Physical products
increasingly have an information context, such as smart cards. Consistency and
timeliness of information assume a greatly increased significance for such products as we move toward greater degrees of sophistication.

At the same time, traditional businesses are being challenged by nimble new
competitors offering cheaper value propositions, bringing them to market more
quickly and attracting large interest from consumers. In order to compete,
established companies are undergoing complex and painful transitions to new
business practices and their supporting technologies (Melinicoff, 1999).
Organizations need to understand where they sit in this spectrum in order to
plan for fully integrated e-business solutions.

1.2.3   The challenges of e-business

1   Time to market The architects, analysts and developers of today are being
   pressed extremely hard to produce critical e-business solutions before some
   competitor does. At the same time, they must realize that short-term thinking today could well result in solutions that lock the organization's hands in
   a year's time.

2 Business fit The sheer reach of e-business throughout the globe, to previously unreachable locations, increases the scope of a business process from an internal focus to a much larger external customer focus. Most systems today were not designed to cater for these demanding business needs, they were often designed as point solutions for internal departmental needs; e-business requires business processes to be rethought – that means the software too!

3 Quality e-Business raises the bar for high quality software. No longer is software designed for single, known individual users; it is designed for vast numbers of anonymous users. No longer are the consequences of poor design painful; they could well be fatal, as a company's image and standing are destroyed by an ill-conceived and poorly integrated website.

4 Cost savings e-Business cannot afford excessive costs for underlying non-value-added processes. There is a need to release energy for concentration on core competencies. At the same time there is a need to reuse not just code, but the business knowledge that is reflected in the code.

5 Adaptability Software must be readily maintainable in timely response to business changes. Yet more significantly, it must enable business innovation and strategic opportunities, while at the same time allowing existing systems and software packages to be integrated where needed.

6 Scaleability Success in the global marketplace presents its own challenges of vast numbers of users and transaction volumes. The customer experience with low-transaction volume websites tends to be more rewarding and less frustrating than on high-transaction volume sites.[1]

7 Consistency Information is accessible from many viewpoints (or 'portals'; see Chapter 2). Increased visibility magnifies the need to keep information consistent and also present it in a consistent manner to the same customer.

8 Integration Back-end systems must be made to integrate with the new web applications. Pressure increases to realize previous IT investments.

1.3   Components in brief

The very term 'component' must be clearly defined and understood. In this section we explain the required concepts in language that should be accessible to business people. Similarly, we explain what we mean by component-based development (CBD) in the context of this book.

---

1. I recently bought an English Pointer as a result of some useful exchanges through a dog-oriented website. I was able to view pictures of dogs, view breeder locations with available puppies and converse by e-mail with various like-minded individuals. All in all a rewarding experience through a low-volume site, which is in sharp contrast to recent frustrations with ordering supermarket goods and trying to by rail tickets, only being asked to submit a fax days later!

1.3.1 Component anatomy

Let us start with the following definition:

> A component is a unit of composition with contractually specified interfaces and explicit context dependencies only. Context dependencies are specified by stating the required *interfaces* and the acceptable execution platform(s). A component is subject to composition by third parties. For the purposes of independent deployment, a component needs to be a binary unit.   Szyperski, 1998

There are three important facets of components that we need to note for the purposes of our introduction. Chapter 3 provides more detail, but the following descriptions will suffice for now.

Interfaces are well-defined sets of software services that provide access points to clients or users of components; a user may be human but may be another component that is dependent on the interface. Interfaces do not depend on the technology used to implement the component. They are 'technically neutral'.

Components are software units that offer sets of interfaces,[2] and whose functionality can only be accessed through those interfaces. A component can be implemented using different technologies to support the same set of interfaces. Components must have software plug points that fit into sockets provided by a component execution environment (CEE).

A CEE is required to provide run-time technical infrastructure services and to hide low-level technology issues from the business solution developer (see Appendix 1, Section A1.1). The CEE offers its infrastructure services through sockets, software written to well-defined and well-known standards, into which components can plug. Figure 1.2 illustrates these concepts.

Figure 1.2
Basic component concepts

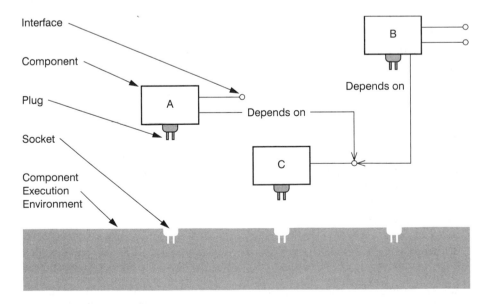

2. Including single interfaces.

We also need to say a little more about services. The services[3] of an interface describe only *what* is offered, regardless of implementation design or executable. How the service is actually performed is hidden from software requesting the service. Services are external facing and should offer a contract with allowable consumers of the services.

1.3.2   Separation of concerns

The anatomy of components allows architects and analysts to concentrate on specifying component interfaces without regard to the environment in which the components that realize these interfaces will run. For example, container technology can be used to host components in run-time environments. Containers also house other components that handle system concerns such as load balancing and transaction handling.

Thus, a component provider can create a business component to handle equipment scheduling without knowing whether it will be used in a back-office operation to assist manufacturing planners or as part of an internet equipment hire system used directly by the public. The consumer organization decides how to deploy the component based upon their own design decisions; for example, the consumer organization's software developers create the components that comprise the container for the scheduling component.

1.3.3   Toward object maturity: How components help

To a large degree, components have grown naturally out of developments in object technology. In fact, my last book (Allen and Frost, 1998) applied object-oriented analysis and design principles more or less directly to CBD. Since then, the concept of interfaces has evolved to central importance.

Components are like objects in that implementation is encapsulated. However, a component is unlike an object in that encapsulation is guaranteed.[4] Yet more significantly, the implementation language can be anything we choose. It can be an object-oriented programming language (OOPL), but it can just as easily be a previous generation structured language like COBOL or PL1.

Providing the interface remains consistent, a component can be replaced with another having different implementation code, without disturbing clients.

---

3. This concept follows the general technological trend, exemplified by Microsoft and others, of separating the services from the hardware on which those services are delivered. This separation will increase as the standards and tools improve. A service is defined as 'A set of functionality that supports activities and/or yields information. A service is accessed through a consistent, published interface. A service represents some computing capability. A description of this capability can be used to represent a contract between the provider of the capability and the potential consumers. Using this description, an arms length deal can be struck that allows the consumer to access the capability' (Microsoft Corporation, 1996).

4. Implementation dependencies are often exposed in OO programming languages. Importantly, this is not true of components.

This feature also allows components to be deployed using different technologies,[5] while retaining the same interface specification. If our approach to abstraction of interfaces is good enough, then a design is achieved such that both business processes and underlying technology can change and adapt with minimal impact.

1.3.4   Business components

Success with user interface and technical components has been common. Business components are distinct from user interface components, such as graphical user interface (GUI) widgets, and technical components, such as database connectivity modules. It is only recently that business components have started to emerge in the commercial marketplace.

> **Business component** A particular type of component that offers services that provide business capability through its interfaces.

What kinds of business component are we likely to find at the centre of e-business solutions? Here are some examples to give a flavour:

- **Customer relationship** A set of services to discover, store, maintain and use customer profiles. This includes all a customer's interactions with the organization, tracking behaviour trends and making these available in real time.
- **Product catalogue** A set of services to allow timely and consistent access of product catalogue information including pricing, special offers, stock levels and lead times.
- **Payment** A set of services providing credit checking and administration of payment transactions; increasingly likely to be provided by an external financial services provider.
- **Order** A set of services to deal with order entry through to delivery, keeping the customer up to date, possibly by e-mail, on order status.
- **Directory** A set of services providing an open, digital version of your internal 'phone' directory that lets customers deal with your organization's people, locations, etc.

1.3.5   Component-based development

One of the problems with CBD is that it is not a precise term and it can take various forms. At one extreme, it is caricatured as a long-winded quality certification process. At the other extreme, CBD is presented by some marketers

---

5. Once delivered as an executable, components are platform specific. However, the component technology masks the actual location from the requesting client, making it appear local to the requesting application.

as snapping together software Lego™ bricks. Realistic approaches lie between these two extremes.

There are three salient characteristics of the term CBD as used in this book. First, the term 'component' used in CBD is used in a general sense; it encompasses much more than software components. Therefore it stretches across the full lifecycle and is not only an implementation activity.

> A software development approach where all aspects and phases of the development lifecycle, including requirements analysis, architecture, design, construction, testing, deployment, the supporting technical infrastructure, and the project management are based on components.   Herzum and Sims, 2000

Second, the term 'development' in CBD is ironic. CBD involves a range of provisioning strategies of which development is one. There is an emphasis on market awareness of available components. Also, the range of CBD across the full life-cycle encompasses a lot more than development, including reuse of requirements knowledge and component models.

Third, it is important to distinguish whether the emphasis is on realizing components or using components. Appropriate architectures, processes and techniques depend on your perspective or mix of perspectives.

Earlier we described three facets of component anatomy: interfaces, components and the CEE. CBD involves three corresponding basic ideas:

1 **Planning, analyzing and designing** at an abstract level in terms of interfaces that offer adaptive business capability to business processes.
2 **Provisioning** in a variety of technologies using implementation techniques that may range from reuse of existing software to outsourcing, and from extending components bought on the open market to creation of new software.
3 **Deploying** to an infrastructure and offering support for managing, executing and upgrading the solution as a set of interacting services.

Much effort and progress has been made in the provisioning and deployment areas. In fact many people who claim to be 'doing CBD' are actually practising component-based implementation not component-based analysis. Much less progress has been made in the planning, analysis and design area. It is to that area that most of this book is addressed.

Although most of the techniques we use involve components, it is important to note that there is nothing religious about this. Of course, it is possible to develop a good software solution, based on sound design techniques and following a useful process, without using components. Conversely, a poor software solution can be developed using components, often because of poor design techniques and process.

1.3.6   A word on modeling

CBD builds on the strengths of established model-based principles like data abstraction and encapsulation, but at the same time introduces further architectural dimensions, process guidance, techniques and specification guidelines that enable the difficulties of previous approaches to be effectively addressed.

Thus far most component reuse has centred on reuse of technical components, especially GUI components. The power of business components, that provides the capability to make real inroads into better productivity, resides in the business knowledge that goes into developing those components. This knowledge is embodied in the component models that are used to architect and specify the business components. This is a major reason why we need to be so interested in effective modeling, a major concern of this book.

1.4   Meeting the challenges of e-business

Perhaps the ultimate promise of CBD is that adaptive e-business systems can be composed from components. Between the promise and the payoff however lie some formidable challenges. Rapidly changing component standards must stabilize. Tools that cater for CBD must replace dated tools geared to development of point solutions. The overall industry issues and trends are eloquently described elsewhere (Brown, 2000). At the same time, software and business folks must acquire new skills and mindsets. Organizational cultures must change toward collaboration and away from departmental self-interest. And, most significantly with regard to the scope of this book, it is going to require new, much more integrated, approaches to business strategy, analysis and software design to address the e-business challenges. Table 1.1 summarizes the relevance of CBD in meeting the challenges we listed in Section 1.2.3.

Here we briefly explain how the approach works in broad terms. Of essence, this has a theoretical feel. Chapters 5 and 6 include a continuous real world example of applying CBD through the different stages of the internet spectrum described earlier.

1.4.1   Top-down: Process and architecture

The shift to e-business fundamentally changes the traditional approach to business strategy that has prevailed for the last three decades, which has rested on the assumption that IT exists to support business (Kalakota and Robinson, 1999). e-Business improvement planning is an incremental and continuous process that recognizes that IT is now integral to the success of the business strategy. This means establishing a clear business case in a way that balances strategy with delivery. Pressure for fast business results has caused many current internet systems to have difficulties with implicit, confused or quickly changing business objectives. Business modeling is therefore applied to help with understanding rapidly changing business contexts. These topics are covered in Chapter 2.

> For those of us working in IT today, the key change is that CEOs will be driving this transition. CEOs don't know about the technology, but they will be demanding results. If IT groups aren't careful, they will agree to undertake development efforts without first putting new architectures, new infrastructures and new component development processes in place. If they do, they will probably doom their companies to obsolescence sometime during the course of the next decade.
>
> Harmon, August 1999

Table 1.1   The relevance of CBD to e-business

Factor	e-Business challenge	Main CBD feature
Time to market	There are rapidly shrinking windows of opportunity.	An assembly process provides **time to market** of e-business solutions.
Business fit	There is a need to reflect, integrate and rethink business processes.	Architectures are used that mirror business needs and establish **business fit** with accuracy. Techniques integrate business and software modeling.
Quality	Consequences of software errors are often catastrophic for e-business systems.	Specification guidelines provide rigour, supported by a provisioning process for engineering of **quality** software.
Cost savings	There is a need to reduce costs, be competitive and exploit niche markets.	Techniques for component reuse result in long-term **cost savings**. Not only that, but business modeling techniques are used to distinguish value-added from commodity processes.
Adaptability	Business can change shape overnight. There is an increase in mergers and acquisitions.	Techniques are employed within an evolutionary process that ensures maximum **adaptability** (components can be reused in 'plug and play' fashion in different business contexts) and effects of changes can be quickly localized.
Scaleability	There are fluctuating and demanding response times across vast numbers of users.	Techniques are applied that address **scaleability**. Components can be deployed using technology appropriate to varying implementation constraints, ranging from hugely demanding peak periods through to quiet times.
Consistency	There is a need for a single organizational view presented to the global village.	An interface-based approach that encourages **consistency** is applied.
Integration	Pressure increases to purchase treadmill software and leverage previous IT investments.	Techniques are applied for **integration** of legacy software, software packages and acquired business components. An evolutionary process helps in legacy migration.

The underlying software needed to realize effective e-business must transcend technology barriers and provide business capabilities that have great flexibility in meeting changing business needs. That in turn requires an architecture, described in Chapter 3, that treats software as integral to business, builds on established design principles and at the same time introduces innovation where it is needed. Techniques are applied that help to identify interfaces and manage dependencies between interfaces.

Precise interface definitions provide a contract between the consumer of the services provided through the interface and suppliers of those services. The quality of outsourcing work, that is so difficult to measure traditionally, becomes much easier to verify against rigorously specified contracts.

Moreover, as we hinted earlier, a software *development* process is no longer appropriate. We no longer have the luxury of a 'clean white slate'. The process is now one of evolution and *integration*.[6] The process must encompass e-business planning, component architecture and legacy integration. It must provide guidance on an increasing diversity of provisioning routes. At the same time, the process must not be bureaucratic. It must include pragmatic timely guidelines, including help with assessing e-business needs against available software. We employ a process framework, described in Chapter 4, that meets all these criteria.

An increased diversity of specialist skills, both technical and business, is needed to realize the process and architecture that are necessary for successful e-business systems. Traditional developers must work hand in glove with a wide range of advertising, marketing, sales, accounting and service specialists. Our approach to CBD therefore integrates organizational guidelines with process and architecture (see Chapter 9).

1.4.2 Bottom-up: Integration

Buying components or software packages, and reusing legacy systems for treadmill processes[7] is one way to minimize the cost of software development. Business modeling is used to help determine which of these software assets serve the treadmill processes. Outsourcing the running of these systems, or indeed whole treadmill processes, promises yet greater cost savings allowing companies to focus on what they are very good at (a key factor in e-business) and subcontract or outsource everything else to others who are very good at their own specialties.

A genuine large-scale software component market has not started to form until recently. Such markets are now becoming viable and reaching critical mass. At the same time, the dividing lines between business components and

---

6. However, it is important to note that we usually integrate to create tightly coupled and centrally managed units, whereas the goal of CBD as understood in this book is loosely coupled and independently managed units. It has been suggested that 'federation' better describes this situation. I am indebted to David Sprott of CBDi Forum for this observation.

7. A treadmill process is a well-established infrastructure process, such as payroll, that adds no direct customer or partner value.

software packages have started to blur. This is partly a result of significant efforts by vendors like SAP, Oracle and Peoplesoft to provide modules with at least some kind of interface and a more open structure.

At the same time, there is growing pressure to reuse internally developed legacy systems and develop plans for migrating them to new technologies. Despite their shortcomings, these systems often provide tried and tested functionality supporting an organization's treadmill processes.

The component architecture provides an integration framework to help identify and design the right interfaces between business processes and the diverse software assets of the organization. Rather than starting each project every time with a 'clean slate', we consider which interfaces (including those open-market components as well as packages and legacy systems) can be reused to provide business capabilities for e-business solutions. Technologies such as enterprise application integration (EAI) tools and code generators are used to deal with as many implementation issues as possible.

1.5 Summary

e-Business demands software that adapts as the business adapts, that provides insulation from technology and business change. Although the latest technologies for distributed systems support and encourage a component view of application integration and deployment, they are actually not the central issues. The significance of CBD is rather that it can provide a model-based approach that is ideally matched to today's eclectic e-business solutions.

Understanding e-business involves considering an 'internet spectrum' of different sophistication levels that range from merely having a web presence to using internet technologies to transform your business processes. CBD is the engine that will drive enterprise-scale e-business solutions and help us navigate our way through the internet spectrum. The remainder of this book provides business-IT alignment guidance, architectures, modeling techniques and enabling strategies for doing just that.

1.6 References

Allen, P., and Frost, S., *Component-Based Development for Enterprise Systems: Applying The SELECT Perspective*, Cambridge University Press-SIGS Publications, 1998.

Brown, A., *Enterprise Scale Application Development in the Internet Age*, Prentice Hall, 2000.

Daum, B., and Scheller, M., *Success With Electronic Business*, Addison-Wesley, 2000.

Haeckel, S. H., *Adaptive Enterprise: Creating and Leading Sense-And-Respond Organizations*, Harvard Business School Press, 1999.

Harmon, P., e-Business Overview, *Component Development Strategies*, Cutter Information Corporation, August, 1999.

Herzum, P., and Sims, O., *Business Component Factory*, Wiley, 2000.

Kalakota, R., and Robinson, M., *e-Business: Roadmap for Success*, Addison-Wesley, 1999.

Melinicoff, R. M, 'The eEconomy: It's later than you think', Anderson Consulting, *Outlook Magazine*, June 1999.

Microsoft Corporation, *Microsoft Solutions Framework: Reference Guide, Version 2.0*, 1996.

Szyperski, C., *Component Software*, Wiley, 1998.

Business-IT alignment 2

2.1   Introduction

It is imperative that the business strategy provides a context for software projects that can evolve as business grows more sophisticated through the range of the internet spectrum (see Section 1.2.2). We will start by outlining an overall approach that involves an e-business process improvement plan that recognizes that the old way of separating business planning and IT development is no longer realistic.

We move on to practical techniques for preparing a business case for applying CBD to e-business. The business case helps gain the investment and trust in IT from the business leaders that is needed for successful e-business. We look at some strategies for creating understanding and commitment to CBD at the business level and consider how to address the organization's current IT capabilities. A major theme is that IT needs to take a very proactive role here in demonstrating the business case for CBD. At the same time, new e-business solutions must be delivered quickly as evidence of productivity.

2.2   e-Business process improvement

In this section we consider the need for e-business process improvement planning and show how this provides an evolving context for software projects. The e-business process improvement plan must identify the main business drivers that are involved in your migration to e-business. In particular, business goals must be determined in order to provide a yardstick against which to measure success. Business process modeling (BPM) provides an important set of techniques that are used in this process.

2.2.1   The concept of e-business process improvement

The need to continually reinvent businesses in the context of a changing technological and sociological world is reflected in sustained interest in business process re-engineering (BPR) originating from the work of Hammer and Champy (1993). Such initiatives flatten organizational structures through the use of empowered teams, remove redundancy and look for new ways to leverage business advantage. Despite some early successes with BPR there were also some major failures. The large-scale changes of BPR were often impossible in the face of internal politics, which often proved a major stumbling block as departmental managers waged turf wars. More modest evolutionary changes were often expedient under the business process improvement (BPI) banner.

The move to e-business is changing this picture. Suddenly almost every employee of a large organization can access internal data. Customers throughout the globe, from previously unreachable locations, can sit at home browsing product catalogues or making purchases. Companies that used to be restricted to a couple of chosen suppliers can use the internet to compare prices of many suppliers in a short time. More than that, companies can partner to shorten the supply chain or to provide hot-links to each other's websites. Such expansion increases the scope of a business process from an internal focus to a much larger external customer focus. Previous BPI efforts have concentrated on streamlining existing corporate procedures, whereas e-business redefines the corporate playing field. To add complexity, the same business process can take different forms for markets that vary with the delivery channel; for example, consider the different customer needs according to whether a travel agency is conducted 'over the counter', using digital TV or via the internet on a PC. In other words, business processes will need to be rethought.

e-Business process improvement is an ongoing commitment that requires guidance in line with business strategy and measures against which the success of resulting software projects can be judged. In other words, we need to consider e-business improvement planning

At the same time most organizations are rightly concerned to minimize risk and maximize reuse of existing systems. Innovative yet practical initiatives are required to migrate the organization forward to e-business. We use the term 'e-business process improvement' to describe these initiatives.

2.2.2   e-Business process improvement planning

The planning cycle should be completed quickly (weeks, not months) and revisited at frequent and regular intervals. Senior executives from both business and IT participate in the effort. There are four types of activity involved in the planning cycle:

1 Envisioning.

2 Reflection.

3 Conception.

4 Organizing.

Typically, the activities operate first in a broad sweep before cycling around again in iterative fashion to zoom in on a particular business area. Once the scope of the business improvement initiative is clear and stable, then software architecture planning and software delivery projects are initiated as illustrated in Figure 2.1. In this way business strategy works incrementally in tandem with software implementation and experience in using the software. This is in sharp contrast to traditional business strategy approaches (Porter, 1985) that tend to take too long and to de-couple business from IT initiatives.

Let us look at the activities of business improvement planning in a little more detail:

● **Envisioning** This activity explores business opportunities and structures these opportunities into a number of e-business improvement options. Some options for ideas generation include the following, though feel free to use your own techniques. One group generates ideas using internet technology to eliminate current business problems. Another group considers how e-business templates (models successfully used by other organizations) can be deployed. Ideas should also be generated using creative thinking techniques. Once the overall change ideas have been generated, the ideas are reviewed and collated into a number of overall change options. A business scope is created for reflection and conception.

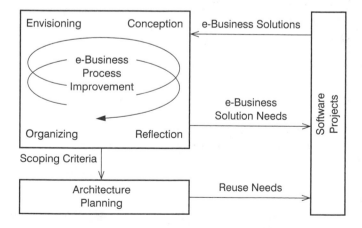

Figure 2.1
e-Business process improvement in context

- **Reflection** This activity[1] analyzes the business scope in terms of existing business processes, organizational structures and information needs. The aim is to broadly understand the existing business processes, identify the major issues and problems. A good set of BPM techniques not only needs to emphasize the order, timing and relationships between business processes and units of work, it must also focus on the organization's structures, people, internal and external technology and customers.

- **Conception** This activity analyzes the business scope mapped out by envisioning in terms of proposed business process, organizational structures and information needs. The aim is to prepare a 'to be' business process model. Again, a variety of business process models can be used including process and organization flow models and business concept models.

- **Organizing** This activity identifies and plans e-business process improvement projects required for transition to the 'to be' model. There are two main parts to this. First, a business change management plan is prepared, describing the roles and responsibilities of the people implementing the new processes. A model of the organization structure is built, showing how the roles[2] in the process team fit together across functions or departments. Second, a technology plan is prepared to provide a scope for the component architecture which will be used to support the proposed e-business systems, and to scope individual software delivery projects.

An important theme throughout is to have a means of quantifying goals and measuring the success of improvement initiatives. The key performance indicators (KPIs) associated with each process are defined within the business process model (see Section 2.2.3). KPIs can be defined at various levels, for the whole enterprise, for specific processes and for specific jobs or roles. Examples are as follows:

- Enterprise – return on assets employed.
- Process – cycle time.
- Job – sales value achieved per period.

The balanced scorecard (Kaplan and Norton, 1996) approach to defining enterprise metrics ensures a balanced strategy, with clearly articulated critical success factors and helps translate strategy into coherent plans. It does this by setting objectives, performance measures and goals for each quadrant shown in Figure 2.2.

The scorecard can be used to record lead indicators (that predict future performance) e.g. rate of innovation, customer retention/loyalty as well as the more

---

1. If starting up a new .com business this does not apply. In other cases, it is often appropriate to build at least an 'as is' organization flow diagram, if only to have an understanding of your starting point for improvement. However, it may sometimes be better to leave this until the 'to be' model has been built in order to avoid prejudicing your thinking about where the business is going with preconceptions based on where it currently is.
2. Team roles are covered in detail in Chapter 9.

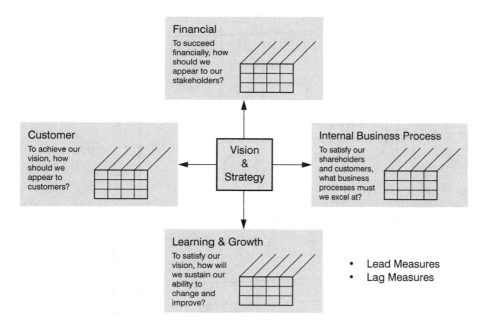

Figure 2.2
The balanced
scorecard quadrants

obvious 'lag' indicators that report past performance. It can also be combined
with other strategic measures such as critical success factor (CSF) analysis
(Henderson *et al.*, 1984) and threats, opportunities, weaknesses and strengths
(TOWS) analysis (Weirich, 1982).

2.2.3   Business process modeling (BPM)

BPM provides business managers with an important thinking tool. It is a means
of graphically exploring their processes and thinking through the possibilities of
new technologies, without incurring the risk of implementation until they are
satisfied that the process 'holds water'. Recall BPM is used in reflection and conception activities of e-business process improvement planning. BPM centres on
identifying and defining three key elements: business concepts, business propositions and business processes. By way of introduction, and to prepare some
ground for our discussion of software architecture in Chapter 3, let us take a
brief look at how business processes are modeled (Rummler and Brache, 1995;
Hunt, 1996). For details of all BPM techniques, the reader is referred to
Appendix 2, Section A2.2.

> A **business process** is a group of related business capabilities that add value to a customer.
> The capabilities are realized by families of tasks, that may collaborate in different event-
> driven groups to fulfil the business process.

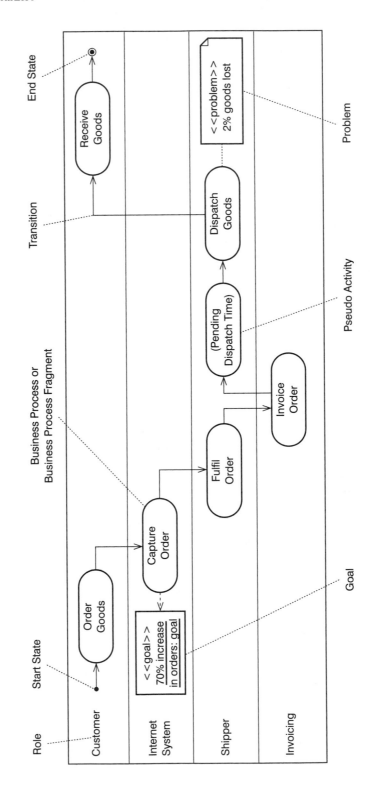

Figure 2.3
Process flow diagram for direct sales process

Business processes are grouped at different levels of abstraction to aid comprehension. A process flow diagram is used to analyze a business process or part of a business process in terms of an event-driven chain of lower level processes as shown in Figure 2.3. Swim-lanes depict roles that are responsible for the processes. Measurable business goals and inhibitors are attached to processes as shown.

There are three types of business process.

A **customer process** provides value-added deliverables to the external customer, for example, Market Vehicle or Service Vehicle.

A **sustaining process** adds value to the external customer, however, it does not exchange information or material directly with the customer, for example Price Vehicle or Administer Warranty.

An **enabling process** has internal customers. It provides the services necessary to support the core processes and manage the business, for example Legal Management or Financial Management.

The different types of processes work in upwardly supportive fashion to interact with the customer through typical customer lifecycles as shown in Figure 2.4.

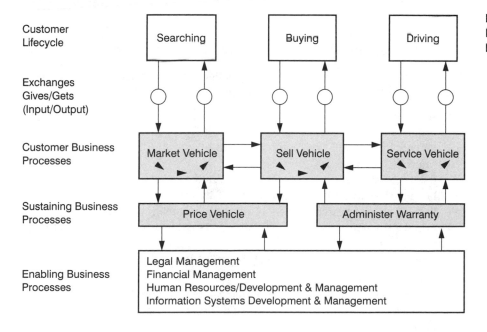

Figure 2.4
Different types of business process

2.3   The business case for CBD

I have visited many organizations where large teams of business process 'experts' have spent many months creating a business process strategy document full of list upon list of business indicators, such as critical success factors, business inhibitors, goals, objectives, directions, threats, opportunities and so on. This is usually accompanied by reams of business process models that sit regally on a shelf doing nothing. This traditional way of separating business planning and IT development is no longer realistic. Let us consider some practical steps for developing a business case for a component-oriented approach.

The business case should be done quickly in weeks rather than months. We will need to identify the business drivers, expected benefits and perceived risks in order to work out the overall approach to CBD that is appropriate. We will also need to address the organization's current IT capabilities. There are three aspects to this: architecture, process and organization. In each case, we will need to look at the strengths and weaknesses and make suggestions for exploiting the strengths and dealing with those weaknesses. In grabbing management attention in today's world of byte-sized information, it is important not to be too purist.

> Your business case must include compelling arguments that support your value proposition. These arguments are grounded on greed, fear or logical reasoning based on the characteristics of the technology … you find yourself in the most unfortunate position, where you cannot convince management based on a greed or fear argument, you will be forced to use logic, a much less powerful means of persuasion.
> Goldberg and Rubin, 1995

2.3.1   Identifying the business drivers

We need to consider the possible business goals and challenges that are going to form the centrepiece of the business case; some examples follow:

- **Business goals**
  - Improve business process efficiency and integration.
  - Remain compatible with approach used by your business partners.
  - Improve customer experience.
  - Use IT for strategic business advantage, new markets, etc.
  - Reduce IT costs and leverage existing IT investments.
  - Reduce time to market: timely IT response to business change.
  - Protect investments in IT against threats of business change (including mergers and takeovers).
  - Protect investments in IT against threats of technology change.
- **Business challenges**
  - Business opportunities are lost or delayed because of IT constraints.
  - Business opportunities incur excessive costs because of IT development.
  - Business is shaped to reflect inadequacies of previous IT solutions.

- Business is unable to exploit e-business because of IT solutions with 'built-in obsolescence'.
- Business thinking is restricted by existing IT mindset.
- Business opportunities are not discussed with IT until it is too late.
- Systems design constrains opportunities to increase business efficiency.
- Costs and benefits of IT systems do not measure up or align with business needs and goals.
- There is ineffective communication between IT and business people and no collaboration or synergy of ideas.
- There is an inability to capitalize on investment in and value embedded within legacy systems.
- IT R&D costs are a 'bleeding edge' and technical innovation an end in itself (not a means to an end).

As we saw in Chapter 1, CBD is not a precise term. It is useful to distinguish three overall approaches[3] to CBD among many variants:

1 'Components in advance' (CAV) is a top–down, architecture-centric approach that aims to significantly improve adaptability of software to match changing business processes.

2 'Components as you go' (CYG) sets out to incrementally deliver business solutions and components in parallel. Each increment must deliver business benefit and at the same time contributes to the evolution of the component architecture.

3 'Components by opportunity' (CBO) involves seeking to assemble solutions by reuse of pre-existing components as the overriding strategy. The approach focuses on providing business solutions using ready-built software components.

The business case should demonstrate how CBD supports the business goals and addresses the business challenges. Correlating the goals and challenges with quality attributes associated with CBD can help

In determining the approach, we will need to weigh up the risk factors against the goals and opportunities. It is important to note that whatever approach is taken, there will be at least some investment in architectures, processes and organizational change. Example risk factors follow:

- Lack of business management support.
- Lack of IT management support.
- Lack of developer support (Not invented here syndrome).
- Lack of effective software methods, metrics and processes.
- Lack of education in CBD principles.
- Cross-departmental political barriers.

---

3. These approaches are described in more detail in Chapter 8.

A certain common sense is needed to work out a strategy. For example, at one extreme, few business goals and challenges might indicate that CBD is not appropriate in any form. Significant business goals and challenges but lack of management support might suggest a CBO approach. On the other hand, significant business goals and challenges and good management support might suggest a CAV approach. CYG is often appropriate as there is a need to produce fast business results, but at the same time to evolve an architecture.

2.3.2   Assessing architecture

Current architectures must be assessed in terms of their strengths and weaknesses. Strengths are important because they represent an investment on which an organization can build. For example, many organizations have a history of migrating to client–server technology and have successfully transitioned to three-tier architectures based upon separation of user interface, business logic and data storage layers. This provides a very good starting point for migrating to

The challenge is not only to introduce an effective CBD architecture, it is to sell the very idea to management who have become disillusioned by the impotence of past efforts

CBD architecture, which shares this basic structure. Other organizations may have experimented with internet projects using client component technologies with bridges to traditional server applications. For example, an insurance broker using a component-based GUI on a workstation with links to a corporate mainframe for fund positions. This kind of approach is sometimes combined with subscriptions to externally provided services, for example, calling a credit checking service over the internet. Such projects help to cut the organization's teeth on new technologies before scaling up to full e-business solutions.

Current weaknesses are important as they help to reveal the challenges that the organization must plan to tackle. Technical architectures are common and there is generally no shortage of diagrams showing software infrastructure and network structure. Business and data architectures are also common, but too often isolated and not used in practice. They are often the result of detailed BPM or data analysis efforts that ultimately result in shelfware.

2.3.3   Assessing process

Current processes, like architectures, must also be assessed in terms of their strengths and weaknesses. Most organizations have at least some experience of rapid application development (RAD). RAD techniques such as Joint Application Development (JAD), prototyping and time-boxing are all useful in CBD, particularly in assembly of business solutions. Other organizations have invested in quality improvement initiatives, which will stand them in good stead if they plan to build components, with their demanding standards of certification. This applies equally to the use third-party interfaces that must be thoroughly assessed before assembly into a solution.

Many organizations use processes geared to development of point solutions in the manner of a linear production line. This does not align well with today's needs for hybrid solutions to support business processes that not only cross divisions and departments, but also transcend organizational boundaries using the internet.

2.3.4   Assessing organization

In the 'old days' authoritarian IT departments would simply tell the users what they could have. Tom DeMarco (1978) once made the following observation: 'Users are not dummies. Some of the methods they work with are far more complicated than structured analysis. Years ago, it was fashionable to look down on users because they had so little knowledge of EDP. Nowadays the user areas we are automating are much more complex and the users are correspondingly more high-powered'.

CBD technologies and techniques are not a magic answer for political and cultural barriers

Although those days are gone, the traditional IT mindset behind them still lingers on in many organizations today.

In the mid-1990s there was a reaction to the entrenched dominance of IT in the form of user-centred design (Winograd, 1996). This approach puts 'technology' second to 'user concerns' and fosters the corporate attitude that IT people only need to come in to build the software after the users have determined their requirements.

Today, it is increasingly suggested that software development within IT departments will end before too long (Clements, 1999). This scenario suggests that the role of the IT department will be to manage the integration of existing solutions, and to provision new solutions from third-party suppliers. Predictions are that the worldwide IT services industry will grow to over $630 million by the year 2003 (Kruchten, 1999).

More worryingly, there is a view of e-business systems as somehow separate from traditional systems. This is exemplified in the existence of the separate e-business systems department that has often grown as an offshoot of the marketing department, who were the first to consider the corporate impact of the internet. The danger here is a lack of integration between the e-business systems and the back-end systems that causes a corresponding lack of business process integration.

Such change calls for a clear organizational change plan. Increased participation of business people, fuelled by a need to align IT much more effectively with business needs, calls for a clear definition of the roles that IT and business people play on a project: the term 'user' is no longer sufficient. We devote Chapter 9 to this subject.

As with architecture and process, current organization structures must be assessed in terms of their strengths and weaknesses. Many organizations are changing toward an organizational model in which value-added software development is carried out by the business units to achieve the benefits of decentralization, but responsibility for software architectures is centralized. At the same time, there is an increase in the outsourcing of treadmill software. This kind of organization actually fits nicely with CBD in that solution assembly can move to the business units, while architecture planning is centrally controlled and commodity components are provisioned externally.

A common organizational weakness is that there is no recognition of software architecture as a discipline that has an important part to play in relation to the business. Too often, where an architecture group exists, it plays the role of custodian of software infrastructure. This problem is usually part of a larger one: IT is seen as a cost, not an asset. Management education is needed to explain the value proposition in clear business terms. To do that it is necessary to find the pain. For example, many organizations suffer an inability to control relationships with partners over outsourcing and packages. CBD provides better control of these relationships via clear specification of interfaces acting as contracts between supplier and consumer. This permits information from various external sources to be interpreted in a consistent manner. Allied to an effective CBD process and architecture this provides help with buy versus reuse versus build decisions, ensuring that software meets the consumer's needs ahead of the suppliers.

2.3.5   Balancing strategy and delivery

How long will it take for the infrastructure necessary for effective CBD to bed down before business can expect a return on its investment? Different organizations have different tolerance windows that can range from a few months to as much as five years in more conservative organizations. With the rise of e-business, this window of tolerance is shrinking fast.

The most appropriate approach is instead one that delivers useful business functionality in incremental fashion, while using the feedback from implementation to evolve an architecture as illustrated in Figure 2.5. Though the graph is an exaggeration it helps to illustrate the point!

Of course the big picture is required in terms of overall goals and directions and software architecture, but it is a mistake to hit too much detail too soon. Think of the e-business improvement plan and component architecture as the bar (macro-level) of a letter 'T' and software delivery as part of the post (the micro-level) of the 'T'. Software delivery is iterative and incremental. Each post will unearth further information that will cause the bar to be revised. So the e-business improvement plan is a living thing and software is part of it!

Ivory tower architecture groups that work in a vacuum and fail to produce tangible business results are anathema to the pressures of internet time: they are embarked on a disaster course

So much for the theory. In Chapters 6 and 7 we will use a practical example that illustrates the approach. As we will see, early increments may actually have nothing to do with true CBD or e-business – they may just be a psychological ploy to 'keep business happy' and 'buy time'.

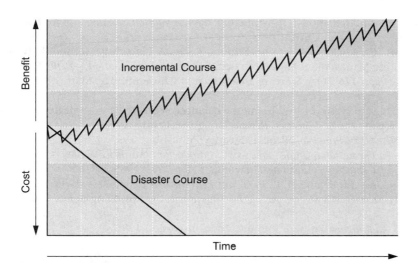

Figure 2.5
Incremental versus disaster courses

In this connection, it is instructive to recall the 80/20 principle that states '80 percent of results flow from just 20 percent of the causes' (Koch, 1997).

Early projects should inspire confidence by hitting the business sweet spots

---

2.4   Summary

Components in themselves do not guarantee successful business solutions. Coupled with an effective e-business process improvement plan, CBD makes it possible to achieve a range of business benefits that have always eluded the software industry. Not only does this require a pragmatic business case, it also requires practical, but imaginative, steps for jump-starting your migration plan.

We need ways of balancing strategic issues with fast results and timely software delivery: IT needs to raise the bar and be more proactive! Successive generations of software technology from 4GLs to objects have fallen well short of the bar in enabling the required shift in mindset. In contrast, component technology presents real opportunities. The foundation of these opportunities is the component architecture. It is to that subject that we now turn our attention.

2.5   References

Clements, P., (ed.) *Constructing Superior Software*, Macmillan Press, 1999.

DeMarco, T., *Structured Analysis and System Specification*, Prentice Hall (Yourdon Press), 1978.

Goldberg, A., and Rubin, K., *Succeeding With Objects: Decision Frameworks for Project Management*, Addison-Wesley, 1995.

Hammer, M., and Champy, J., *Reengineering the Corporation: A Manifesto for Business Revolution*, Allen and Unwin, 1993.

Henderson, C., Rockart, J. F., and Sifonis, J. G., A Planning Methodology for Integrating Management Support Systems, *Centre for Information Systems Research Working Paper 116, Sloan School of Management*, MIT, Cambridge, Matt. 1984.

Hunt, V. D., *Process Mapping*, Wiley, 1996.

Kaplan, R. S., and Norton D. P., 'Using the balanced scorecard as a strategic management system', *Harvard Business Review*, January–Febryary, 1996.

Koch, R., *The 80:20 Principle*, Nicholas Brearley Publishing, 1997.

Kruchten, P., *The Rational Unified Process: An Introduction*, Addison-Wesley, 1999.

Porter, M. E., *Competitive Advantage*, Macmillan Free Press, 1985.

Rummler, G. A., and Brache, A. P., *Improving Performance*, Jossey-Bass, 1995.

Weirich, H., *The TOWS Matrix: A Tool for Situational Analysis*, Long Range Planning, 1982.

Winograd, T., *Bringing Design to Software*, Addison-Wesley, 1996.

Component architecture   3

3.1   Introduction

This chapter presents the main principles of an interface-based approach to e-business solutions. We introduce the concept of component-based architecture and explain its different dimensions. A key element in this is to foster business-IT alignment through business capabilities. We therefore spend some time looking at the anatomy of business processes and how this relates to component architecture.

We consider how the architecture provides overall structure and sets of rules for managing scale and complexity and for providing the flexibility and agility to meet new e-business needs. At the same time, we show how the architecture provides a framework for reuse and integration of existing software assets and external components, helping to provide a platform for smooth low-risk migration.

The approach draws on work at Sterling Software (now Computer Associates) by John Dodd in developing Advisor™ (Dodd *et al.*, 1999) and on work by John Cheesman and John Daniels (Cheesman and Daniels, 2000) in component meta-modeling.

3.2   An interface-based approach

3.2.1   The separation of interface and implementation

Recall that a component offers services through its interfaces. Given knowledge solely of the interfaces, any potential user or client of those interfaces can focus on its part of the overall solution without concern for how those interfaces are

Figure 3.1
An interface in
context

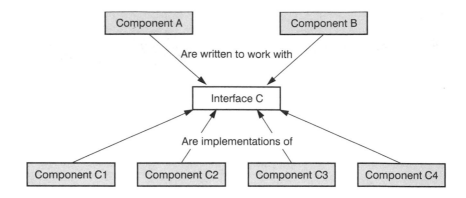

actually rendered. The services are rendered by a developer who provides an implementation for a component that is guaranteed to meet the specification. The implementation may be written in a different programming language or executed on a different technology platform from the language and platform used by the client program, as illustrated in Figure 3.1. One component may be replaced by another, as long as both implement the same interface.

The split between specification and implementation is the key to effective encapsulation

Figure 3.2
Different
implementations of
components

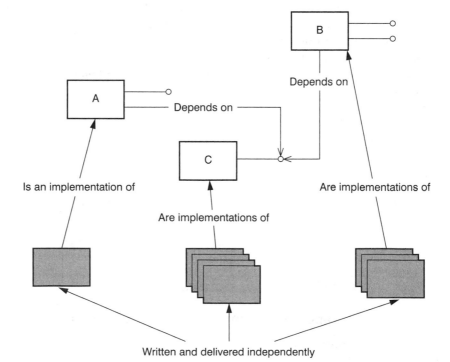

Interfaces are grouped into component specifications that may themselves depend on interfaces offered by other component specifications. In the example shown in Figure 3.2, component specifications A and B are dependent on an interface offered by the component specification C; note that B offers two interfaces.

3.2.2   Interface-based design

Focusing on interfaces as the key design abstraction leads to much more flexible designs. For example, the implementation of the component specification may be developed internally by the user organization. On the other hand, a component specification can serve as a definition of the requirements for some externally acquired implementation. In this case, the user does not implement the component, but offers the component specification as a complete and unambiguous contract (Meyer, 1997) to be met by an external provider of that implementation. In between these extremes are various mix and match approaches. For example, an interface provided by an external component framework containing its own implementation might be extended or specialized to meet the specified requirements.

The interface-based approach involves an evolution in analysis and design techniques. These techniques are not applied in a vacuum, but in the pragmatic context of everyday constraints and in balance with a need to assess and reuse available components. The iterative series of steps can however be usefully summarized as follows:

- Understand the business needs in terms of strategy, organization, process and information.
- Scope and identify the business context of the software behaviour.
- Identify and describe business concepts to be managed by the software, and evolve to help identify candidate interfaces.
- Examine dynamic interplay between software concepts to realize required behaviour. Identify and partition the behaviour to be exhibited by the software, assign responsibilities to and evolve candidate interfaces.
- Understand software dependencies and adjust responsibilities of interfaces. Verify technical feasibility, exploring how to group interfaces into possible components and how to partition the software into deployable units.
- Specify the interfaces in terms of behaviour and information. Specify groups of interfaces to be implemented as components, in the form of component specifications, include constraints. Enroll and publish specifications in catalogues.
- Develop or acquire component implementations.

We will return to this basic set of steps in Chapter 4 as we develop our understanding of the concepts involved.

3.3 Integrating business processes and components

In Chapter 2 we emphasized that business modeling provides business managers with an important thinking tool. It is important that business models are integrated with their software counterparts. One of the great pitfalls of past efforts has often been that because the business models are detached from the software models they soon start to bear little relation to reality. The essence of e-business is that business and software are no longer separate entities. There is a fusion here that calls for effective integration of different models. At the same time it is important to keep things as simple as possible. The means must justify the end.

3.3.1 The service-oriented view

A business component provides interfaces that offer business capability.

> **Business capability** A set of services that work as a coherent family toward a defined business purpose.

The concept of business capability sits at the bridgehead of e-business process improvement planning and CBD. It helps in moving from a functional view of a closed traditional enterprise to a service-oriented view of an open e-business-enabled enterprise. The de-coupling of business process and business capability provides the organizational flexibility that is so important in adapting processes to change and in preserving processes against the threat of technological changes, most dramatically exemplified by the shift to the e-business.

e-Business systems are designed as configurations of defined services, provided through interfaces, to meet the needs of business processes as illustrated in Figure 3.3. In this example, the Make Rental Reservation business process invokes the services Establish Requirement, Take Customer Details, Schedule Vehicle and Secure Reservation. Each service provides business capability to the business process. These services are provided through interfaces as shown. The interfaces are realized by software components. A Reservations e-business system is composed using components that satisfy these specifications. Components can be 'moved around' at execution time and deployed in a way that optimizes the technology in order to deliver the appropriate business capability. Not only that, but new interfaces can be introduced and redundant ones removed as the business changes.

3.3.2 The criticality of architecture

One of the benefits of using the service-driven approach is that business processes are addressed in relation to a unifying component architecture. Getting this architecture right is critical if we are to move from applications that are designed as tightly coupled, inflexible software islands to loosely coupled,

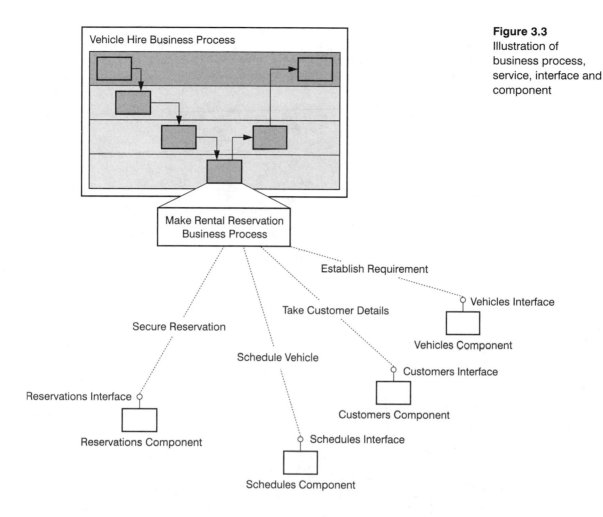

Figure 3.3
Illustration of
business process,
service, interface and
component

flexible families of interfaces that facilitate sharing of business capabilities as depicted in Figure 3.4.

If a business process changes, the component architecture should enable us to demonstrate how to handle the change by unplugging unwanted interfaces and plugging in new interfaces.

The service-oriented view reflects the way that e-business is changing the overall manner in which information systems are viewed as exemplified in the upsurge in portals. Portals can be likened to virtual keyholes in cyberspace that aggregate services.

From a business process viewpoint, we can imagine the different roles (or actors) that are involved in a business process having their own portals as depicted in Figure 3.5, in which the shaded components represent portal servers that aggregate the business capabilities; see Appendix 1, Section A1.2.1 for a discussion of portals and portal servers.

Figure 3.4
Business processes
as families of
interfaces

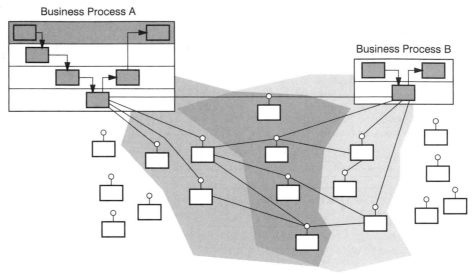

Figure 3.5
Portal views
serviced by
component
architecture

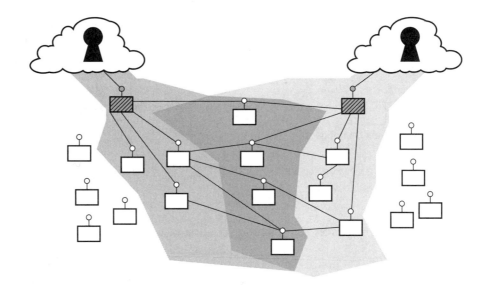

3.3.3   Structuring the business process model

Let us look at three particularly important structuring principles of the business process model. The reader is referred to Appendix 2, Section A2.2 for a more detailed account of the concepts and notations of BPM overall.

Function decomposition approaches, based upon top-down analysis of business processes as function blobs that must be divided and conquered, are not conducive to identifying business capabilities. Instead, business processes are 'time-sliced' by events that denote essential constraints imposed by the business, not by technology. This helps in 'knowing when to stop' modeling and achieving good granularity at the lowest level of business process (known as 'atomic process'; see Appendix 2, Section A2.2.1). Equally important, that will help us with our goal of arriving at well-defined sets of interfaces providing services.

Atomic business processes are constrained by the business need, not the limitations of a particular implementation. For example, many organizations suffer delays and errors in processing transactions because the transaction impacts multiple applications and must be manually re-keyed into each downstream application, or must sit in a queue waiting batch transfer. The objective of straight through processing (STP)[1] is to capture the transaction at source and then automate processing, without manual intervention, across multiple applications and people, increasingly across multiple companies. Analysis in terms of atomic business processes encourages and supports this view.

It is important to organize the business process model in a way that promotes identification of shared processes

The concepts of customer business process, sustaining business process and enabling business process map naturally to the layers of business components as illustrated in Figure 3.6.

3.3.4   Value-added versus commodity components

e-Business is forcing large organizations to become smaller and more specialized as they focus on what they do best and on what differentiates them from the competition. Legacy software, software packages or purchased business compo-

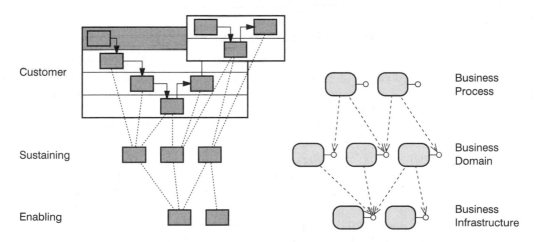

Figure 3.6
Business and component architecture correspondences

1. In the finance sector, STP is exemplified by automatic processing of securities trades across multiple placement, execution and settlement systems. We see the concept again in telecommunications in the shape of automatic processing of a service activation order across multiple order management, provisioning and network management systems.

nents increasingly perform treadmill work. The running of this software may be outsourced to an application service provider (ASP) (see Chapter 8). On the other hand, the whole process may be outsourced to others who are better equipped to deal with it efficiently.

The enabling processes of an organization are examples of such treadmill processes. It may be that a payroll software package is purchased and run by an ASP or perhaps a recruitment process is outsourced.

In shaping our component architecture to mirror the different types of process, we create a framework for managing the provisioning of components in line with business direction

In contrast, an organization will often want to concentrate its resources on its customer processes in an effort to retain and attract customers through value-added activity. For example, in Figure 2.4 the marketing, selling and servicing of vehicles may well be processes that the vehicle hire company wants to resource and nurture itself.

Sustaining processes probably sit somewhere in the middle. An organization might outsource where there is little need for differentiation, but resource the process itself where differentiation is required. The vehicle hire company might want to buy a component for warranty administration but develop their own special pricing component, if they see pricing as a strategic activity.

To recap, at one extreme are value-added components that we might want to build ourselves, while at the other extreme are commodity components that can be outsourced or purchased. In the middle are components that might require a mix of approaches. For example, we might purchase a component and extend it to fit a particular need.

3.3.5   Architecture and e-business

Upper levels of our component architecture will often feature large grained components, such as customer relationship management (CRM) components as well as smaller grained components, such as product catalogues, shopping carts and credit card components. Often these components are particularly appropriate for customer facing solutions. Smaller grain components may well be deployed on a web server, though the larger grained ones would typically be deployed on an application server.

Lower levels of the component architecture may also include large grained components, such as shipping logistics components as well as smaller grained components, such as a partnership component. These components are usually most appropriate for partner facing solutions and would typically be deployed on an application server (see Appendix 1, Section A1.2.1).

As customer facing applications become more integrated with the supply chain, we find that many of the smaller grained components required are appropriate to both customer and partner facing functionality. Examples include tax calculation and currency conversion components that become increasingly necessary as business 'goes global'.

Components may be implemented in a variety of ways as shown in Figure 3.7. Some components, providing well-established functionality, such as

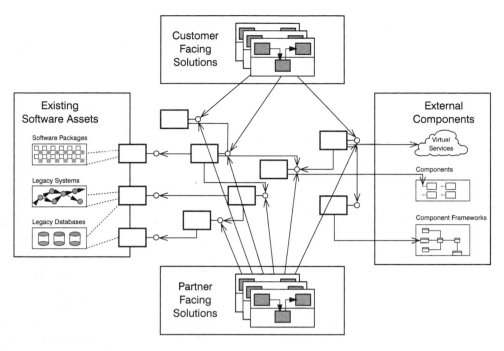

Figure 3.7
Component architecture in context

shopping carts and credit card components may be available for purchase from component suppliers. Others may be specialized using component frameworks. Legacy mining tools may be used to harvest existing code. Adapters and wrappers may be used to access services of existing systems, databases and packages; EAI tools may be used to provide the required middleware (see Section 5.3.1).

It is the component architecture that provides the underpinning structure for effective integration, at the business level

As technology moves forward that provides three big advantages:

1 Components can be deployed using different platforms according to implementation constrains and business needs.[2]

2 Component implementations may be replaced providing the component specification remains the same, so today's legacy adapter can be replaced with tomorrow's new component.

2. The target technology will typically provide some form of deployment support to assist with this activity. For technologies supporting EJB, this is managed through the concept of a deployment descriptor. A deployment descriptor is a description of the deployment-specific characteristics of the application that may vary from one installed instance of the system to another (e.g. security, access control and transactional behaviour). Use of deployment descriptors allows customization of application behaviour at run time without having to change the software itself.

3 Designing our components independently of the implementation, in an abstract way, puts us in a good position for supporting web applications in mixed technologies (for example, Enterprise JavaBeans (EJB) or COM+).

3.4   Dimensions of component architecture

In abstract terms, a software architecture 'involves the description of elements from which systems are built, interactions among those elements, patterns that guide their composition, and constraints on these patterns. In general, a particular system is defined in terms of a collection of components and interactions among those components' (Shaw and Garlan, 1996).

There are many aspects to this characterization that we do not have the scope to go into detail here, for example, architectural patterns, analysis of non-functional requirements and physical design topics such as capacity planning; the reader is referred to Bass *et al*. (1998), Hofmeister *et al*. (2000) and Shaw and Garlan (1996) for comprehensive accounts.

Software architectures that worked well for handcrafted, stand-alone applications are ineffective for the heterogeneous distributed systems upon which effective e-business depends. For that we need a service-based component architecture that offers the designer several dimensions of abstraction.

Many architectural initiatives fail because they are too theoretical, complex or unachievable. There is an unfortunate misconception that architects are somehow like policemen who set bureaucratic rules by which everyone else must design their systems. Unfortunately, in some organizations this myth has become a reality. The result is that developers become resentful, ignore the architects and possibly quit in frustration at their stifled creativity. At the same time, architects become increasingly desperate in their attempts to exert authority. This is not the way of good architecture. At the same time, without some standard setting, we have software anarchy. As in city planning, someone has to define the infrastructure. Achieving a good balance is a matter of pragmatism.

Architecture is not a set of box diagrams that constrain all software development

Practical help is above all what is needed. The rapid pace of change of web-based technologies poses difficult questions for the beleaguered Chief Information Officer (CIO). Which technologies should I adopt and when? If I wait too long for the market to decide on an obvious long-term technology direction, then we will lose customers to our more advanced competitors. If I choose too soon, we risk selecting a dead-end technology. In this section, we consider how an effective component-based architecture provides an integration model for addressing these challenges in the form of a backbone for future distributed systems.

Good architecture is meant to help, not hinder

3.4.1   Level of abstraction

A mistake that is commonly made in many IT departments is to treat the architecture of a set of related systems and the architecture of all systems across the enterprise at the same level of abstraction. So, for example, just as detailed component models are used to specify a set of purchasing and procurement systems, attempts are made to use the same models to specify the complete portfolio of systems and their relationships within a manufacturing enterprise. Apart from impossibility of managing the sheer scale of such a detailed enterprise model, there is also the problem of diversity. Most enterprises typically use a mix of disparate types of software built at different times by different internal and external development groups, each often operating independently using different tools. It is simply not practical to try to re-engineer all of these to eliminate redundancy.

   This distinction between system and enterprise level abstraction has been likened to the difference between the architecture of a building and city planning (Gartner Group, 1998). CBD 'City planning' is all about setting integration strategy and overall guidelines, such as providing different design patterns (Gamma *et al.*, 1995), analysis patterns (Fowler, 1997) and standards for different types of system, for example, message brokers, data warehouses and data integration strategies. The task is one of integration not development. 'Only summary-level models that focus on interfaces (city planning models) will apply to multiple, independently developed applications' (Gartner Group, 1998).

3.4.2   Project versus enterprise architectures

A project component architecture provides an overview of the software parts from which the envisioned software will be built, and describes how these parts inter-relate. The software parts may be encapsulated components, non-component assemblies, software packages, legacy systems and utilities. The objectives of this architecture include the following:

The distinction between project architecture and enterprise architecture is akin to the distinction between building or district architecture and city planning

- Identify opportunities for using or adapting pre-existing components.
- Identify which new components can be shared or reused, so the requirements of other consumers can be considered. A component gallery can be used to publicize the components over an intranet. This enables other projects to consider the appropriateness of the components for their own use.
- Estimate project effort, elapsed time and cost.
- Establish a 'big picture' for analysts and developers to work to; this is particularly important for incremental and parallel work and when the software is enhanced or corrected.
- Plan and visualize provisioning strategy; see Chapter 7.

An enterprise component architecture models the component requirements for all the planned component-based solutions for an enterprise or, more commonly, for a significant sub-set of the enterprise.[3] Individual project architectures should conform to the enterprise component architecture. The objectives of the enterprise component architecture include the following:

- Describe a vision for the component-based software within an enterprise.

- Understand how components relate to one another across projects.

- Investigate and recommend standard patterns and mechanisms.

- Recommend architectural policies, for example, policy for implementing cross-component associations[4] in a way that maintains the integrity of the associations and policy on backward compatibility of interfaces.

- Plan and visualize provisioning strategies across projects; see Chapter 7. Dependencies declared on the enterprise architecture help determine the provisioning strategy. Conversely, the provisioning strategy may actually constrain the enterprise architecture. For example, it may be corporate policy to use a certain software package for all personnel applications.

3.4.3   Architecture as integration model

The architecture provides a framework for reuse and integration of existing software assets. The latter typically consist of a mix of externally provided components, software packages, previous generation design models linked to code, legacy systems or databases. Such software assets are drawn into the big picture. Existing assets are integrated in terms of the interfaces they must provide, and not just at the technology level using proprietary application programming interfaces (APIs). The latter is unfortunately often the case with

The process of architecture is one of progressive refinement

some of the EAI vendors' products. The most successful business components are those that can be 'rewired' in many configurations in effective response to business change (top-down) and existing software capability (bottom-up) as illustrated in Figure 3.8.

It is important to understand that this is not a static picture. Architecture is a living artifact: it is not done once and then forgotten. The architecture may undergo considerable metamorphosis as new details are revealed, as business changes occur and as design ideas evolve.

---

3. We will still use the term 'enterprise architecture' for the more common situation where a sub-set of the enterprise is actually meant. The sub-set could be an organization unit, subsidiary or family of organization units that collaborate in a business process that runs through all those units.
4. Mechanisms for implementing cross-component associations include relationship management components or call-back mechanisms.

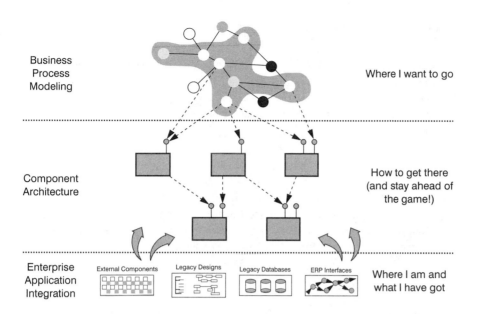

Figure 3.8
Component architecture as integration model

Business Process Modeling

Where I want to go

Component Architecture

How to get there (and stay ahead of the game!)

Enterprise Application Integration

External Components   Legacy Designs   Legacy Databases   ERP Interfaces

Where I am and what I have got

3.4.4   Forms of a component

Before going further, we need to understand the meaning behind the term 'component' and to be more precise in our definition. In this section, we follow the work of John Cheesman and John Daniels in defining component forms and their relationships (Cheesman and Daniels, 2000) as illustrated in Figure 3.9.

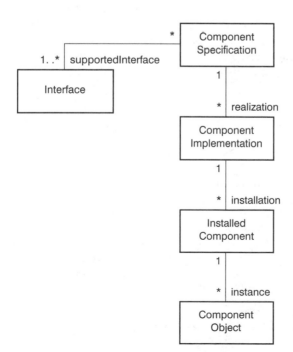

Figure 3.9
Component forms (Cheesman and Daniels, 2000)

Let us look at the different component forms in more detail:

A **component implementation**[5] is a realization of a component specification, which is independently deployable. This means it can be installed and replaced independently of other components. It does *not* mean that it is independent of other components – it may have many dependencies. It does *not* necessarily mean that it is a single physical item, such as a single file.

A **component object** is an instance of an installed component. A run-time concept. An object with its own data and a unique identity. The thing that performs the implemented behaviour. An installed component may have multiple component objects (which require explicit identification) or a single one (which may be implicit).

A **component specification** is the specification of a unit of software that describes the behaviour of a set of component objects, and defines a unit of implementation. Behaviour is defined as a set of interfaces. A component specification is realized as a component implementation.

An **installed component** is an installed (or deployed) copy of a component implementation. A component implementation is deployed by registering it with the run-time environment. This enables the run-time environment to identify the installed component to use when creating an instance of the installed component, or running one of its operations.

An **interface**[6] is the definition of a set of behaviours that can be offered by a component object.

Note that the run-time environment is a CEE as described in Appendix 1, Section A1.1.1.

5. Note: The UML (OMG, 1999) definition of component is very general encompassing both implementation and executable level concepts, including executable programs, static and dynamic libraries, database tables, and source code files or documents. The UML definition is 'an executable software module with indentity and a well-defined interface'. The above definition of component can be thought of as a specific kind of UML component.
6. More precisely, Cheeseman and Daniels refer to an interface as a 'component interface'

3.4.5   Specification versus implementation

Architecture models are used to focus on different dimensions. There are two basic types of component architecture: specification and implementation. Component specification architecture (CSA) operates at the logical level to group interfaces into component specifications and expose interface dependencies. Component implementation architecture (CIA) works at the physical level[7] to model how specifications are realized in terms of actual component implementations and to expose the dependencies between those component implementations. Table 3.1 itemizes the main differences between these architectures.

The overall approach therefore is to start by identifying interfaces that will provide desired business capabilities. We model dependencies between these interfaces, but then move straight to a first-cut CIA by initially assuming one component specification (with a corresponding component implementation) for each interface. This is adjusted within the context of the enterprise CIA to maximize reuse. The dependencies included in the CIA are reviewed to determine whether they should be specification level dependencies. Only then, having tested that the end product is realizable, are the results actually recorded in the CIA.

Conversely, specification rules requiring that certain interfaces be invoked, restrict implementation possibilities, and may cause the CIA to change. At the same time, despite the restriction, this facilitates an important feature of CBD: the substitution of one consumed component by any other offering the requisite interfaces.

Whether we begin with one or the other of the two architectures is not the issue here: we must consider both, as there is a dynamic interplay between the two architectures. In fact many organizations choose to employ a single 'combined' view[8] focusing on components and interfaces (as opposed to component specifications and interfaces). Other non-component software units, such as legacy systems and external packages may also be included. The combined view is essentially a CIA that includes dependencies on interfaces that are by definition specification dependencies. Unless we specifically state otherwise, we will employ this combined view, known simply as the component architecture, throughout this book.

---

7. Additionally, it may be useful, especially if you want to examine platform distribution issues, to model run-time dependencies between installed components or component objects as described in Appendix 2, Section A2.5.
8. For example, if the policy is to make all the implementation dependencies into specification rules, then there is little point building the CSA, since it will be identical to the CIA.

Table 3.1 **Component specification and implementation architecture characteristics**

	Component specification architecture	Component implementation architecture
Intent	Explore and describe a technically neutral and adaptable software framework that mirrors business needs.	Explore and describe the choices made in a particular realization of the CSA.
Content	Component specifications, their interfaces and any dependencies on other component specifications or interfaces.	Component implementations and how these component implementations depend on one another, including dependencies on interfaces.
Dependencies	Dependencies are specification rules.	Dependencies are implementation rules.
Inter-relationship	Dependencies constrain how *any* implementation of the component is built.	Influences what is technically feasible in the component specification architecture.

3.4.6 Architecture layering

Many organizations are adopting a layered architecture pattern in which reusability and stability increase downward through each layer, as shown in Figure 3.10. This pattern also sits well with the need to distinguish value-added from commodity components (described earlier in Section 3.3.4) and to help visualize provisioning strategy.

Let us look in more detail at the different layers:

● **User interface layer**
  – The solution assembly supports all facets of the solution that are not supported by components. It typically supports the solution's user interface. The solution assembly is not usually a formal component itself, although there is nothing to stop it being so.
  – User interface controls provide user interface graphics and event handling. For example, a hierarchical scrollable list or a histogram.

● **Business layer**
  – Process components provide local business process functionality and persistence[9] independent of the user interface. The solution assembly software invokes the process component. Process components may provide

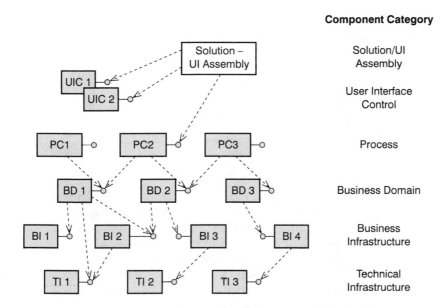

Figure 3.10
Component
architecture and
component
categories

Component Category

Solution/UI
Assembly

User Interface
Control

Process

Business Domain

Business
Infrastructure

Technical
Infrastructure

significant reuse of local business rules (including sequencing logic) across solutions running within the same business process (or part of a business process). For example, an underwriting or claims component.

- Business domain components provide functionality and persistence[10] needs across different business processes within the same domain or industry, for example, a policyholder component in the life insurance domain. Domains may be further layered according to commonality; for example, finance components may provide interfaces used by insurance components that are in turn used by the life insurance components.
- Business infrastructure components are used across different domains. For example, currency conversion services, address reformatting operations or an organization calendar.

● **Technical infrastructure layer**
These components provide technical services such as error message handling, access control, security and recovery. Where there are complex data management issues typically associated with existing databases, this layer may include persistence services to control data integrity and provide unified data services to the business components.

9. Note: persistence services may be further split out into the technical infrastructure layer.
10. Again, persistence service may be handled by separate data service components, in the infrastructure layer. This is a popular strategy where legacy data has to be maintained, the data service components acting as wrappers for relational databases.

It may sometimes be expedient to compromise the layered structure in the face of implementation constraints; treat it as an ideal

The price paid for a pure layered architecture can be increased numbers of calls across the layers. This problem is exacerbated in the case of a highly constrained implementation, where services are fragmented across several platforms. These issues together with non-functional requirements, such as performance or security, must be balanced against the flexibility, maintainability and reuse that come with a layered approach.

3.4.7   The main sequence

It is useful to consider components in terms of the number of dependent components they serve and the number of components upon which they depend. We can plot this on a graph as shown in Figure 3.11. The band that extends from upper left to lower right is where most components should sit; we refer to this band as the 'main sequence' (Martin, 1995).

Components that are both independent and responsible are stable – in other words they are unlikely to change. These components should sit in the lower regions of architecture diagrams. Conversely, components in the lower right of the main sequence are very unstable. These components should sit in the upper regions of architecture diagrams.

Traditional approaches do not conform to the main sequence. It is common in structure charts and function hierarchies to find that changes to the modules or functions appearing at lowest levels propagate upward to the highest levels. This forces changes in all the intervening modules or functions. For example, in a traditional application, a main loop calls several other functions. The main loop is a control structure that defines the architecture of the system, yet it depends on the functions that contain the implementation details. Changes to implementation detail ripple through the system. This leads to the absurd situation where basic architectural decisions are easier to change than the implementation details!

Figure 3.11
The main sequence

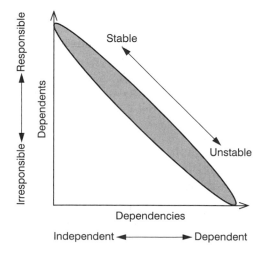

In contrast, if the component architecture follows the main sequence, the generalities are stable and the details are unstable. Changing the details is easy, changing the generalities difficult. Although it might appear that this leads to inflexible designs, remember that a design that is hard to change is not necessarily difficult to extend. And this is the whole point about interface-based design.

Well-designed interfaces allow components to be extended without changing the internals of the components

The position of a component with respect to the main sequence provides a useful check on the quality of the component architecture. While it is possible to do this in general terms, Martin also provides workable metrics for quantifying the relative stability of components.

3.5   Summary

In this chapter, we have considered the main principles of an interface-based approach to e-business solutions and how a component-based architecture helps put those principles into practice. A key element in this is to foster business-IT alignment through business capabilities.

While the component architecture provides a structural context in which to apply component-oriented modeling techniques as they are used through the software process, it is more than merely a set of diagrams. Other important aspects include non-functional requirements, patterns, design guidelines and architectural policies and mechanisms. We looked at the different dimensions of component architecture such as enterprise and project dimensions and specification and implementation dimensions and considered how to put those to work. For example, the architecture provides a framework for reuse and integration of existing software assets, and external components, helping to provide a platform for smooth low-risk migration.

3.6   References

Bass, L., Clemens, P., and Kazman, R., *Software Architecture in Practice*, Addison-Wesley Longman, 1998

Cheesman, J., and Daniels, J., *UML Components*, Addison-Wesley, 2000

Dodd, J., *et al.*, *Advisor 2.4*, Sterling Software, 1999.

Fowler, M., *Analysis Patterns: Reusable Object Models*, Addison-Wesley, 1997.

Gamma, E., Helm, R., Johnson, R., and Vlissides, J., *Design Patterns: Elements of Reusable Object-Oriented Software*, Addison-Wesley, 1995.

Gartner Group, *IT Architecture vs IT Planning, Confererence Presentation*, R. Schulte, ESC101Tarch1198, November 1998.

Hofmeister, C., Nord, R., and Soni, D., *Applied Software Architecture*, Addison-Wesley, 2000.

Martin, R. C., *Designing Object-Oriented C++ Applications Using The Booch Method*, Prentice Hall, 1995.

Meyer, B., *Object-Oriented Software Construction*, Prentice Hall, Englewood Cliffs, New Jersey, 2nd edn, 1997.

OMG, *OMG Unified Modeling Language Specification*, V1.3, June 1999.

Shaw, M., and Garlan, D., *Software Architecture*, Prentice Hall, 1996.

Process guidelines 4

Introduction

Organizations today do not have the luxury of starting each project from scratch using a clean white slate, as is commonly still assumed. Many organizations use processes geared to development of point solutions in the manner of a linear production line. This does not align well with today's needs for hybrid solutions to support e-business processes that not only cross divisions and departments, but also transcend organizational boundaries using the internet. There is a growing need to solve these complex business problems by reusing and acquiring as much of the functionality as possible. Traditional software engineering processes were not designed to do this. New approaches are needed which are better suited to the new challenges, while building on lessons that have been learnt in streamlining software development in response to business needs.[1]

This chapter sets the context for putting component-based modeling techniques to work using a practical component-oriented process framework, so conspicuously lacking in most methods. Most current processes are too overwhelmingly detailed to be applied in practical enterprise settings. Our aim is rather to provide a workable project management framework for applying the modeling techniques described, largely by example, in this book. Our focus is on patterns and checklists, hints and tips.

1. For example, as conceived by James Martin (Martin, 1991) and others, rapid application development (RAD) brought with it many useful techniques such as Joint Application Development (JAD), prototyping and time-boxing. More recently, the Dynamic Systems Development Method (DSDM) consortium has forged good practical guidance on the responsible use of RAD (DSDM Consortium, 1997; Stapleton, 1997) and the use of CBD with DSDM (DSDM Corporation, 2000).

4.2   The CBD process framework

Development of e-business systems involves collaborative work of several different types of specialist with different areas of expertise, for example, business
process consultants, software architects, legacy specialists, graphic designers and
server engineers. We will need a coordinating framework for dealing with these
diverse skill sets and introduce a track-based pattern to help. It is also important
to have a good idea of the kinds of deliverable that we can expect to produce.
We describe a broad set of deliverables that work well on CBD projects.
Techniques can then be applied in flexible fashion within our overall process
framework of track-based pattern plus deliverables.

4.2.1   A track-based pattern

A track-based pattern provides a coordinating framework for control of CBD
and for organization of staff according to the roles played. In Chapter 9, we will
see how different team roles fit into the track-based pattern.

It is helpful to consider solution assembly and component provisioning
working in parallel fashion as indicated in Figure 4.1. This is often called 'twin
track development' (Allen and Frost, 1998). Consumers and producers follow
separate processes geared to their respective needs of fast business solutions and
high quality components. Solution developers seek to harvest components produced by the provisioning track. At the same time, component provisioners
seek to sow solutions as a basis from which to grow components.

Looking at the figure, we can see that the twin track process is triggered in different ways. The assembly track is triggered by the need to produce a timely
business solution, for example, direct sales over the internet. Assembly involves
searching for available components and, where necessary, raising requirements
for new components from the provisioning track.

In contrast, the provisioning track may be triggered independently of specific
solution requirements, by business reuse needs that provide the requirements
for reusable components, for example, commonly required business infrastructure components such as a product rule engine.

Increasingly there is pressure to reuse existing systems, packages and databases. Integration projects (Linthicum, 2000) use EAI software to remove data
and process redundancy and introduce consistency across families of existing

Figure 4.1
The twin track
process

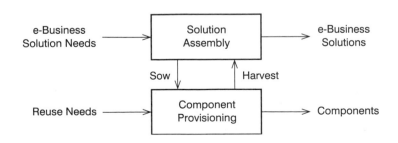

systems and packages, often implemented using diverse technologies. Note how reuse requirements are effectively filtered down to make use of legacy software as shown in Figure 4.2.

The track-based pattern does not operate in a vacuum. e-Business process improvement provides the right business context for CBD, as shown in Figure 4.3. Of particular importance for transitioning to e-business using CBD are the overall e-business improvement plan (see Section 2.2.2), which provides business direction for architecture planning and the business models, which focus on understanding specific processes requiring e-business solutions.

Note that the process is evolutionary and ongoing. Results from software projects are fed back to e-business process improvement for reassessment in the light of experience with e-business. Change must be managed. Similarly, components are assessed with respect to architecture planning, in a process of progressive refinement. Architecture planning covers the high-level enterprise component architecture that provides a 'big picture' for projects to work to.

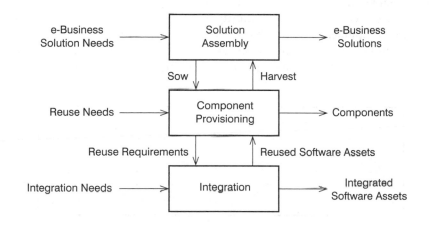

Figure 4.2
The twin track process and integration

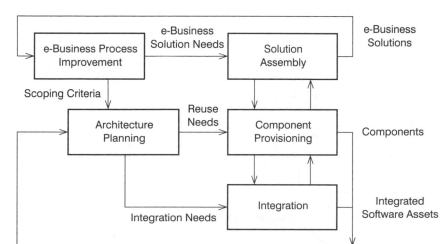

Figure 4.3
The track-based framework

Underpinning the track-based framework are effective infrastructure facilities as shown in Figure 4.4. These include support for component and internet standards (see Appendix 1, Section A1.1) and configuration management. Some component management tools now provide component catalogues that hold component information within a repository and provide the ability to browse, install and register the components in harmony with model-driven approaches.

4.2.2 Deliverables

There are many software processes that make the mistake of identifying prescriptive series of tasks that at the end of the day bear little relation to realities of everyday project life. The reason for this is that these kinds of process focus on the 'how' before understanding the 'what'. Before considering techniques and activities, we need therefore to focus on expected deliverables. Later in this chapter, we will show which types of models (described in Appendix 2) are expected within each type of deliverable.

Deliverables are needed to provide targets for projects, to measure progress and to ensure common understanding along the road to software delivery. There are 'n' number of deliverable sets and accompanying techniques that we might identify across different organizations according to culture and industry type. Nevertheless, we provide a generalized set in order to provide a context for

Figure 4.4
The track-based
framework and
component
infrastructure

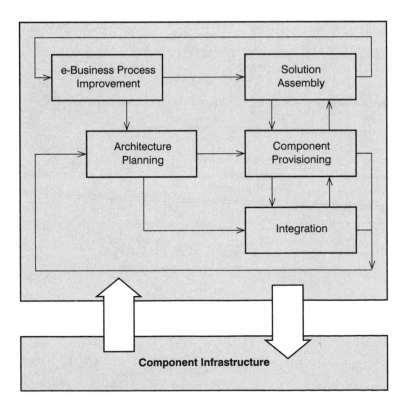

the modeling techniques discussed in the succeeding chapters – feel free to adapt these to fit your own organizational needs. Five types of deliverables[2] can be identified on typical CBD projects:

1 E-business process improvement plan.

2 Software requirements.

3 Component architecture.

4 Behaviour specification.

5 Implementation.

Implementation covers a number of further deliverables, the details of which are outside the scope of this book. However, we cover component provisioning strategies in Chapter 7.

An **e-business process improvement plan** is produced as described in Section 2.2.2. Business modeling is used to understand the business requirements in a way that is easily understood by business people, but at the same time usable with as little translation or rework as possible into a set of functional and non-functional requirements for some new software. The plan must include the business case for software requirements projects and scoping criteria for architecture planning (enterprise architecture).

Software requirements documents capture the scope of the proposed software together with enough information to enable a broad development schedule to be devised. The software requirements are usefully prototyped to facilitate user involvement and verification of correctness. Existing analysis patterns and software assets that might be used to meet the requirements are assessed. The latter includes existing systems, databases and available software packages, components and interfaces. This is important for early identification of reuse opportunities and for understanding requirements and for assessing integration needs.

Component architecture documents work at two levels (project and enterprise) as described in Chapter 3 (see Section 3.4.2). The underlying project and component architectures are progressively refined in the light of project experience and software delivery.

Behaviour specifications[3] provide a full and precise definition of the required software behaviour. The externally visible software behaviour is described, without dictating the internal design. However, constraints on the internal design are described. Such constraints can take the shape of interface dependencies, non-functional requirements and invariants (see Appendix 2, Section A2.7).

---

2. It is often convenient to split a project into separate stages, which reflect the deliverables involved, but there is nothing sacrosanct in this.
3. Here we are focusing on the component-related aspects of the behaviour specification. It is important to note that a typical behaviour specification document may well include traditional 'external design' information, such as screen layouts, report formats, examples, screen validation rules and non-functional requirements on the solution (for example, 'online and/or batch', 'single processor or distributed').

There are two types of behaviour specification. **Interface specifications** specify the behaviour of the interface from the point of view of its consumers. They include contractual specifications of services offered by the interface and a catalogue of the information that the interface deals in (an 'interface type model').

Component specifications specify behaviour of sets of interfaces that provisioners are contracted to implement as software units.[4] They include the interface dependencies, invariants and non-functional requirements that constrain the provisioner. The component specification can be likened to a compliance document; any implementation must comply with its component specification.

Interface and component specifications should be enrolled in catalogues and published using a component management tool.

4.2.3   Integration

Integration projects may exist at a tactical level and involve reuse of isolated legacy systems. Such projects may be non-invasive, seeking only to identify existing services that can be wrapped or adapted for use in component provisioning. On the other hand, a legacy renewal project may be invasive and involve re-engineering parts of legacy systems in preparation for exposure of interfaces which are used in component provisioning projects.

Other integration projects are more strategic. However, the basic pattern of activities (planning, requirements, architecture, specification and implementation) remains the same. A strategic integration project should be looking to offer the integrated services for use in component provisioning projects. Legacy models may be used to assist in either tactical or strategic integration work, a subject to which we return in Chapter 6. Tools that connect modeling capabilities with EAI middleware are extremely useful here.

4.2.4   Organizing deliverables within the track-based pattern

Figure 4.5 shows the relationship between deliverables and track-based pattern. Software requirements, project architecture and behaviour specification apply in a project context in any of the three delivery tracks. However, as we will see a little later, de-scoping may occur at regular points through the lifecycle, resulting in hybrid projects. So, for example, a solution assembly project could branch into separate smaller assembly, provisioning and integration projects.

For example, software requirements techniques may also be used within a business process improvement project. They are especially useful in conjunction

Remember we are describing guidelines here, not rigid laws of nature

with prototyping, as a means of scouting ahead to explore different designs. This is particularly appropriate for e-business systems where software becomes part of the very fabric of business and the distinction between business process improvement and solution assembly becomes naturally rather blurred.

4. That is, the 'component implementation' form described in Chapter 3.

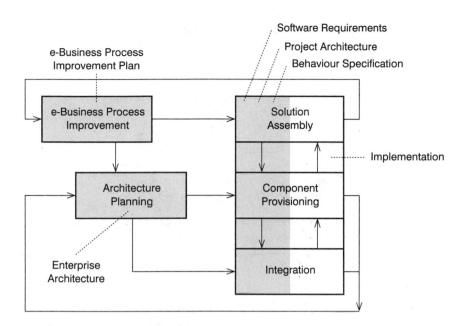

Figure 4.5
Deliverables within
the track-based
framework

4.2.5 Reuse checkpoints

Rather than the 'Should I build or buy software?' choice that is presented in traditional processes, the questions in a CBD process now are:

- *Which* components should I buy and which do I develop?

- How do I scope and identify business components that align with my business needs?

- Is 80% of the solution (using pre-built components) at 20% of the cost/time acceptable to the business?

- Are there software packages that I can reuse and integrate to solve the problem?

- Are there legacy software assets I can reuse and integrate to solve the problem?

- Are there legacy models I can use to help address the problem?

- Are there component frameworks[5] I can extend to solve the problem?

- Are there opportunities for outsourcing a component implementation?

- How can I pick and choose the best products, and integrate them in a mix and match manner?

---

5. A component framework is a set of component interfaces and dependencies designed to be extended and/or specialized by its users. It may be that a user selects just one interface to specialize. On the other hand, the whole framework could be used as the architectural basis for a user's systems.

It is useful at this point to consider some general guidelines for building reuse checkpoints into the track-based framework as shown in Table 4.1.

Table 4.1   Reuse checkpoints

Deliverable	Solution assembly	Component provisioning
e-Business process improvement plan	Has the business problem been tackled before? Search for business templates, common business models.	
Enterprise component architecture	Are there cost-justified opportunities to reuse or genericize existing software assets[6] or build frameworks, as part of the overall enterprise architecture? Consider architectural fit of identified software assets; consider architectural patterns. Examine dependencies and investigate overall feasibility.	
Software requirements	Has the software problem been tackled before? Search for possible existing models, and frameworks that might help solve the problem. List candidates.	Can the problem be stated in more general terms? Conduct comparative studies with similar projects. Identify opportunities to generalize common features. Ensure analysis caters for sufficient diversity of contexts.
Project component architecture	Can existing software assets or frameworks be used to solve the problem? Consider architectural fit of reused asset. Examine dependencies and investigate overall feasibility.	Are there further opportunities to generalize software assets or build frameworks? Consider architectural fit of generic components or frameworks; consider architectural patterns. Examine dependencies and investigate overall feasibility.
Behaviour specification	Can existing interfaces be used to solve the problem? Extend and specialize interfaces.	Can generalized interfaces be provided? Generalize interfaces, consider analysis patterns.
Implementation (internal design and acquisition)	Can existing implementations be used to solve the problem? Reuse implementation designs. Purchase implementations. Outsource implementations. Subscribe to virtual run-time services	Is the design flexible enough to cater for change? Design, purchase or outsource implementation for flexibility, consider design patterns. Ensure test plans cater for sufficient diversity of contexts

6. Software assets may be existing software systems, databases or software packages. They may also be existing components developed internally or provided externally.

4.3   CBD process themes

Another key feature of e-business systems is that, unlike traditional systems, they are subject to rapid change. Charles Schwab, for example, releases a new version of its electronic brokerage website each month and evolves the underlying infrastructure to meet the demands of growing traffic. A balance must therefore be struck between the need for process guidance and the demands of rapid solution delivery. An effective process needs to exploit best practices but not constrain in an overly bureaucratic way, as is unfortunately often the case.

Good processes are meant to help, not hinder

What is needed is an 'adaptive' rather than an 'optimizing' framework (Highsmith, 1999): 'Rather than processes the model needs to focus on patterns. We need to move from a 20th century "Command-Control" model to a 21st century "Leadership-Collaboration" one'. In this section we take a look at some themes of successful software process that help with the adaptive approach: iterative and incremental development, hybrid development and gap analysis. This provides a context for mapping the families of techniques, coming up in detail in Chapter 5, to the process framework described above.

4.3.1   Iterative and incremental integration

Iterative incremental processes are characteristic of object-oriented development projects and have been well documented elsewhere (Kruchten, 1998; Jacobson *et al.*, 1999). Our deliverables also evolve in iterative and incremental fashion as shown in Figure 4.6. At the same time there is an important gear shift.

CBD for e-business is neither a point solution driven nor a *development* process. It is an ongoing change management and *integration* process

The process must recognize that architecture evolves in harmony with changing business needs. Also, you can only do as much architecture as the business will tolerate as reflected in the business case for CBD. Harvesting and sowing of reuse run right through the process from requirements to implementation as described in the previous section. A diversity of implementation options are involved, from bespoke design to outsourcing, from existing system integration to component purchase and from framework extension to service subscription.

e-Business process improvement planning sets scoping criteria for enterprise architecture and provides the business case for software requirements projects. Feedback is assessed on a regular basis from implementation of e-business solutions.

Refinement of software requirements, specification and project architecture is essentially iterative, with de-scoping at points of stabilization, providing a new context for drilling-down. Enterprise architecture provides an overall context that governs the evolving project architecture.

Once software requirements have stabilized, it may be that the project moves directly to implementation by incremental assembly. This is sometimes known

Figure 4.6
Iteration and de-
scoping of CBD
activities

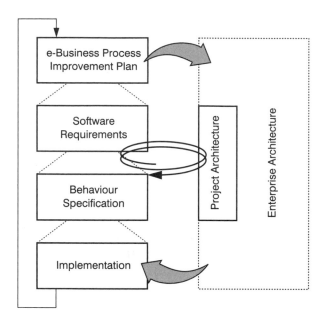

as 'fast-track' and is an evolution of RAD. Otherwise, specification moves to more detail, usually on a further scoped sub-set of requirements.

The refinement of specification and project architecture is again iterative. Once both have stabilized, the project then moves to incremental implementation according to the provisioning strategy.

4.3.2   Hybrid integration

Let us look at how the process supports a particularly key feature of CBD: hybrid integration. Suppose for example, that the first iteration of a complex project results in a software requirements document that gives rise to two sub-projects (P1 and P2), as illustrated in Figure 4.7. P1 is a RAD project for fast-track assembly to serve one sub-set of requirements. P2 is a specification project to further investigate the architecture and specify components. P2 results in five implementation projects, say one for each of five components:[7]

1 P2.1 is another assembly implementation, though this time to provide a set of interfaces, in the form a process component (see Section 3.4.6) rather than direct user facing functionality.

2 P2.2 involves legacy integration work and the creation of adapters[8] to implement components.

---

7. More typically increments will be triggered for each interface of a component.
8. An adapter is a component that calls non-component software, typically a legacy system, transforms the information received and provides new functionality through its interfaces. Adapters often form a layer of components between new components and legacy software and are very useful for easing legacy migration.

3 P2.3 is a straightforward wrapper on to a small legacy system.

4 P2.4 involves internal design of a component that the organization decides to build itself.

5 P2.5 is an outsourcing project.

Once a component is implemented, further interfaces may be added or existing interfaces extended. For example, the fast-track assembly might be evolved to component status or further interfaces added to the adapter. This is an important feature of CBD: it is an evolutionary approach. Mixed implementations like this are an increasingly common feature in software development today.

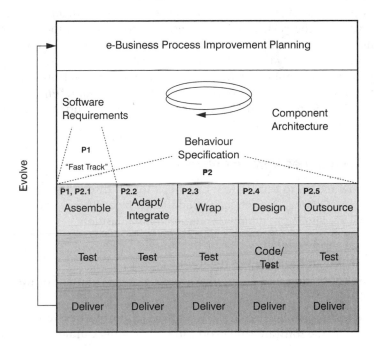

Figure 4.7
Hybrid implementations within the CBD process

We have already seen that applying CBD for e-business systems involves treating the interface as the unit of analysis and design. It should now be clear that the interface provides a natural delivery mechanism for incremental and parallel development.

Interfaces are also a very convenient means of evolving an e-business solution. Early increments might involve incomplete and tentative interfaces designed largely to kite-fly the solution. New, more complete and stabilized interfaces can be introduced, as the requirements become clearer. Client systems can be switched to the new versions of interfaces, as they become ready. Interfaces that are no longer used can be phased out. We must also address configuration management issues as the number of interfaces grows. Versioning of interfaces becomes a small discipline in its own right.

4.3.3   Gap analysis

An important feature of CBD is the application of gap analysis to assess the difference between stated requirements and existing components. A gap analysis results in a provisioning strategy: as we saw in the previous section, recommendations that may include a hybrid of different options.

It is important to understand that the gap analysis might involve realigning the stated requirements, making a compromise to requirements in order to deliver the solution faster and cheaper. Even in an extreme case where use of a package is mandated as part of the e-business improvement plan, a gap analysis is still important if only at a high level in order to understand possible shortcomings of the package and to manage expectations, particularly of business people. After all, the package may severely constrain the component architecture forcing integration of business components around its capabilities as opposed to those ideally required by the business!

Gap analysis is applied at decreasing levels of abstraction through the process, not just once at the specification phase as is sometimes mistakenly thought. CBD affects software's entire lifecycle. We will return to the subject of gap analysis in Chapter 7.

4.3.4   Techniques versus deliverables

We can now return to our basic set of steps for an interface-based approach introduced in Chapter 3. Each step is addressed by a different family of techniques that are applied in iterative and incremental fashion:

- **Business modeling** Understand the business needs in terms of strategy, organization, process and information.
- **Use case modeling** Scope and identify the business context of the software behaviour.
- **Business type modeling** Identify and describe business concepts to be managed by the software, and evolve to help identify candidate interfaces.
- **Interaction modeling** Examine dynamic interplay between software concepts to realize required behaviour. Identify and partition the behaviour to be exhibited by the software, assign responsibilities to and evolve candidate interfaces.
- **Architecture modeling** Understand software dependencies and adjust responsibilities of interfaces. Verify technical feasibility. Group interfaces into components and partition the software into deployable units.
- **Specification modeling** Specify the interfaces in terms of behaviour and information. Specify groups of interfaces to be implemented as components in the form of component specifications; include constraints. Enrol and publish specifications in catalogues.
- **Internal design modeling** Develop or acquire component implementations.

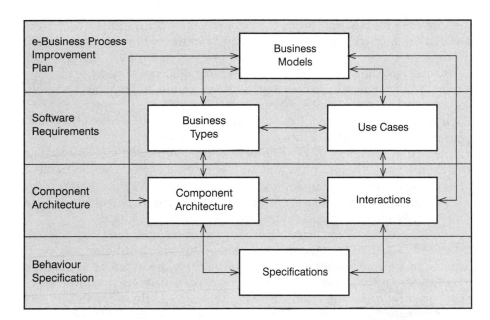

Figure 4.8
Technique types in relation to typical project deliverables

Figure 4.8 illustrates the overall relationships between the techniques and shows how techniques relate to typical project deliverables. Internal design modeling is not shown here as it is outside our scope.

4.3.5   Technique overview

We provide an overview of how the techniques work together, with reference to Figure 4.8, in preparation for the case study that follows in Chapters 5 and 6.

The business models provide a context for modeling business types and use cases. Business process flow diagrams help to identify use cases. Business concept models provide an initial pathway toward developing business types. The business models help to scope the component architecture and set a context for interaction modeling. Conversely, information unearthed as a result of any of the four software-related techniques may result in a revision to the business models.

Modeling of use cases and business types is two-way. Both help in understanding software requirements. The business type model must support the use cases. Use cases help unearth new business types, attributes and associations. At the same time, the business type model should reflect requirements not covered by use cases, such as business policy, business rules and information requirements.

Business type modeling drives architecture modeling (and vice versa). Interfaces are initially declared by consideration of the business type model. An interface should manage cohesive sets of business types. Dependencies between

If you are unfamiliar with any of the modeling techniques, you are advised to refer to Appendix 2 where you will find a catalogue of concepts, notations, quick starter guides and tips and hints

the interfaces must be reflected in the component architecture. Interfaces are declared on interaction models, which help to further refine understanding of the interfaces.

Use case modeling drives interaction modeling (and vice versa). Use cases are refined into lower level use case steps and the required types, and interfaces, declared on interaction models. (Note: In fact it is possible to proceed direct to the interactions without prior use case modeling.) Thinking through interactions in this way may also cause use cases to be adjusted.

Interaction modeling drives architecture modeling (and vice versa). The architecture provides interfaces that are declared on the interaction models. Conversely, the interactions (and use cases) are 'played through' and test out the architecture, causing adjustment of interface responsibilities, questioning of dependencies and new interfaces and dependencies to be identified.

Interaction modeling drives specification modeling (and vice versa). Operations required to support the interactions and attributes and types required by the interactions are declared in interface specifications. Interaction modeling also helps identify constraints and dependencies recorded in component specifications. Conversely, thinking through specifications in this way may also cause the interactions to be adjusted (for example, perhaps an operation is moved to a different interface).

Architecture modeling drives specification modeling (and vice versa). The interface specifications and component specifications must support dependencies identified in the architecture. Conversely, thinking through interfaces in this way may also cause the architecture to be adjusted

4.4   Summary

In this chapter, we have summarized the key features of an effective process for e-business. We have not attempted to catalogue or structure this information more comprehensively. This is partly for reasons of scope and partly because CBD for e-business is a highly skilled, creative and adaptive process. Too often processes are produced for projects that ignore this fact and attempt to rigidly prescribe the development process to an extreme level of detail.

Nevertheless, some structure is essential for planning CBD and for managing the diversity of potential provisioning routes and skill sets. A process framework and set of deliverables provide a good starting point together with checklists and guidelines such as those we looked at for reuse. The deliverables also help to provide a context for using the different CBD modeling techniques, a subject we consider so important that Appendix 2 is devoted to it.

4.5   References

Allen, P., and Frost, S., *Component-Based Development for Enterprise Systems: Applying The SELECT Perspective*, Cambridge University Press-SIGS Publications, 1998.

DSDM Consortium, *DSDM Version 3*, Tesseract Publishing, 1997.

DSDM Corporation, *DSDM and Component-Based Development*, DSDM White Paper, 2000.

Highsmith, J., 'Adaptive management: Patterns for the e-business era', *Cutter IT Journal*, vol. 12, no. 9, September 1999.

Jacobson, I., Booch, G., and Rumbaugh, J., *The Unified Software Development Process*, Addison-Wesley, 1999.

Kruchten, P., *The Rational Unified Process: An Introduction*, Addison-Wesley Longman, 1998

Linthicum, D., *Enterprise Application Integration*, Addison-Wesley, 2000.

Martin, J., *Rapid Application Development*, Macmillan, 1991.

Stapleton, J., *DSDM-The Method in Practice*, Addison Wesley Longman, 1997.

5 Migrating to e-business

5.1 Introduction

Many organizations are faced with hybrid software and hardware environments that have evolved over a number of years. Most of these organizations are not early adopters: there is a need to minimize risk and maximize business return from existing software assets, both internally developed and externally acquired. An effective online presence requires tying together these hybrid software units with new web-based front ends; it means integration, significantly it means business process integration.

This chapter explores the issues many organizations face in migrating to e-business and emphasizes the use of component architecture to help manage this change. We use an example scenario to illustrate how to put the principles, described in the first part of this book, into practice. We explore some initial measures for transitioning to e-business at minimum risk by leveraging existing system services and evolving early solutions to component status. In the next chapter we will develop the example to address more sophisticated requirements, looking at new and extended business processes.

5.2 Legacy renewal and EAI

5.2.1 First generation e-business

First generation e-business systems are familiar to most readers. Static web pages are used mainly as a promotional aid for customers to browse. Product information is re-keyed by website administrators. Or perhaps electronic versions of marketing brochures are replicated on the internet.

Orders are placed by completing a form that looks very similar to its printed counterpart. Submission of the order to the sales department may take place via e-mail, printed output or fax. Integration with existing systems is wholly manual by re-keying of data. Orders placed via the internet go in the same queue as those arriving by post.

Some first generation e-business systems use web-server databases to help manage content and provide limited customer-related information. Nevertheless, these first generation solutions are essentially standalone. The consequences of manual re-keying of information at any point in an e-business process are not difficult to visualize in terms of incorrect information. Readers will no doubt have their own unfortunate experiences with products that were wrongly priced or unavailable despite assurances to the contrary, or orders that somehow got lost. Equally important, if the same manual steps are required to process orders as they are for an existing channel, such as mail order sales, then a web front-end is not a way to improve efficiency and reduce operational cost. On the contrary, the web front-end becomes an additional overhead.

In short, first generation e-business solutions, while providing useful ground for cutting the organization's teeth on new technology, often pose more problems than they solve, for example, in terms of decreased customer service and increased cost to the organization. The attraction of exposing existing tried and trusted functionality for use by e-business solutions promises much in the way of addressing the problems of these first generation systems.

5.2.2   Legacy renewal

Exposing functionality from existing systems, databases and packages in the form of services delivered through component interfaces for use by employees (intranet), customers (internet) and partners (extranet) is an approach sometimes referred to as web-enablement. However, except in the simplest of cases, a lot more is involved than simply putting your legacy application on a web browser to make it more widely available. Many companies have discovered this to their cost in the rush to ensure a presence on the web. Indeed I have struggled to buy airline tickets recently through such ill-conceived websites.

In all but the simplest cases, exposing existing business services for use by e-business systems raises integration issues. Even in apparently simple cases, work is often required on the existing software if only to create the necessary plug points or 'componentized interfaces'. At the

Business process integration issues are commonly not thought through. It is important to address existing systems and software packages with respect to their context within business processes

other extreme, we may need to repartition and rework existing systems in order to maintain integrity and ensure the right services are exposed. Yet more significantly, if we are really serious about adaptable software for the internet, we will need to migrate effectively to a set of flexible components; we will need a good component architecture. We use the term 'legacy renewal' rather than web-enablement to convey the fact that this is not a mere 'quick fix'.

5.2.3   Exploiting legacy systems

Let us look at some of the driving forces behind the use of legacy systems as a basis for exposing business services:

- Many organizations want to protect and reuse their existing investments in legacy systems. This often includes significant resources in developing various types of data models and process models. Harvesting of the resultant 'knowledge base' makes good business sense, rather than having to start over.

- The relational databases that underlie most core systems are set to stay for the foreseeable future. Therefore, like it or not, it is important to understand the database structures that will form the storage foundation for any new components, in order to design an effective set of data services as a buffer between the two worlds.

- Costly Y2K projects have produced up-to-date inventory of applications and data that often make use of legacy models. Such organizations are looking for ways to maximize this investment.

- Existing systems and packages that have stood the test of time 'do a job'. They may not do it in the most adaptable and efficient manner. They may be a maintenance nightmare. Nevertheless, they are tried and tested. There is a comfort factor embodied in the slogan 'Better the devil you know'.

In legacy renewal of software, we work to realize value by exposing business services free from the clutter of existing implementation constraints

The fact is that 'legacy' is not a bad term despite the fact that it is often read that way applied in the context of software. A legacy represents something bequeathed by a predecessor that has a value not commonly apparent. There is an onus on the inheritor to do some work to realize the value.

5.2.4   Exploiting software packages

Software packages fall into two categories: legacy software packages and new software packages. Legacy software packages are a special case of legacy systems, but are notoriously more difficult to 'open up'. Package vendors are increasingly recognizing the need to expose interfaces to their products using component standards such as Corba, COM+ and EJB. For example, SAP, Peoplesoft, Oracle and Baan all have initiatives to provide various standard interfaces to existing packaged applications. Many of these packages are themselves following a transition path that means their initial components are in fact wrapped legacy systems. The data models and function catalogues that often accompany the documentation are an important tool for organizations seeking to integrate packages within the context of their application architectures.

Many organizations are still irresistibly attracted to purchasing software packages. This is seen as the only viable alternative to developing from scratch. As more standard interfaces are provided and as their functionality grows richer and customizable, this trend will doubtless continue. However, we need to understand the rationale for e-business improvement and not simply the current technology if the package is to fit the business process, rather than vice versa (Ulrich, 2000).

This reminds me of a situation that I encountered in a large energy company, while analyzing some of their business processes. I came upon a small army of clerks who were busy at their workstations. They would inspect data in one window, drag it on to another window, make some calculations and finally submit the data through another window. On closer analysis, it turned out that what they were actually doing was to extract data from a software package and push it through into various systems. They were not actually producing anything. Their job was to ensure integrity between the packaged applications and the other applications. And the software package had been purchased four years previously on the assumption that it would hugely increase productivity! It is vital that we learn from such lessons.

> Those who cannot remember the past are condemned to repeat it.
>
> George Santayana

5.2.5   Enterprise application integration

EAI technologies have their roots in much earlier techniques for developing integrated systems, explored in domains such as application tool integration (Linthicum, 1999). The key concept is connectors.[1] Connector technologies offer mapping and translation facilities that allow different legacy systems and packages to communicate and share data. A common way to achieve this is to apply an exchange notation such as XML (see Appendix 1, Section A1.1.6), together with agreed data definitions for the information exchanged.

The attraction of EAI for e-business is exposure of tried and tested shared information and services. For example, a bond trade may touch up to twenty different systems before it is cleared.

However, true EAI, as opposed to use of an EAI tool, involves more than buying an EAI product to supply message broking services.

> Our new millennium's resolution should be 'to stop writing legacy systems'. While EAI tools do make legacy applications more easily accessible, it does not make them any more maintainable or allow them to be upgraded and replaced piece by piece.
>
> L. Wilkes January, 2000

Information must flow from legacy systems and software packages to an e-business system such that the customer receives accurate, up-to-date information. Yet more challenging, information entered via the web must be captured such that integrity of existing systems and databases is ensured. More than that, the e-business system soon extends the scope of what is currently possible with existing systems. For example, customers need the ability to track the status of orders or amend them without having to telephone the call centre. Again, a key element of the e-business solution has to be an effective payment mechanism.

---

1. In fact, there are a number of approaches to application integration (Gilpin, 1999), though connectors are the most typical.

Traditional payment mechanisms will no longer do. Competitors may have much faster turn-round that forces the organization to partner with third parties for inventory supplies. This raises issues with integration of the supply chain to the e-business system.

At the same time, new offerings from the maturing component marketplace from component frameworks to virtual services cannot be ignored. These too must be integrated into the overall software landscape, such that the lessons learned from prior installations are gleaned for current projects. The integration overall issues are well treated elsewhere (Brown, 1999).

With the escalation of such concerns paralleling the rapid pace of change of technologies, the CIO is, once again, in the classic dilemma. EAI tools may provide useful 'gluing' technology, but do not help me choose which systems to integrate and when? If I wait too long to decide, then we will lose customers and market share to our more advanced competitors. If I choose too soon I risk selecting the wrong legacy systems or software packages. This will result in wasted effort, expensive maintenance and delays while the systems are integrated.

5.3   Approaches for integration

5.3.1   Architecture for integration

In Chapter 3 we considered how a component architecture provides a framework for addressing integration issues and for handling change. The component architecture provides a frame of reference for integration projects which work 'under the covers' to provide business capability to fit the business process, rather than vice versa. And at a more tactical level, techniques such as wrapping and adapting help to reuse existing functionality, but in a way which is adaptable to unforeseen change.

The EAI software provides the middleware, the tactical wiring to hook disparate systems together. Figure 5.1 illustrates the role of the EAI software with respect to our earlier view of architecture (see Section 3.3.5). The component architecture provides the strategic set of interfaces that are to provide business capabilities and identifies implementation dependencies to invoke the integrated legacy and package services. An insurance policy is provided for future possible replacement of the EAI solutions with newer solutions, perhaps provisioned as virtual services from a service provider or maybe extended from interfaces provided by a component framework, subjects to which we return in Chapter 7.

The separation of interface and implementation allows the legacy software to be unplugged in graduated fashion, and new solutions plugged in, as they become available

5.3.2   Strategic versus tactical integration

The e-business process improvement plan identifies 'to be' business processes that are strategically important and determines the degree of commonality across those business processes. At the same time legacy systems and software packages

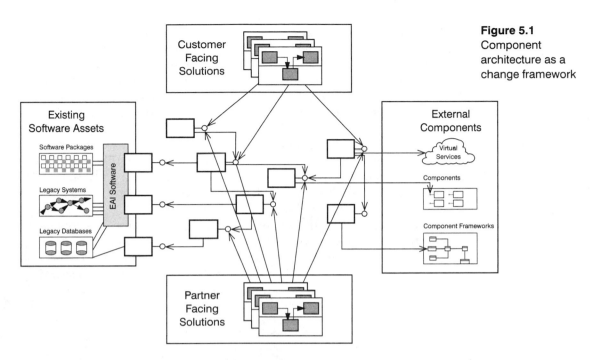

Figure 5.1
Component
architecture as a
change framework

are pinpointed and catalogued as part of the 'as is' business process model. The e-business process improvement plan should outline how the organization intends to migrate from existing to target business models, and the part that existing legacy systems and software packages are to play in this process.

Architecture planning provides the overall context for integration projects. Integration projects may be driven in two ways: strategically, top-down from architecture planning, or tactically, as a result of reuse needs identified in solution projects and filtered down through component provisioning, as indicated in Figure 5.2.

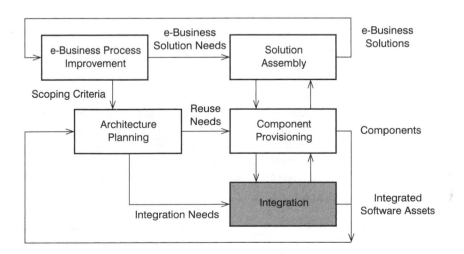

Figure 5.2
Integration in context
of the track-based
process pattern

The strategic approach drills down into the existing software architectures that support the 'as is' business models and analyzes the differences with the proposed enterprise component architecture. The amount of work involved depends on the size and complexity of the organization, but can be significant and therefore requires careful justification. The strategic approach should therefore be reserved for key legacy systems likely to yield fruitful business capabilities.

The tactical approach works bottom-up in response to requirements identified in solution projects. It emphasizes the need to try to maximize return on investment from integration projects. For example, it might be the case that several solution projects identify a need for a common client access service. The tactical approach to integration is lightweight and incremental and therefore lends itself well to fast time to market needs of e-business.

Regardless of whether the approach is strategic or tactical, the component architecture provides the overall context for the integration project. The gaps between current and target models are assessed at increasing levels of detail as the project unfolds. New and changed services are added where necessary to meet the needs of our target models. Depending on the results of the gap analysis, there are two basic approaches to the integration project:

1 Non-invasive Existing business services are abstracted from the legacy system for use by business processes. EAI software is used to integrate existing legacy services via connectors. Wrappers or adapters may also be used, normally as part of a more tactical solution.

2 Invasive Legacy system candidates for migration to CBD are pinpointed and partitioned with respect to our overall CBD architecture into candidate high-level components. Business rule mining techniques and legacy models (Allen and Frost, 1998) are used to extract the required functionality.

5.4   Example: Migrating to e-business

Imagine a vehicle hire firm that can see distinct advantages of using the internet to improve its business. The firm has an established clientele but is threatened by new leaner and meaner internet start-ups. At the same time Harry's Vehicle Hire (HVH) has considerable investments in previous generation technologies in the form of back-end systems, including packages and databases. The business leaders at Harry's are keen to preserve their investments in these existing assets in a way that allows them to move forward with e-business. EAI software is viewed as a tactical measure for leveraging this objective within the overall strategic umbrella of a component architecture. At the same time, there is increased recognition of the importance of component frameworks and virtual services provided over the internet. Overall Harry's business leaders understand the need for an approach to e-business process improvement that balances long-term need for sound software architecture with short-term demand for fast results.

The case study is illustrative of the steps involved in migrating in low-risk fashion to increased e-business capability using component-based techniques.

Illustrative is the keyword here. In particular, we attempt to show how the modeling techniques described in Appendix 2, can be applied in a real-life setting. Many variations from these steps are possible as dictated by the specific context within which the project takes place, for example, goals, skills, timescales and available assets. In particular, in this case study we concentrate on the earlier stages of the project from business modeling to interface specification. These stages are emphasized because they provide the groundwork for a CBD project, yet are frequently the most misunderstood and misapplied.

If you are unfamiliar with any of the modeling techniques employed in this case study, you are advised to refer to Appendix 2 where you will find guidance and help

5.4.1   e-Business process improvement planning

Let us start with some background on the business context:

- Harry's Vehicle Hire (HVH) is part of Harry's Enterprises.
- Currently there are ten HVH branches with expansion plans for four more in the next eighteen months.
- Other services within Harry's Enterprises involve valet and chauffeur services, as well as fleet hire.

There is a good overall business case for introducing e-business solutions. IT, particularly e-business, is recognized as a central enabler of the business strategy. The main business drivers are:

- Increased sales.
- Increased profit ratio of operation.
- Provide competitive edge.
- Cost savings.

The e-business process plan identifies the following supporting goals and underlying business strategies:

- Process efficiency and operational service to the customer
  - Streamline dated business processes.
  - Gain and present consistent view of customers.
- Agile adaptation to business and technology change
  - Outsource commodity business processes.
  - Nurture value-added business processes.
- Improved market reach and growth
  - Extend scope of business processes to capture new markets.
  - Partner with other firms to provide total services.

The organization flow diagram shown in Figure 5.3 indicates the context for business improvement.

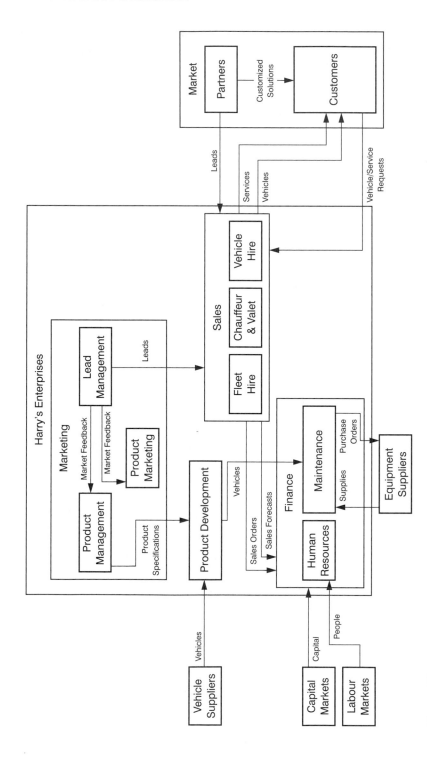

Figure 5.3
Organization flow diagram

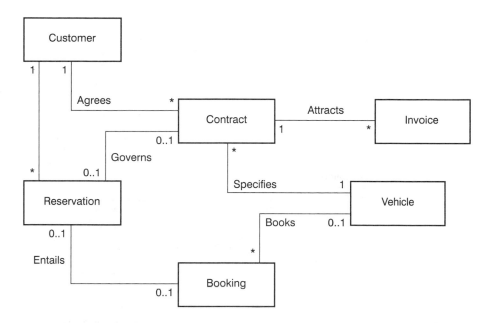

Figure 5.4
Business concept
diagram

It is decided to focus on Vehicle Hire, the core business of HVH as well as the one in most need of improvement.

The main concepts in the business domain are sketched out as shown in Figure 5.4.

A business process flow diagram is created for the current hiring process, as shown in Figure 5.5. The objective is to remove any inefficiencies from the current process, but to leave it intact. At the same time, we will look at how a new internet solution can be built in parallel. This is seen as a low-risk strategy.

Note that had we wished to adopt a more radical approach, we might have built the current business process flow diagram after creating a future business process flow diagram. The advantage with that approach is that it does not run the risk of constraining thinking about new business solutions in existing terms – particularly key, in radical re-engineering projects.

The existing process can be immediately improved by consolidating the verification activity within the sales activity, thus removing the reservation clerk from the process.

Introducing a new internet process to enable customers to reserve vehicles directly is obviously in line with the business case. This opens up the market as well as by-passing the manual selling process, thus improving process efficiency. The future hiring process is shown in Figure 5.6.

5.4.2   Scoping software requirements

The business process analysis provides an excellent starting point for scoping use cases. In the majority of cases, atomic processes will map to single use cases.

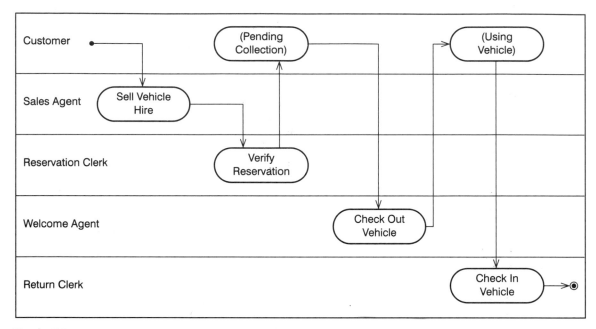

Figure 5.5
Process flow diagram for existing vehicle hire process

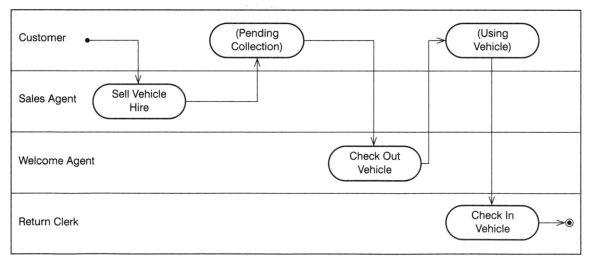

Figure 5.6
Process flow diagram for future vehicle hire process

We simply add another swim-lane depicting the software and add use cases to that lane as shown in Figure 5.7.

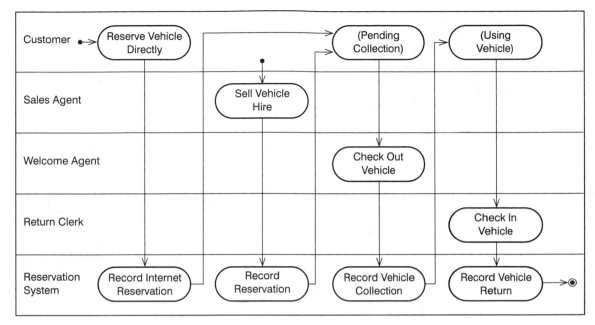

Figure 5.7
Process flow diagram for future vehicle hire process, showing software services

We document software requirements for Vehicle Hire as shown below:

- **Functional requirements:**
  - Accurate booking of vehicles hired by customers, in particular there have been problems with booking failures and double bookings.
  - Accurate and timely operation of telephone reservation, collection and return of vehicles, currently this takes too long and is inefficient.
  - Immediate access to quotations and hire rates for sales agents.
  - Adaptability to cater for internet reservations.
  - Capability of extension to hire business in general.
- **Non-functional requirements:**
  - Business: reduce reservation call time by half.
  - Availability: maximum 60 minutes downtime per month during opening hours.
  - Performance: response time < 5 seconds for all transactions.
  - Integrity: 100% accuracy of financial data.
  - Security: only authorized employees can update or view account and customer information.
- **Project requirements:**
  - Must be built incrementally, with tested increments delivered every four months or less.

The main actors and use cases are identified and diagrammed as shown in Figure 5.8. Each use case is described in terms of its intent and its steps; examples follow.

Figure 5.8
Use case diagram

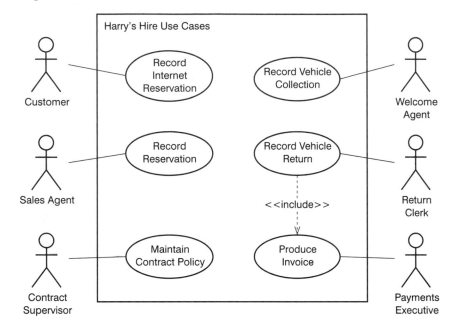

Use case 5.1   Record reservation

Use Case Name	Record Reservation
Use Case Intent	To reserve the most appropriate and available vehicle for a customer.
Use Case Description	

1. Establish party

   A party search is used to find customer details and check credit (using existing databases) for confirmation with customer.

   If the customer wishes, the customer details are entered for future internet access.

2. Establish hire requirements

   Vehicle types are listed by requested location and a vehicle type selected. Vehicle type details including hire rate are agreed. The reservation period is entered and suitable vehicles are shown for the period.

3. Secure reservation

   A vehicle is selected and booked for the requested period. A reservation is made, securing the vehicle for the customer. The reservation number is displayed.

Use case 5.2   Record internet reservation

Use Case Name	Record Internet Reservation
Use Case Intent	To reserve the most appropriate and available vehicle for an internet customer.
Use Case Description	

1. Establish hire requirements

   Vehicle types are listed by requested location and a vehicle type selected. Vehicle type details including hire rate are agreed. The reservation period is entered and suitable vehicles are shown for the period.

2. Establish customer

   A customer password is used to find customer details for confirmation with customer.

   Otherwise new customer details, including password, are entered.

3. Secure reservation

   A vehicle is selected and booked for the requested period. A reservation is made, securing the vehicle for the customer. The reservation number is displayed.

Use case 5.3   Record vehicle collection

Use Case Name	Record Vehicle Collection
Use Case Intent	To support collection of a vehicle by a customer according to reservation.
Use Case Description	

1. Identify reservation

   Reservation number is used to find reservation for customer.

2. Stipulate contract

   Contract details are agreed and set up. Contract number is displayed.

3. Agree handover details

   An entry sheet is printed showing vehicle mileage, service details, valet and safety details. The contract is agreed and the entry sheet printed for signing by customer. The contract is closed.

Use case 5.4   Record vehicle return

Use Case Name	Record Vehicle Return
Use Case Intent	To support return of a vehicle by a customer according to contract.
Use Case Description	

1. Identify contract

   Contract number is used to find the contract.

2. Check compliance to contract

   A return checklist (keys, documents) is checked. Return information is entered, including any damage or accident details.

3. Calculate settlement amount.

   The return mileage and deposit is used to calculate the final balance for invoicing.

4. Produce invoice

   An invoice creation service is invoked. The invoice is printed.

Note that the traditional and internet reservation use cases are in fact very similar. This should come as no surprise as what we are concerned with here is largely an online presence based upon existing functionality. However, the internet reservation is sequenced differently and contains no online credit check at this stage; credit is checked off-line prior to vehicle pick-up. We will need to address that shortcoming in a subsequent iteration.

Knowledge of system requirements and use case descriptions is used to refine the business concept diagram to a business type diagram adding attributes and responsibilities (see Figure 5.9).

Because of the amount of detail on the above diagram, it is often useful to suppress detail for presentation purposes (see Figure 5.10).

5.4.3   Building an enterprise component architecture

We build an initial enterprise component architecture both top-down using business knowledge within the scope identified as part of the e-business process improvement plan, and bottom-up using knowledge of possible legacy assets and software packages impacted by the e-business process improvement plan.

The top-down approach is aimed at achieving maximum adaptability for the business processes, in this case the Vehicle Hire process, within the constraints of the overall provisioning strategy. The complementary bottom-up approach

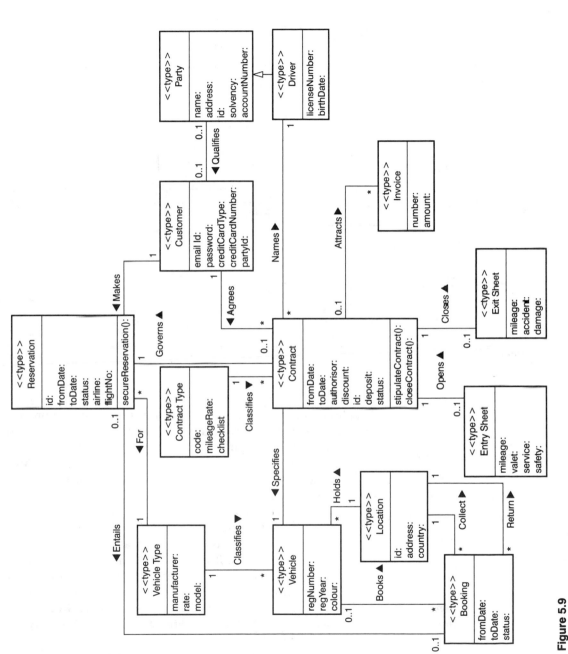

Figure 5.9
Business type diagram

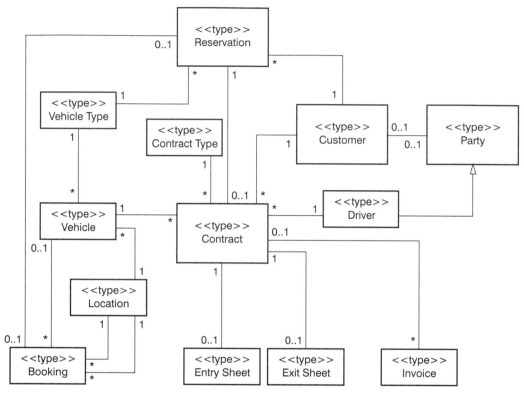

Figure 5.10
Business type diagram

aims for ease of application integration. In this case, a customer integration project has been initiated from the e-business process improvement plan with regard to the requirement for a unified view of customers.

In order to obtain results quickly and avoid 'analysis paralysis', it is important to keep the enterprise component architecture to a reasonably high level.

The enterprise component architecture works at 'city planning' level, in contrast to the project component architecture, which works at individual building level

We focus on components that are likely to be shared between Vehicle Hire and other solutions. The scope can be extended and evolved as practical project feedback is received. Invoices, Requisitions, Parties and Vehicles are core business domain components that we declare as part of the enterprise component architecture as shown in Figure 5.11. Schedules, Code Tables, Address Formatting and User Security are business infrastructure component frameworks. Error Handler and Recovery are technical infrastructure components.

Address Formatting is used exclusively by Parties, at this stage. The other infrastructure components (shown along the bottom of the diagram) are used globally by any business component; by convention their client dependencies are omitted from the diagram.

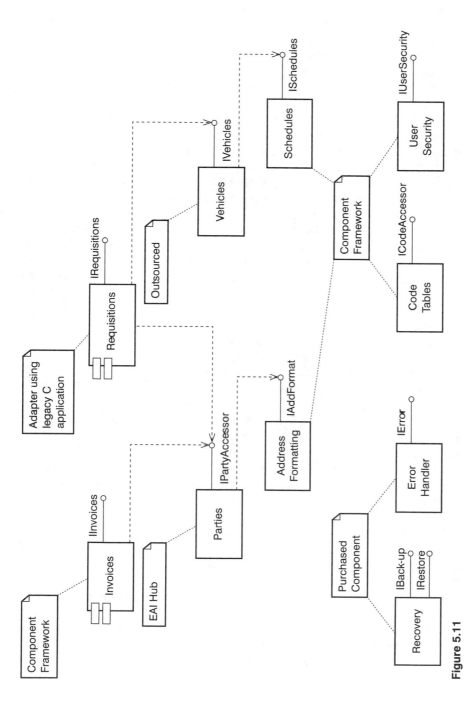

Figure 5.11
Enterprise component architecture diagram

Note that, at this early stage, we want to keep our design as open as possible. Component implementations, rather than component specifications are used for the dependent components, which are the ones most likely to change. These can always be 'promoted' to component specifications later on if and when things have stabilized. We only settle on component specifications for the really stable base infrastructure components.

In parallel, we also approach bottom-up by assessing existing software assets. In particular, if reuse of a particular legacy database or software package is mandated up-front, then it is important to declare this within the overall architecture. In the example, the overall provisioning strategy is to reuse existing applications and to purchase package software where possible. Software is only to be custom-built where there is a significant business advantage to be gained. For example, Parties is an existing EAI project that will integrate Party information using two existing customer data management systems and a separate customer database as shown below.

In order to keep our design as open as possible it is decided to restrict parties to a single simple inquiry interface (IPartyAccessor). Further interfaces can be added as necessary later on, once the wider picture becomes clearer in the light of project delivery and business feedback. In particular, it is anticipated that Harry's Enterprises may well use customer relationship management (CRM) software (see Chapter 6) to personalize its e-business, but is postponing a decision until the market for these packages has matured somewhat! The organization remembers only too well its experiences with an ERP package that had to be abandoned because of the disruption it caused.

If the EAI software can provide standard component interfaces then, it can be modeled as a component implementation that conforms to a component specification. On the other hand, where the EAI software uses non-component APIs, then a further component implementation may then be designed to present the unified service through a standard interface within the component architecture. The example shown in Figure 5.12 assumes the latter case. Note that it may equally be decided to use the APIs of the EAI software directly, as non-component interfaces. In certain circumstances that may be a good approach, especially short term. However, in this book we are interested in a component-based approach.

There are several other integration requirements. The Invoices and Schedules components offer interfaces acquired (for possible extension) from an external component framework. Requisitions is to use a single legacy C application, for which a bespoke adapter is to be designed.

The remaining components shown in the enterprise component architecture are to be provisioned externally. The Vehicles component is to be outsourced to a component supplier. Address Formatting, Code Tables and User Security are to be extended from a component framework. Finally, Error Handler Recovery is to be purchased as a standard component.

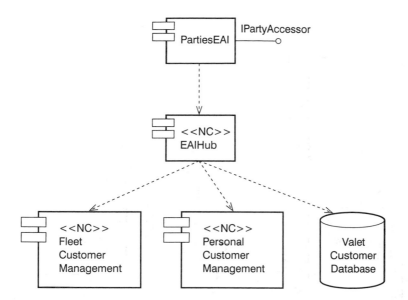

Figure 5.12
Parties component
dependencies

5.4.4   First increment: Rapid delivery

The first solution increment is aimed at streamlining the reservations business process and establishing reuse of existing system services. However, there is no internet implementation involved – at this stage we are preparing the ground to minimize risk. The example assumes that an application is to be developed with maximum reuse of existing components, but with no requirement to deliver the solution itself as a component. The prime driver of such projects is a tight deadline in which to deliver useful business functionality. There is simply no time to engineer interfaces for the application itself. This is a situation many developers find themselves in today.

However, even on such 'tight projects', it is still useful to perform a limited degree of component-based analysis to ensure the right components are being reused and as an insurance policy for the future. Such applications are commonly the subjects of upgrades, extensions and further variants. Once the application has been delivered successfully, it may be possible to upgrade the application to the status of component. The next section describes that situation.

We need to identify all the interfaces that will be used to assemble the solution. This involves identifying the dependencies between these interfaces, and scoping the part of the solution that must be 'hand-built', either as new components or simply as client code, in the interests of rapid development.

In our example three existing interfaces (IVehicles, IInvoices and IPartyAccessor) are identified, leaving the business types Contract Type, Reservation, Contract, Entry Sheet, Exit Sheet and Customer within the scope of the solution build. A useful technique is to correlate business types with candidate interfaces, using overlays to suggest interfaces using an interface responsibility map, as illustrated in Figure 5.13. The reader should understand this is not a formal diagram – it is intended to illustrate the thought process involved in the manner of a whiteboard discussion.

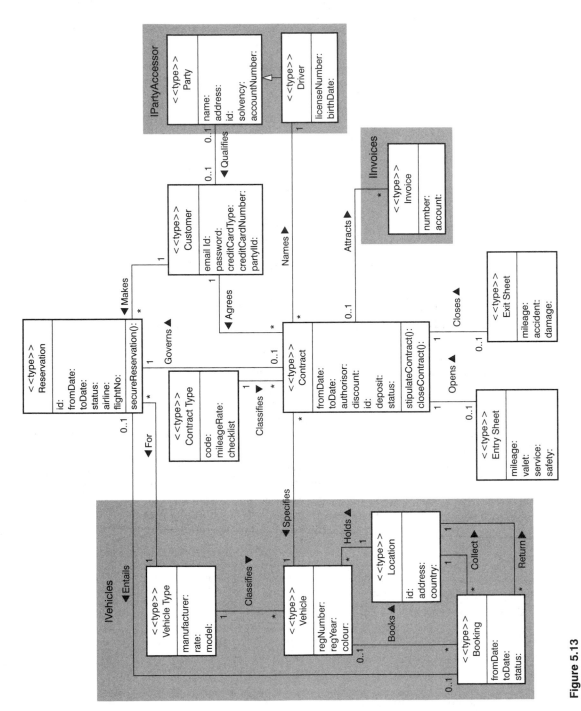

Figure 5.13
Interface responsibility map

The three interfaces shown are suggested from the enterprise component architecture and provisioning strategy. We will be applying gap analysis to make sure these interfaces are adequate for providing the first increment with appropriate information and services.

Use cases and use case refinement maps are used alongside the business type model to help identify interface responsibilities. They are also used to help identify associated existing systems and interfaces and assist with gap analysis. Reusing prototypes from previous projects and modifying these to meet the requirements under study can also be particularly fruitful for identifying existing interfaces.

A use case refinement map, shown in Figure 5.14, is used to analyze the use case steps of the non-internet reservation with respect to the interfaces identified on the responsibility map.

The use case steps can be refined a little more to expose the need for specific services as shown in Figure 5.15. Establish Party invokes the listParties and identifyParty services from the existing IPartyAccessor interface, but also requires a way to set up the customer details (for future internet usage). The Customer type is the logical home for this service, but we do not have any existing services here. Customer lies within the scope of the solution build.

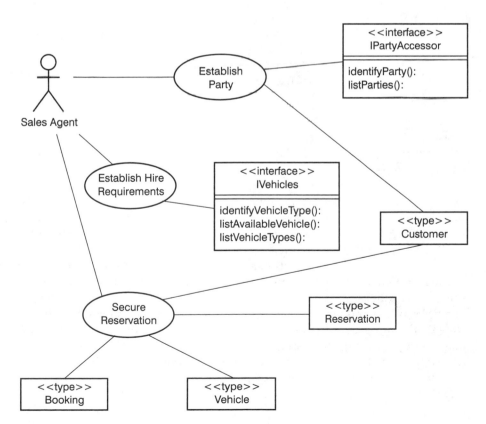

Figure 5.14
Use case refinement map (non-internet reservation)

Figure 5.15
Further refinement of
non-internet
reservation

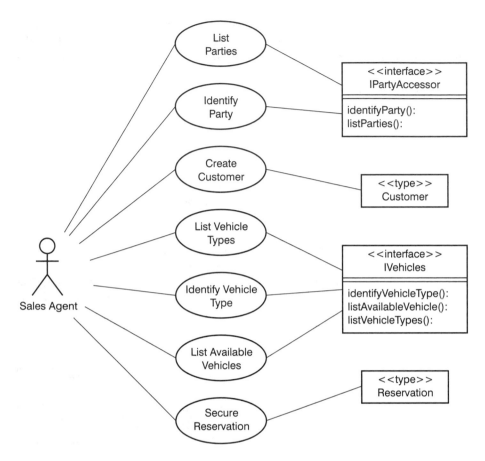

Establish Hire Requirements is supported by the listVehicleTypes, identifyVehicleType and listAvailableVehicles services from the existing IVehicles interface.

Secure Reservation requires a corresponding service and although there is no existing interface to supply it, we did in fact identify secureReservation as a possible service of the Reservation type when we scoped the software requirements and created an initial business type diagram. Analysis of the use case has thus confirmed the need for the secureReservation service!

To summarize, Secure Reservation and Create Customer lie within the scope of the first increment solution build. Further analysis and design is required on these to help develop the increment. We recommend using object-oriented principles (Allen and Frost, 1998), but exclude the details for reasons of scope. Note that in using an object-oriented design the types within the solution scope map to implementation classes; the implementation classes Customer and Reservation supply createCustomer and secureReservation respectively.

A first-cut project architecture is prepared, as shown in Figure 5.16.

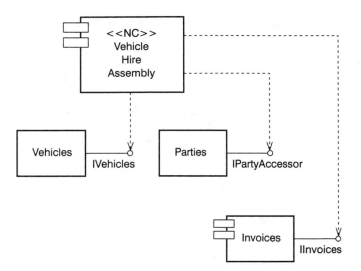

Figure 5.16
Project architecture diagram

User interface prototypes are created. The implementation involves user interface design, coding, assembly and various testing stages, including integration testing with Parties, Vehicles and Invoices components.

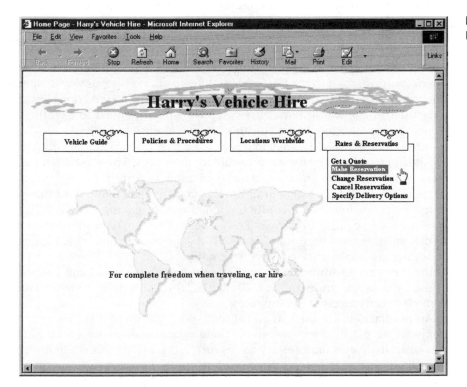

Figure 5.17
HVH home page

5.4.5   Second increment: e-Business solution

An increasingly common approach in organizations that do not want to run the risk of provisioning components from scratch is to evolve software to component status Recall from Section 2.3.1, this is sometimes referred as the 'bottom-up' or 'components as you go' approach.

In other cases, projects may start with a much broader brief: to expose common requirements across several business areas without the benefit of previously developed software. Again recall from Section 2.3.1, this is sometimes referred as the 'top-down' or 'CAV' approach.

Our example illustrates a typical mix of the top-down and bottom-up approaches that evolve the first solution iteration to component status.

We will focus again on reservations. A parallel project (to which we will return at the end of this section) is initiated to ensure that contracts are sufficiently generic for use in wider (as yet unknown) contexts; for example, in Chapter 6 we will consider e-business solutions for vehicle collection and return.

The home page for HVH is shown in Figure 5.17. We have kept the design deliberately simplified and Spartan so as not to distract from the modeling issues. This figure is based on the models created thus far. Within Rates and Reservations, the user is invoking Make Reservation which represents the Record Internet Reservation use case.

We construct an initial web page for the internet reservations use case as shown in Figure 5.18. This figure illustrates an existing customer securing a reservation after establishing the hiring requirements (step 1 of the use case) and customer's details (step 2).

We draw a use case refinement map for the internet use case as shown in Figure 5.19. As a first cut, two new interfaces ICustomers and IReservations are introduced to supply the createCustomer and secureReservation services. These interfaces correspond to the Customer and Reservation types already defined in the previous increment. The interfaces ICustomers and IReservations are similarly used in the non-internet use case. We will now need to examine the component architecture to see how this idea works out.

Interface responsibility modeling is applied to refine the initial component architecture and arrive at a set of candidate interfaces. These candidate interfaces will be refined into interface type models. Interface responsibility modeling is far from a mechanical process that involves some hard thinking, weighing up various, often conflicting, factors and making trade-offs. Let us consider how we might improve our example architecture to be more adaptable. In particular, we will need to think about how previously built client assembly code might be engineered to component status.

Interfaces are identified using both the business type model and knowledge of use cases as shown in Figure 5.20. Earlier, three interfaces were identified: IVehicles, IPartyAccessor and IInvoices.

An interface, ICustomers, is added for capture of internet customer details (for example, e-mail id and password). There are two main reasons for this. First, it is unrealistic and unnecessary to capture full party details – a lightweight interface is needed to support the new e-business system and data capture needs

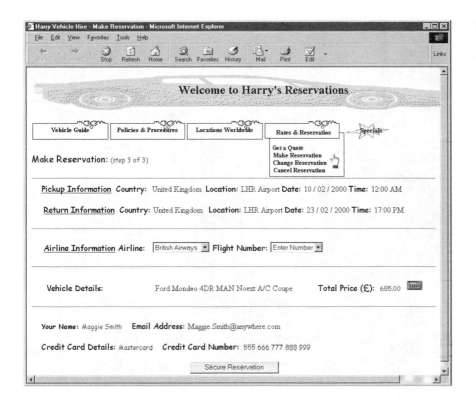

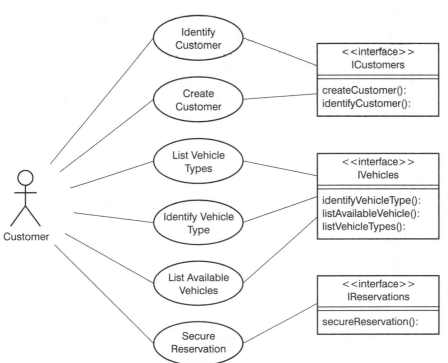

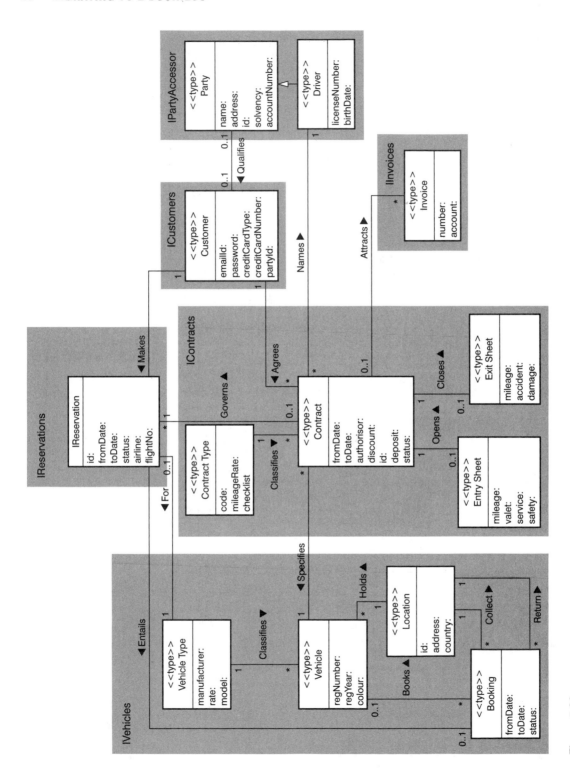

Figure 5.20
Interface responsibility map

to be minimal. Second, as more is learnt about e-business, so further interfaces can be added to support the customer focus that is so important for e-business; for example, in Chapter 6 we will look at personalization.

A separate interface, IReservations, is introduced to cater for all types of reservation, including the new requirement to process reservations over the internet. Although there is just one business type, Reservation, that needs to be managed here, it is very much a core type of the Vehicle Hire business. Any business rules that are local to the reservation business are well catered for by a separate reservation interface. Reservation has structural dependencies on Vehicle Type and Customer that are reflected in single multiplicity associations to these two types. It is therefore worth considering including reservation management as a responsibility of the IVehicles or ICustomers interfaces. However, it is decided not to do this, as it would compromise the stated requirement for flexibility.

Contract has structural dependencies on Vehicle, Driver and Reservation that are reflected in single multiplicity associations to these types. It is therefore worth considering including contract management as a responsibility of the IVehicles, ICustomers or IReservations interfaces. Using IVehicles or ICustomers would place a circular dependency (something to be avoided) on IReservations. So it is decided not to do that.

We might instead consider including contract management as a responsibility of IReservations, either collapsing the IContracts interface into IReservations or allowing IReservations to delegate responsibility to IContracts. However, the structure of the business type model suggests a separate IContracts interface to cater for the use cases Collect Vehicle, Return Vehicle and Maintain Contract Policy. Note that although Collect Vehicle and Return Vehicle are superficially 'about vehicle', their main intent centres on contractual matters. Moreover, Contract Type, Entry Sheet and Exit Sheet are all exclusively related to Contract: the four types are cohesive within the domain of contracts. Finally there is an extensibility requirement to cater for all types of hire suggesting a de-coupling of contract and reservation management. Any business rules that are local to the contract side of the business can be encapsulated through a separate interface. So, on balance it is decided to create a separate IContracts interface.

Note that the responsibilities secureReservation (that we had allocated to Reservation) and closeContract and stipulateContract (that we had allocated to Contract) have been removed from the interface responsibility map as these are now provided by the IReservations and IContracts interfaces respectively.

Interface dependencies can be usefully modeled using an interface dependency diagram, prior to packaging into component specifications. However, in this example it is decided to group interfaces 1-1 with component specifications so the component architecture is modeled directly. Note that on a real project, it is likely that each component specification will provide at least two interfaces as we are likely to need both instance and manager interfaces (see Appendix 2, Section A2.5); the example assumes only manager interfaces.

Clearly, the decisions made in creating the project architecture have an impact on the enterprise architecture, which must be assessed and verified. The enterprise component architecture evolves as shown in Figure 5.21. Note in

Figure 5.21
Refined enterprise
architecture diagram
(partial)

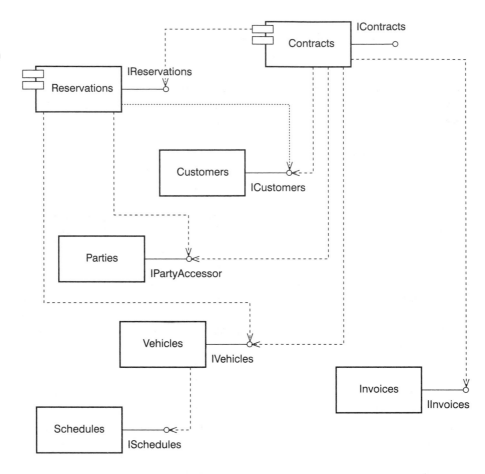

particular that if design and implementation of Vehicles is to be outsourced as indicated in the first pass of the enterprise component architecture, then the company designing the Vehicles component must understand they are constrained by the dependency of Vehicles on ISchedules.

Collaboration diagrams are used alongside the interface responsibility maps and architecture diagrams to examine how best to allocate responsibilities to interfaces. Let us look again at the traditional reservation. The new Reservations interface will take responsibility for handling service requests from the sales agent as shown in Figure 5.22. Responsibilities previously allocated to IPartyAccessor, ICustomers and IVehicles still apply, but as far as reservations are concerned, they are now delegated via IReservations. This provides for centralized control of reservations, while at the same time retaining the flexibility of IPartyAccessor, ICustomers and IVehicles for use in other contexts.

In addition, IVehicles now delegates determining availability and scheduling to ISchedules, though from the point of view of clients of the interface, its behaviour is just the same as before. This provides a good, even distribution of responsibilities.

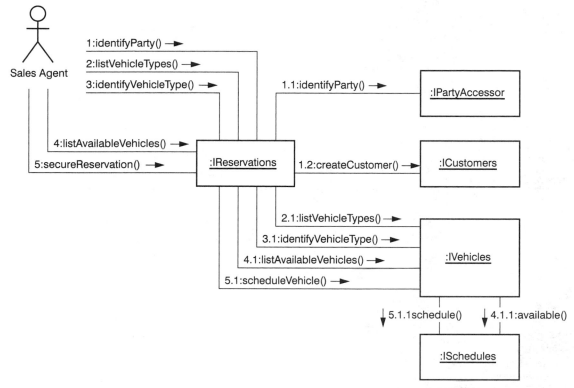

Figure 5.22
Collaboration diagram for non-internet reservation (normal course)

Similarly, a collaboration diagram is constructed for the internet reservation normal scenario as shown in Figure 5.23.

A sequence diagram can be used to examine messaging details, particularly where responsibilities are distributed across different components. For example, secureReservation involves invoking the schedule service from IVehicles, and an internal operation, createReservation (which is implemented using a Reservations class as shown in Figure 5.24).

Recall from our earlier discussion (at the start of this section) that a separate project was to work in parallel with the reservations project on the contract-related use cases. The collect and return use cases were examined for generic use case steps which were highlighted with <<include>> relationships as shown in Figure 5.25. These use case steps invoke corresponding services on the IContracts interface.

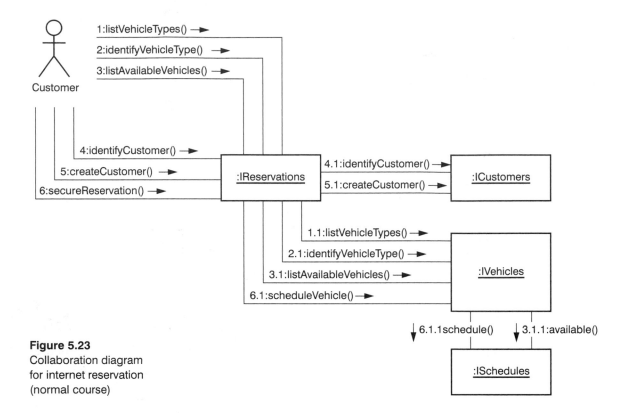

Figure 5.23
Collaboration diagram
for internet reservation
(normal course)

Figure 5.24
Sequence
diagram for
secureReservation

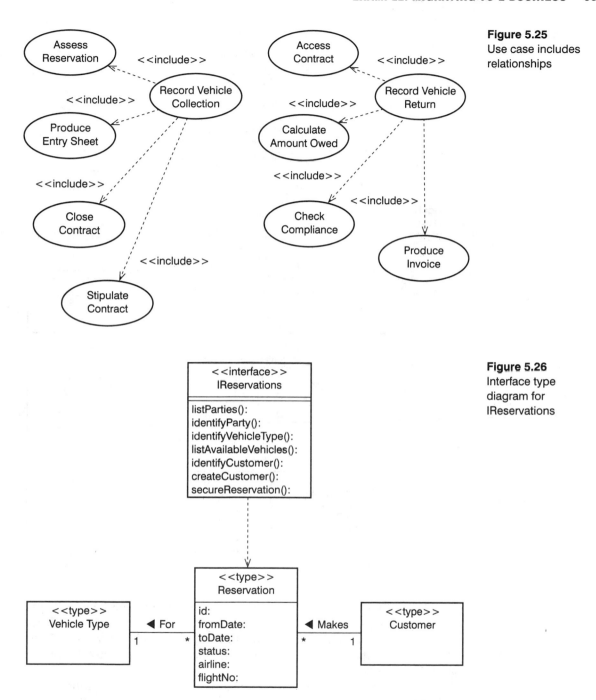

Figure 5.25
Use case includes
relationships

Figure 5.26
Interface type
diagram for
IReservations

Interfaces are specified with the help of interface type diagrams as shown in
Figures 5.26 and 5.27. The interface type diagrams act as information catalogues
of the interfaces.

Figure 5.27
Interface type
diagram for
IContracts

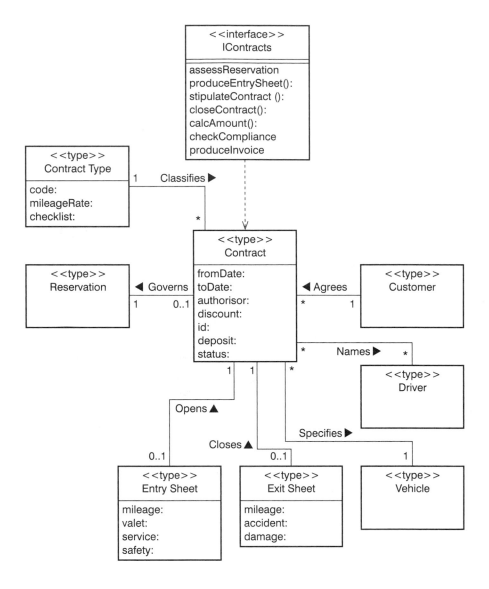

It turns out that contract type maintenance services are used exclusively by a Contract Supervisor role. Also, the Contract Type stands alone without dependencies on any other types. Therefore, an IContractType interface (see Figure 5.28) is added to the Contracts component specification to provide contract maintenance services.

Each interface operation is specified using pre- and post-conditions as illustrated in Figure 5.29.

The Contracts component implementation (see Figure 5.30) conforms to a component specification that offers both the IContracts and IContractType interface specifications.

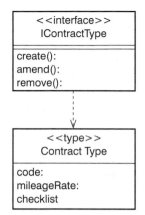

Figure 5.28 Interface type diagram for IContractType

```
createContractType(in n:string, in id:number, s:number, return r:Result)

pre    NO contractType q EXISTS IN contractTypes WITH q.code = id
post   contractType p is CREATED IN contractTypes WITH
       p.code = id
       p.mileage = s
       p.checklist = n

pre    contractType p EXISTS IN contractTypes WITH p.code = id
post   r. errorCode = 12
```

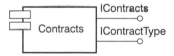

Figure 5.29 Example specification for createContractType

Figure 5.30 Contracts component implementation

The Contracts component specification also includes non-functional requirements and invariants as follows:

- **Non-functional requirements:**
  - Availability: maximum 60 minutes downtime per month during opening hours.
  - Performance: response time < 5 seconds for all transactions.
- **Invariants:**
  - An object of the ContractType type occurring in the interface type model of each interface is always one and the same object for any occurrence of the Contracts component object.

5.5   Summary

In this chapter we have looked at how existing legacy assets, as well as open market components and frameworks, can be used to help migrate the organization toward e-business.

The case study illustrated that we must be prepared to be very pragmatic in allowing existing components and legacy systems to play their part in shaping the component architecture. While we need to fully address business goals and strategies and plan for adaptability, any attempt to create too purist an architecture will almost certainly come to grief on the rocks of reality. We also want to ensure that our component architecture is in fact implementable!

The second major point to note about the case study is that it was based on an evolutionary approach. Deadlines always dominate and strategy has to be balanced with efficient software delivery. By trying to anticipate what might lie around the corner and planning our solutions in architectural context we give ourselves a reasonable chance of evolving solutions to component status when the time is ripe.

It is important to understand that this is not a panacea for all ills; it is one, albeit very useful strategy, in a whole bag of techniques. Perhaps the most important lesson here is to minimize risk by evolving the things we do best.

5.6   References

Allen, P. and Frost, S., 'Using legacy models in CBD', *Component Strategies* November, 1998.

Brown, A., 'Enterprise scale solutions for the internet age: Part 1', *Sterling Software White Paper*, 25 October 1999.

Gilpin, M., 'Internet application integration', *Application Development Trends*, October 1999.

Linthicum, D. S., 'EAI without the hype', *Enterprise Development Journal*, July 1999.

Ulrich, W. M., 'Information Architecture Integration Strategies', *Business-IT Alignment Advisory Service, Executive Report*, vol.3, no.2, Cutter Consortium, January, 2000

Wilkes, L., 'A new millennium resolution – no more legacy systems', *Interact*, www.cbdiforum.com, January 2000.

Realizing e-business 6

6.1   Introduction

One of the characteristics of the early e-business solutions designed to leverage existing services, discussed in Chapter 5, is that manual processes often become replicated as internet processes. New technology is used within the context of an existing mindset. The next 'wave' of e-business systems break this mould. There is a need to rethink the business process and more than that, there is a need to rethink the customer's experience.

This chapter considers how to evolve early e-business systems in the context of the e-business process improvement plan. It is vital to understand this is not a mechanistic process! Our focus is therefore on practical examples. We continue the Harry's scenario to illustrate how to use component modeling techniques to move eastward through the internet spectrum to business process transformation. In particular, we will consider personalization and improving the customer's experience. Finally, we take stock of the Harry's scenario, in terms of 'things to watch' such as adaptability, process integration, CRM and external service integration.

6.2   Welcome back to Harry's

Recall that Harry's Vehicle Hire (HVH) made an early entry into the world of e-commerce by introducing an internet capability for capturing vehicle reservations. HVH achieved this as part of an initiative to improve the existing vehicle hire process. The approach was low risk in that the core of the business process was left intact and iterative development techniques were used to gradually bed the new internet piece in to the overall process. The work was done within the context of a component architecture and solid business analysis allowing for future migration to adaptable e-business.

If you are unfamiliar with any of the modeling techniques employed in this case study you are advised to refer to Appendix 2 where you will find a catalogue of concepts, notations, quick starter guides and tips and hints

It is important to understand that thus far HVH's move to the internet has been very much constrained by existing business processes. In the next phase of activity that proviso no longer applies. Nevertheless, if our analysis in terms of business components was done well, we should expect to build on it. Let us now look at some examples of how HVH, is able to use CBD to build upon this foundation.

6.2.1   e-Business process improvement planning

Following the successful introduction of internet reservations, the e-business process plan is reviewed. The following strategies (shown in italics) are added to the original strategies identified in Chapter 5:

- Process efficiency and operational service to the customer
  - Streamline dated business processes.
  - *Guarantee internet payments.*
  - *Partner with vehicle brokers to enhance scheduling of vehicles.*
  - Gain and present consistent view of customers.
- Agile adaptation to business and technology change
  - Outsource commodity business processes.
  - Nurture value-added business processes.
  - *Personalize service (e.g. Reservations).*
  - *Capture and analyze market feedback.*
- Improved market reach and growth
  - Extend scope of business processes to capture new markets.
  - Partner with other firms to provide total services.
  - *Partner with travel agencies and infomediaries.*[1]
  - Enhanced information access.

At first sight, a sensible strategy appears to be to design e-business solutions in roughly sequential fashion: improve service, adapt it and then grow it. However, the real world is not so kind. The pace of technology change opens up possibilities for adaptation that directly effect operational efficiency. The ability to partner affects the organization's ability to adapt to new situations. Moreover,

---

1. An infomediary helps its internet customers by acting as an information collector to enable them to make decisions; for example, www.autobytel.com.

there may be great organizational pressure to use packages, (for example, CRM products) that directly affects operational service.

In other words, as we saw in Chapter 2, we need to balance strategy with delivery. It is recognized that customer needs are changing and though there are some impressive looking CRM packages that appear to address this area, currently they are expensive and involve considerable compromise to Harry's business processes and component architecture. It is decided therefore to rapidly develop a basic e-business personalization capability and build upon the results. This forms our third increment and addresses the two new strategies in support of the second goal ('Agile adaptation to business and technology change') of the e-business process improvement plan.

As things are changing so fast, we will keep our options open for increment 4 but be mindful of the other goals and strategies, keeping the component architecture as adaptable as we can. We also need to be prepared to change the e-business process plan as the business changes, technology develops and we gain insight from implementing the previous increments.

We need to stay light on our feet: moving to e-business is like re-engineering an airplane while in flight!

6.2.2   Third increment: Personalization

Our third increment focuses on the gap (described below) between the reservations and customer relationship processes. The goal is to provide capture and analysis of customer requirements through the internet in a way that integrates the business processes. At the same time, it is important to prepare the ground for the future with minimal risk, evolving the component architecture, with the business goals of agile adaptability in mind.

Process flow analysis of the reservations process shows that if a vehicle of the right type is not available, that is the end of the process as shown in Figure 6.1.[2] It is also important to question the exceptions. For example, 'Why does the reservation not go any further'? Well, it may be that the customer wants a service that needs a little personalization. For example, a customer wants a different kind of vehicle. Significantly customers are willing to pay a premium for that kind of tailoring. Maybe special terms can be negotiated for such customers. These are certainly questions that at least need to be asked as the company seeks e-business differentiation in a competitive marketplace.

We also need to look at connections across processes as well as within processes. For example, suppose a market analyst is responsible for deciding the vehicle types, which are updated on a regular basis, based on contracts history. Market analysts are provided with information about vehicle types already available that have sold, but do not discover the demand for anything that is not already available! Neither do they find out about those customers who go away when they are told the rate. Significantly, it also turns out that the market

2 This example is based on a similar example drawn from a paper by Richard Veryard (Veryard, 1998).

Figure 6.1
A gap between
processes

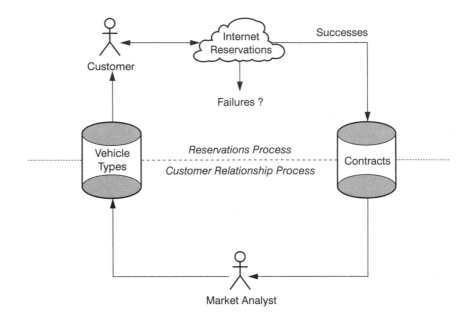

Figure 6.2
Enhanced use case
diagram (internet
reservation)

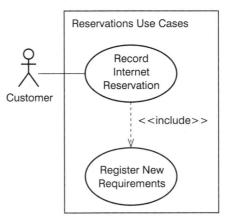

analyst does not find out that there is a huge demand out there for vehicles delivered to the customer's location. How can the reservations and customer relationship processes be better integrated?

Clearly, the requirement capture use case should not be restricted to the reservations process, but should be available in multiple contexts. We therefore model it with an 'includes' relationship as shown in Figure 6.2.

A further use case diagram illustrates the required integration with the customer requirements process as shown in Figure 6.3.

Considering a business as a network of unfolding collaborations, as opposed to a production line, helps with creative thinking. This helps to gain an understanding of inter-process connections, in addition to the intra-process view provided by process flow analysis. Use case modeling used in this way is a useful technique in achieving business process integration.

We also need to make it attractive to customers to tell us what their requirements are. One approach might be to offer the customer options for registering their requirements through the reservations web page offering discount vouchers and free prize draws for registering as illustrated in Figure 6.4. This figure represents the capture of customer information and requirement category. A separate page is used to capture the detailed customer requirements depending on the requirement type.

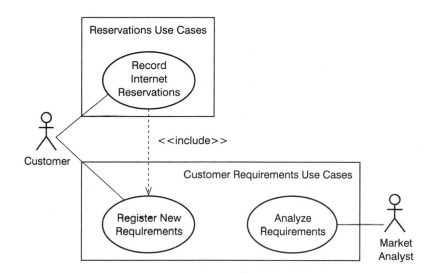

Figure 6.3
Use case diagram showing dual use of requirements capture

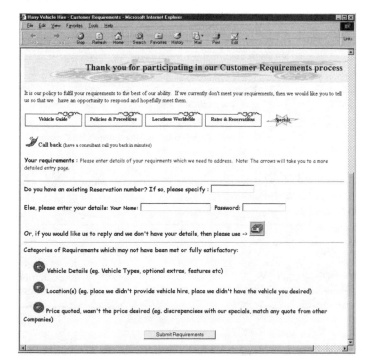

Figure 6.4
Customer requirements web page

The actors customer and market analyst play different roles with respect to the domain of customer requirements. This suggests a separate interface for each, as shown in Figure 6.5.

How would the proposed interfaces fit within the component architecture? Iteration 2, discussed in Chapter 5, revealed the need for a Customer component for e-business solutions. Further analysis on the related area of customer requirements, reveals two further business types, Customer Requirement and Requirement Type, as shown in Figure 6.6. In addition, the type, Vehicle Req Type, records the demand for existing vehicle types.

Interface responsibility modeling is used to examine how the two new interfaces relate the business types, as shown in Figure 6.7.

An interface type diagram for the IRequirementTypes is shown in Figure 6.8. This interface needs to support the Market Analyst with fairly extensive information, even though the example is deliberately simplified in that in reality, a lot more customer information would be required to support sophisticated analysis of requirements. Note in particular that the Customer type is depicted in its entirety, not just its identifying reference, in order to supply the interface with the customer information required.

An interface type diagram for ICustomerRequirement is shown in Figure 6.9. Note that this is an instance interface responsible for capturing instances of CustomerRequirements.

Figure 6.5
Use case diagram
showing possible
interfaces

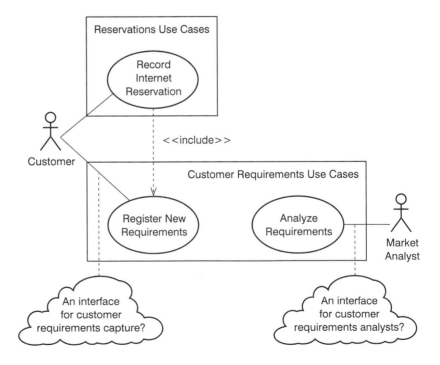

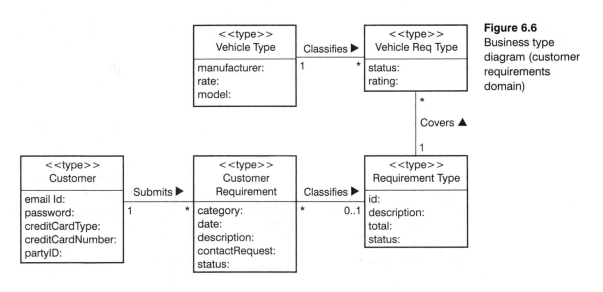

Figure 6.6
Business type diagram (customer requirements domain)

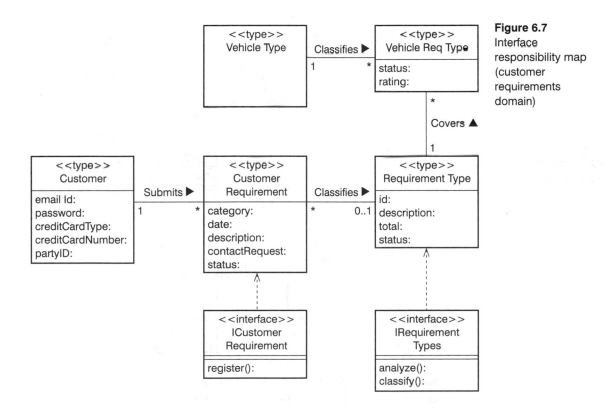

Figure 6.7
Interface responsibility map (customer requirements domain)

Figure 6.8
Interface type
diagram for
IRequirementType

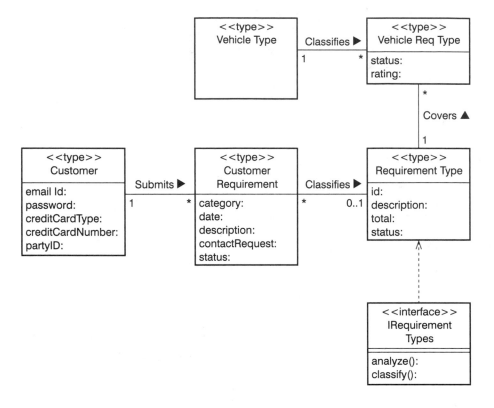

Figure 6.9
Interface type
diagram for
ICustomer
Requirement

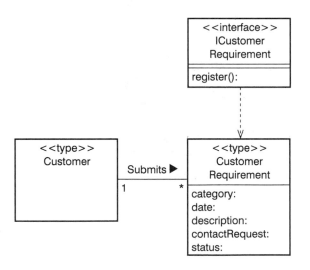

We would like to offer the above two interfaces along with the ICustomers interface within the Customers component specification. By doing that we will achieve a high degree of integration.

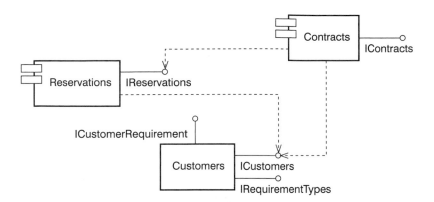

Figure 6.10
Enhanced enterprise component architecture diagram (partial view)

However, we will need to be careful about managing the integrity of information between the different interfaces. For example, the CustomerRequirement type appears in both the IRequirementType and ICustomerRequirements interface diagrams. In the Customers component specification, we will need to state that an object of the Customer Requirements type occurring in the interface type model of each interface is always one and the same object for any occurrence of the Customers component object. Similarly, note that the Customer type is depicted in its entirety in IRequirementTypes, and is referenced in ICustomerRequirement. The Customer type also appears in its entirety in the ICustomers interface type diagram (though this is not shown here). We will therefore need to state that this is always one and the same object for any occurrence of the Customers component object in each of the three interfaces if information is to be kept consistent between interfaces.

The impact on the enterprise component architecture diagram is illustrated in Figure 6.10. Note that the two new interfaces do not constrain either the Reservations or Contracts components. This keeps the architecture open for possible future changes in line with the increment objectives.

6.2.3   Fourth increment: Improving the customer's experience

The personalization increment reveals an interesting business need: customers are willing to pay a premium for vehicles delivered to their door. Delivery drivers are to be equipped with the latest internet-enabled palmtops to record the necessary transactions.

The fourth increment needs to address the delivery requirements as well as the two operational service requirements:

1 Streamlining and guarantee of payments using a credit card.

2 Partnering with vehicle brokers to enable efficient acquisition of vehicles, where not available internally.

We first need to consider how the concept of delivery effects the business type diagram as shown in Figure 6.11.

Figure 6.11
Partial business type
diagram showing
Delivery type

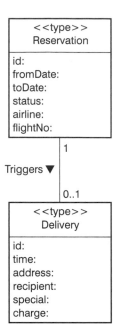

A business process flow diagram is created for the improved internet hiring process as shown in Figure 6.12. Note that the diagram represents a single thread or scenario. Although this diagram shows the process quite well from the customer's viewpoint, unlike the business process flow diagrams based around the existing business processes back in Chapter 6, this diagram does not actually tell us very much about the business process itself. To understand that, we have to start to consider the software requirements. This is because we are crossing the threshold into new terrain.

Software is an integral part of the business process in an e-business system

Again, our business process analysis in terms of atomic processes provides an excellent starting point for scoping use cases. In the majority of cases, atomic processes will map to single use cases. We simply add another swim-lane depicting the software and add use cases to that lane as shown in Figure 6.13.

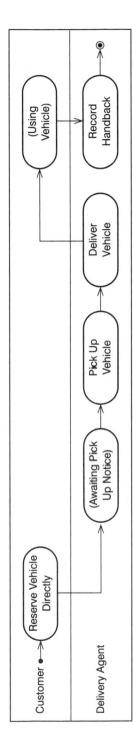

Figure 6.12
Process flow diagram for proposed vehicle hire process

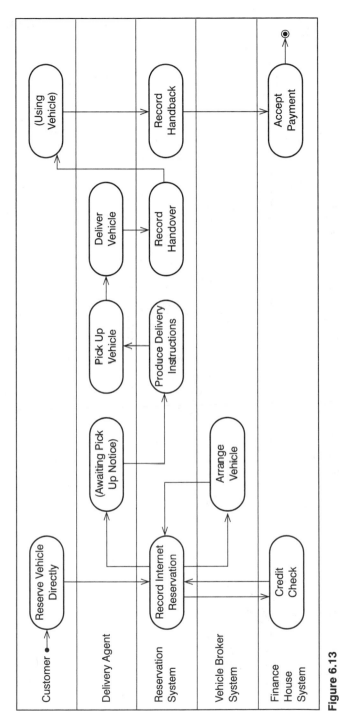

Figure 6.13
Process flow diagram for proposed vehicle hire process showing software services

The main actors and use cases are identified as shown in Figure 6.14.

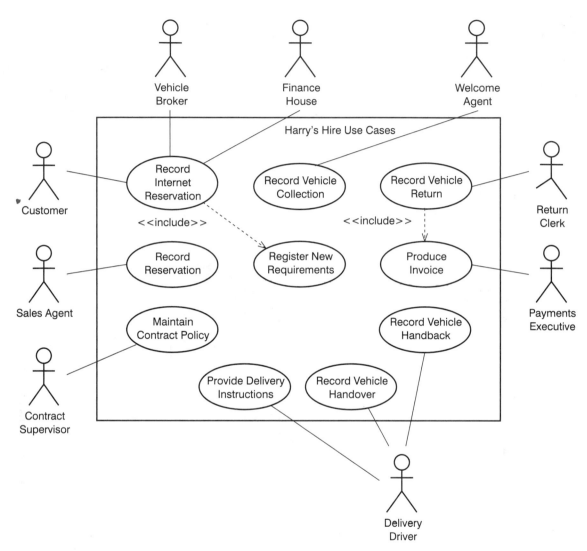

Figure 6.14
Use case diagram for vehicle hire process

The Record Internet Reservation use case from Chapter 5 is changed to reflect the new requirements to accept credit card and delivery instructions. Where deliveries are required, the entry sheets are now printed at the start of the day for the delivery drivers to take to the customers for signing.

Use case 6.1   Record internet reservation

Use Case Name	Record Internet Reservation
Use Case Intent	To reserve the most appropriate and available vehicle for an internet customer.
Use Case Description	

1. Establish hire requirements

   Vehicle types are listed by requested location and a vehicle type selected. Vehicle type details including hire rate are agreed. The reservation period is entered, and suitable vehicles are shown for the period.

2. Establish customer

   A customer password is used to find customer details for confirmation with customer.

   Otherwise new customer details, including password, are entered.

   A credit card transaction is created for the reservation to be secured.

3. Secure reservation

   The vehicle is booked for the requested period. A reservation is made, securing the vehicle for the customer. The reservation number is displayed.

4. If delivery is required

   Delivery address, time and driver's name are entered. The delivery charge is calculated and if acceptable the delivery is submitted.

An option is provided for the customer to enter specific requirements or preferences.

Use case 6.2   Produce delivery instructions

Use Case Name	Produce Delivery Instructions
Use Case Intent	To produce a daily schedule of vehicle delivery instructions.
Use Case Description	

1. At the start of the day

   Identify deliveries to be made for the day.

2. For each delivery identified

   Contract details are set up, including contract number.

   The delivery instruction (together with entry sheet for signing) is printed.

Use case 6.3   Record vehicle handover

Use Case Name	Record Vehicle Handover
Use Case Intent	To support handover of a vehicle by a delivery driver using a palmtop to customer according to reservation.
Use Case Description	

1. Identify reservation

   Reservation number is used to find reservation for customer.

   Contract number is found and contract details displayed.

2. Agree handover details

   Entry sheet details (vehicle mileage, service details, valet and safety details) are agreed for signing by customer. The contract is closed.

Use case 6.4   Record vehicle handback

Use Case Name	Record Vehicle Handback
Use Case Intent	To support handback of a vehicle by a delivery driver using palmtop to customer according to contract.
Use Case Description	

1. Identify contract

   Contract number is used to find the contract.

2. Check compliance to contract

   A return checklist (keys, documents) is checked. Return information is entered, including any damage or accident details.

3. Calculate settlement amount.

   The return mileage and deposit is used to caloulate the final balance for invoicing.

4. Agree payment details

   An internet payment transaction is posted and the contract marked as paid.

A use case refinement map, shown in Figure 6.15, helps to understand the impact on service requirements of the Record Internet Reservation use case.

The use case refinement map reveals that most of the existing services from the IReservations interface can still be reused. However, we need to consider the new requirements to create an internet credit imprint and accept delivery instructions. Create credit imprint is a separate 'virtual service' provided by a finance house. The createImprint service of the pre-stipulated ICreditCard interface allows a credit imprint to be created online. The Price Delivery and Book Delivery steps are less clear. We associate both of these with the Delivery type for now. Booking a delivery should be as generic as possible; for example, it may be that a customer decides to have a vehicle delivered a couple of days after making a reservation. Therefore, we make this an 'includes' use case as shown in Figure 6.16.

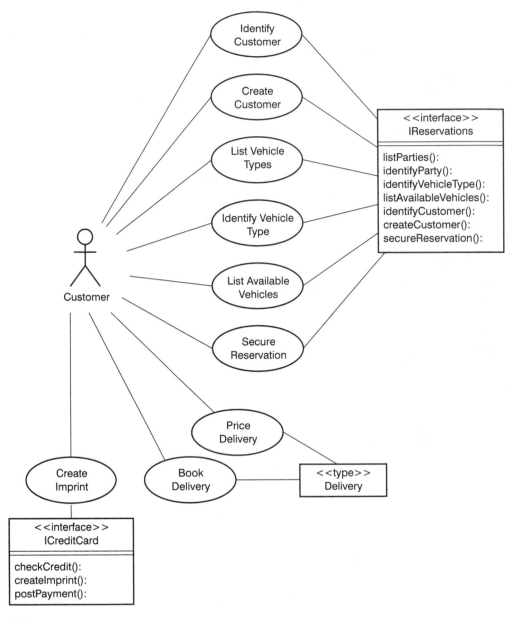

Figure 6.15
Revised use case refinement map (Record Internet Reservation)

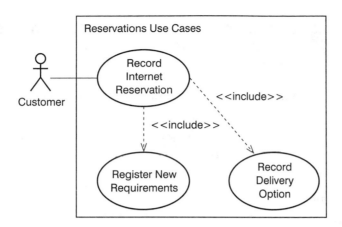

Figure 6.16
Applying includes
use cases

Let us consider the web page design. An additional menu option 'Specify Delivery Options' which allows the customer to interact with the delivery options process is added to the reservations page as illustrated in Figure 6.17.

Figure 6.18 illustrates step 2 of the delivery options process and captures the information illustrated in Figure 6.11. Step 1 establishes the reservation number dependent on the context of the customer's session.

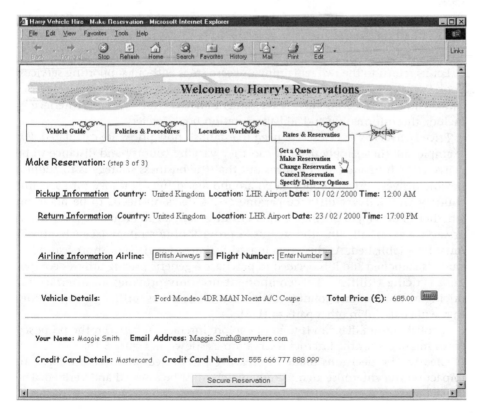

Figure 6.17
HVH reservations
page with delivery
option

Figure 6.18
HVH Vehicle delivery
options page

Let us return to the two remaining use case steps without supporting services. Book Delivery looks fairly straightforward. The Delivery type is exclusively associated with the Reservation type. We can enhance the IReservations interface to include this information and add an operation bookDelivery.

Price Delivery is less clear. We need to establish how prices are calculated. For example, are they simply fixed or can they vary by country and distance to be delivered? On investigation it turns out that the business strategy is to adopt a flexible delivery pricing policy based around algorithms that take into account country and delivery distance parameters. A decision needs to be made on whether to develop a pricing component internally or to acquire a component or service externally. In other words, a provisioning strategy (see Chapter 7) must be established. As this is such a critical area for HVH, a short feasibility study is launched and it is decided to purchase a generic pricing utilities component (Pricing Utilities). This component not only provides an interface for pricing by distance and country (IDistance), it also offers further pricing utilities that will be useful in other parts of HVH.

A collaboration diagram is used to explore interaction between the proposed set of interfaces for the internet reservation as shown in Figure 6.19.

Clearly, the decisions made in creating the project architecture have an impact on the enterprise architecture, which must be assessed and verified. The impact on the enterprise component architecture is shown in Figure 6.20.

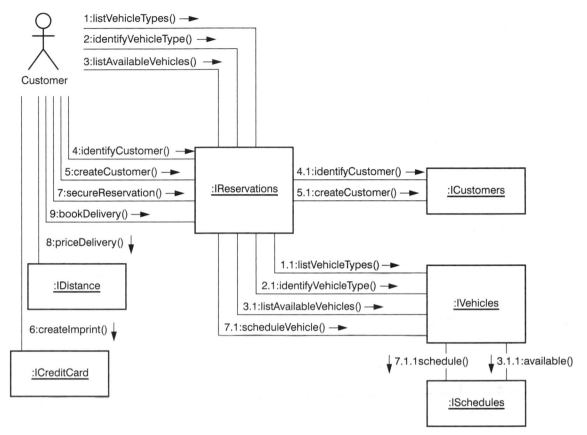

Figure 6.19
Collaboration diagram (internet reservation)

Note that whether the vehicle is acquired internally or via the vehicle broker is of no interest here. That decision is encapsulated behind the ISchedules interface. Schedules will decide if a suitable vehicle can be found internally. If a suitable vehicle cannot be found internally, the Schedules component will poll the vehicle broker and issue a requisition if a vehicle is available through the broker.

The decision to include the recording of delivery information as part of the secureReservation operation means that we must either change the IReservations interface and publish a new version, or create and publish a brand new interface. The new functionality is to be used globally, both using the internet and the traditional process. Moreover, the new version will be backwardly compatible with the previous one. This means that there is little advantage of creating a new interface. Therefore, we decide to publish a new version of the IReservations interface. The revised interface type diagram is shown in Figure 6.21.

Figure 6.20
Refined enterprise
component
architecture

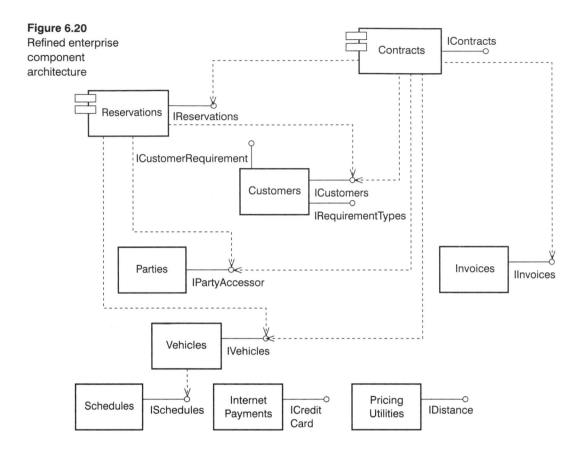

Business transformation

In this section, we take stock of the Harry scenario and consider some of the factors that will need addressing as the organization progresses forward through the internet spectrum. Note that overall e-business trends are well covered elsewhere (Amor, 2000; Fellenstein and Wood, 2000; Kalakota and Robinson, 1999; Rosen, 2000). Our objective is to raise awareness with respect to our example. We begin by making some observations about adaptability: the business components achieved thus far should provide a good foundation for moving further forward. The subject of business process integration is undoubtedly one for a book in its own right: we look at some of these issues with respect to the Harry scenario. CRM has become something of a hot topic. Having already introduced a personalization increment to 'test the water', we take a look at what CRM might mean to Harry's. Finally, make some comments about external services, particularly subscription to virtual services.

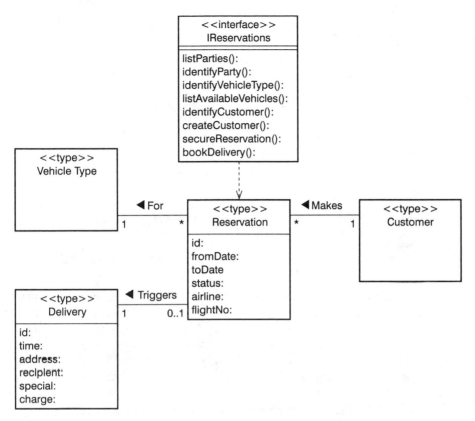

Figure 6.21
Revised interface
type diagram for
IReservations

6.3.1   Adaptability

It is important to realize that the use cases focus on fixed sequences of user-system interactions. This helps to expose software scope. Where it is less useful is in bringing out the flexibility of the user interactions. For example, it is usually possible to think of many alternative sequences. Having established the scope, it is important not to get distracted and overwhelmed with the many variations. A more productive strategy is to concentrate on abstracting the business capabilities that are needed both to support alternative paths within single use cases and to provide common functionality across different use cases.

The use case <<include>> dependency can be used to highlight common services. Some examples follow.

Recall from our discussion in Chapter 5 (about anticipating generic services in increment 2) that the IContracts interface provides Access Contract,[3] Calc Amount, Check Compliance services for use by the vehicle return use case. These can be reused by the vehicle handback use case as shown in Figure 6.22. This use case also requires services Register Payment and Post Internet Payment. The

---

3. Note that an interface can by definition provide access to all information depicted in its interface type model; by convention there is no need to list these services.

Figure 6.22
Use case includes
relationships for
return and handback

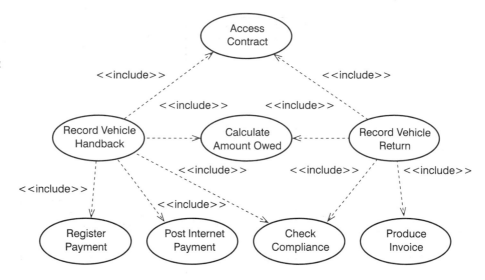

former is added to the IContracts interface; the latter is a virtual service provided by the ICreditCheck interface provided by the finance house mentioned earlier.

Similarly, the IContracts interface provides Assess Reservation, Produce Entry Sheet, Close Contract and Stipulate Contract services for use by the vehicle collection use case. The first three of these can be reused by the vehicle handover use case as shown in Figure 6.23. Stipulate Contract is reused by the Provide Delivery Instructions use case.

Keeping the business component interfaces as generic as possible within the business context not only helps ensure process integration by de-coupling process flow from business logic, it also stands the organization in good stead for exploiting new business opportunities.

As we have already seen in our limited four increment scenario, e-business systems can be rapidly adapted and extended to cover new business requirements. Three of the e-business process improvement strategies in our case study were:

1 Ability to reach rapidly growing global markets especially by partnering with travel agencies.

2 Ability to partner with informedaries.

3 Enhanced information access.

The enabling technology issues are important, particularly XML for ensuring consistency of data exchange (see Appendix 1, Section A1.1.6). At the same time, we need creative thinking and imagination too. For example, we will need to anticipate possible partnering scenarios that will expose the need for web hot-links.

To ensure that the software can adapt to possible changes in the business, future scenario playing is immensely useful. When Royal Dutch Shell applied the technique back in the 1970s, one scenario suggested that in certain circumstances OPEC might unilaterally raise oil prices. How painful it was when we

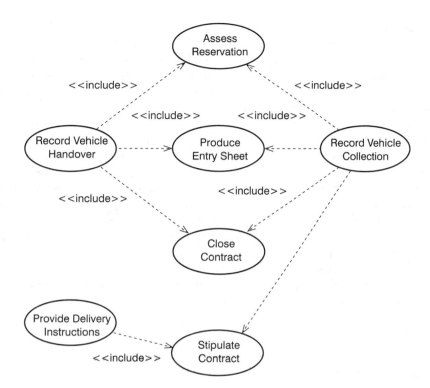

Figure 6.23
Use case includes relationships for collection and handover

learned about that! Shell, however, had thought the scenario through extensively. As a result, they were able to respond more effectively than other larger firms, becoming the first to move millions of barrels of oil a day through the spot markets, rising in the process to the third largest oil company (from seventh). The value of individuals able to apply this kind of imaginative thinking increases by an order of magnitude for anticipating the changes that can occur in internet time.

6.3.2   Business process integration

The examples shown in the Harry Enterprises case study have been deliberately simplified in order to provide a comprehendible illustration of how to employ component-based techniques in graduated fashion through the internet spectrum.

There are many technical integration issues that must be addressed. Our four-part scenario, for example, includes EAI hubs to existing functionality (Parties), outsourced functionality (Vehicles) and extension of component frameworks (Schedules). There are many connections, protocols and standards that must be carefully planned, controlled and tested.

In our present context, however, it is vital to understand that increasingly, e-business systems work within the context of a business process. It is imperative to clarify how the business process as a whole will operate with the new internet piece. We have briefly touched on how a business process might have links to internal processes (customer relationship), external processes (vehicle broker), internal components (reservations) and external virtual services (credit check).

Such hybrid processes that are typical of e-business systems raise a plethora of business process integration issues. For example, vehicle reservations over the internet and direct delivery to the customers by drivers equipped with palmtops present some interesting challenges.

If there is a problem with the vehicle itself, for example, if for some reason the vehicle fails to arrive or is damaged and there is no replacement available, we need to have a way of warning the customer about this. The customer should be given an alternative choice and also the option of canceling the credit transaction.

The introduction of direct payment by credit card, in the internet solution will still need to generate journal entries to the existing accounts system. The Register Payment service needs to include this facility.

The decision to outsource vehicle supply introduces possible weak links in the process. We will need to consider how to handle the internet reservation if links to the vehicle broker are down.

Exceptions must be identified, for example, if the Customer component is down. Prototypes, storyboarding and scenario playing (and the people who create and run them) are essential to ensure that the correct requirements are addressed and the entire process runs smoothly.

6.3.3   The role of CRM

Increment 3 of the case study began to address two other important objectives from the e-business process improvement plan:

1 Personalization of vehicle reservations: quotations and vehicle preferences.

2 Capture of market feedback from customers to enable business to adapt.

CRM is an important, but often misunderstood, element in the move toward fully enabled e-business and has received lots of attention in the trade press (Prime Marketing, 1999). The received wisdom is that winning new customers is six times as costly as retaining existing ones, that instead of looking at market share, companies need to be looking at customer share (Peppers and Rogers, 1997).

The CRM software vision is of everyone in an organization able to look at the history of customer contact, including purchasing patterns, complaints and inquiries. By analyzing this information an organization can provide more efficient customer service and better product design. Most importantly, it should be possible to anticipate the need for new products based on market feedback and to adapt to these needs with great agility.

Cross-selling and up-selling by personalizing the sales cycle is another promised benefit of CRM; for example, cross-selling a study chair to a customer who has just purchased a bookcase or up-selling insurance to a customer who has just purchased an automobile.

CRM software comes in different varieties, but typically integrates across three key business areas:

1 Sales: software to improve the field sales and telesales operations.

2 Customer service: software to improve response to customer queries and to support after sales service.

3 Marketing: software to support campaign management and market analysis.

The theme of consistency of service is an important one here in that the business services provided should be channel neutral.

Information must be kept consistent regardless of where it is stored. The customer's experience across channels to market must reflect this consistency; for example, the customer is quoted the same hire rate irrespective of whether they use the internet, call centre, or visit the agency. The price quoted is related to the type of car, season and customer purchasing history. At the same time, we need to be able to vary core services by channel. For example, internet customers are given a special discount. And building personalized offers into the sales cycle demands a significant degree of information aggregation. Not only that, but the information must be provided in real time for internet users. In order to achieve these goals, CRM software must be effectively integrated within the component architecture.

The CRM vision is a holistic view of the organization by the customer and a holistic view of the customer by the organization

The more basic issue however is whether and how to use CRM to improve your business processes. Moving from a call centre to an internet strategy may sound exciting and make apparent financial sense. However, it may not be well received by the CEO upon finding that most of your customers have defected to your main competitor en-masse because they happen to be technophobic. There is a basic need to understand your customer base before making such moves!

The internal challenge is also as much cultural as logistical. The sales, services and marketing departments in most large organizations often exist in a state of mutual denigration. Sales resent the fact that services is a cost centre. Services complain that sales are always selling products that do not work. Both look down on marketing. Marketing criticizes sales for not being proactive enough, and so on!

Well chosen CRM causes the business process itself to be transformed: sales, services and marketing are made part of one integrated customer-facing process. The sharing of customer information across the marketing – sales – servicing lifecycle increases the value of interaction between the different factions. Effective change management becomes imperative as responsibilities change. There is simply no time for historical and personal differences. For example, no longer does the request for an overdraft get pushed up the hierarchy chart by the call centre clerk. Instead the request is treated proactively. Perhaps the customer needs a personal loan? The customer service representative can now use the CRM software to make these decisions in dialogue with the customer. The internet takes this a step further, the customer having the option to ask for a personal loan as part of the dialogue and CRM software used to support the process and validate the request.

Whether to 'Go CRM' is therefore a non-trivial decision. That is why it has been left until reasonably late in the overall process before considering it.

Commitment to CRM, in the true sense of the term, also has important implications for our approach to enterprise component architecture. Ideally, an architecture is constructed first and package software is evaluated against it using gap analysis at some point in the software process, as discussed in Chapter 7. In that sense, CRM is no different to any other package. Sometimes, however, use of a software package is mandated in advance of any architecture work. In that case, the architecture is shaped to a degree by the structure of the package itself, which clearly can be a high-risk strategy as evidenced by the shortcomings of many of the ERP solutions of the mid-1990s. Integration around the capabilities of the package has left many organizations that bought heavily into ERP ill-equipped to deal with the flexibility needed for e-business. CRM software is yet more challenging in that it is not just invoked as a server component, but also requires and assumes a number of services, in the manner of a front-end client component!

By treating the CRM package as a set of services, we can design interfaces around it, as required often by employing connector technology using EAI software. However we will also need to understand the services required and identify interfaces to support them so that the necessary sockets can be 'filled in' within the CRM package itself. For example, much of the information required by the CRM package will almost certainly be provided by existing data warehouses. Clearly, we will need to understand the relationship of the CRM package to these existing assets (Hall, 2000).

For example, future releases of the Reservations and Contracts components might use CRM services to up-sell other Harry products, perhaps maps or hotel vouchers to those hiring vehicles. We can employ a CRM Services component to provide the necessary CRM Sales interface. Other interfaces will almost certainly be needed for marketing and customer servicing.

6.3.4   External services integration

Supply chain integration has been high on the business agenda for a number of years. However, until recently it has centred on optimizing the operation and logistics of supply chains, typically in manufacturing applications. The internet changes this picture dramatically in that there is now a need to integrate the capabilities of different organizations in real time within new e-business processes.

Until recently, one of the main barriers to successful supply chain integration has been the closed nature of the communication mechanisms used. EDI was the first formal approach, but has often proved costly and complex, requiring specialist skills. However, extranet business-to-business exchanges using XML-based message exchange are increasingly pervasive. This technology is used to make online links to suppliers' systems enabling business to share production plans, pricing and delivery schedule information.

More interestingly however the exchanges can contain service requests; for example, increment 4 used external services to address the questions:

- What types of vehicle are available tomorrow?
- Is the customer's credit ok?

We will need to increase awareness of possible external services within the context of business processes and to model these external services as part of our component architecture. In Chapter 7 (see Section 7.4.6), we take a look at a more recent trend to use the internet to sell, broker and implement extremely generic services known as megaservices.

At the same time, new business partnerships triggered at the click of a hot-link, add a further dimension of complexity. This model has been referred to as 'Collaborative Commerce' (C-Commerce) by Gartner Group (1999) and achieves dynamic collaboration among employees, business partners and customers throughout a trading community or market: a dynamic 'virtual enterprise'.

6.4   Summary

In this chapter, we continued our journey through the internet spectrum. We looked at some examples of how to apply CBD modeling techniques to evolve the early solutions toward effective e-business solutions. Such systems extend the scope to full business process integration and on to business transformation. We looked at using internet-enabled technologies to improve the customer's experience and the personalization of that experience. An important underlying theme that emerged was the need for business process integration, especially integration with third parties and the use of external components including virtual services.

At the same time, this is not a mechanistic process. The need for long-term adaptability must be balanced with the inevitable opportunist use of technology for business advantage.

6.5   References

Amor, D., The E-business *(R)evolution: Living and Working in an Interconnected World*, Prentice Hall, 2000.

Fellenstein, C., and Wood, R., *Exploring E-commerce, Global E-business, and E-societies*, Prentice Hall, 2000.

Gartner Group, 'C-Commerce: the new arena for business applications', *Administrative Application Strategies*, SPA-08-5311, 1999.

Hall, C., 'Intelligent transaction mining for real-time CRM', *Business Intelligence Advisor*, Vol. 4, No. 2, Cutter Information Corp., February 2000.

Kalakota, R., and Robinson, M., *e-Business: Roadmap for Success*, Addison-Wesley, 1999.

Peppers, D., and Rogers, M., *The One to One Future: Building Relationships One Customer at a Time*, Bantam Doubleday Dell, 1997.

Prime Marketing, www.conspectus.com, Customer Relationship Management Systems, *Conspectus*, Prime Marketing Publications Ltd, October 1999.

Rosen, A., *The e-Commerce Question and Answer Book*, Amacom, 2000.

Veryard, R., *Scipio Case Study: Liam O'Croder Mail Order Co*, www.scipio.org, March 1998.

Provisioning strategies   7

7.1   Introduction

The separation of specification from implementation means that components may be realized in different ways. It is important to consider a diversity of realization routes and choose the most appropriate from the different alternatives. In other words, we need to think about provisioning strategy.

In this chapter, we begin by considering two important factors that are often neglected, with disastrous consequences, in the rush to innovate using the internet: the roles of gap analysis and component architecture in shaping the provisioning strategy. We also consider the importance of business specification standards and the influence of component granularity in assisting the provisioning process.

We look at an increasingly diverse range of different options for realizing components. Again, a keynote is that IT and business need to work through the issues together. This is especially important in CBD with such a variety of provisioning routes that need to be considered.

7.2   Gap analysis

Gap analysis assesses the difference between stated requirements and existing components. A gap analysis results in a provisioning strategy: recommendations to either do some development work on the one hand or to reuse/buy an existing component on the other. Doing some development work might involve developing from scratch or extending an existing component to meet the stated requirements. Outright purchase or reuse of an existing component might involve realigning the stated requirements, making a compromise to requirements in order to deliver the solution faster and cheaper.

7.2.1   A world of choice

Provisioning strategy involves choosing from an increasing diversity of different options for components and services that may be mixed and matched in various combinations, for example:

- Develop a component from scratch.
- Extend an existing interface.
- Outsource a component design and implementation.
- Reuse an existing component.
- Wrap or adapt an existing system.
- Purchase an external component.
- Subscribe to an external service.
- Outsource to an ASP.

Component markets mean that an organization can buy the more generic features of a desired solution and focus on the more specific features that make the solution truly valuable to the customer.

As we depart the software development era, so we enter a world of increasing choice: a world of mix and match for business advantage

Ideally, the analyst should be able to browse a component catalogue for existing interfaces that exactly match those identified from component modeling. However, in real life compromises must often be made. The analyst might reuse the interface that 'comes closest' to the ideal. In fact sometimes it may be that things are compromised so much in the interests of saving money and time, by reusing what is already in the bag, that the original business process is significantly changed. OK it is not perfect, but maybe it is cost justified and practical to settle for less than perfect business process and maybe upgrade it later by rewiring in interfaces that better match the ideal. So, gap analysis involves making trade-offs between what the business would ideally like, and what it is realistic to expect.

7.2.2   Revisiting the CBD process

Let us consider the role of component provisioning with respect to the track-based process pattern from Chapter 4 (repeated in Figure 7.1).

Looking at the figure we can see that the twin track process is triggered in different ways. The assembly track is triggered by the need to produce a timely e-business solution, for example, direct sales over the internet. Assembly involves searching for available components and, where necessary, raising requirements for new components from the provisioning track.

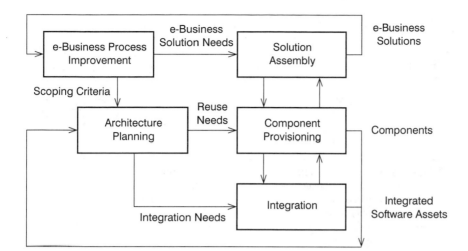

Figure 7.1
The track-based
process pattern

In contrast, the provisioning track may be triggered independently of specific e-business solution requirements, by reuse needs identified in architecture planning, for example, commonly required business infrastructure components such as a product rule engine, to guide provisioning strategy. Provisioning needs are often best addressed by legacy software assets made available through an integration project.

Development work is minimized through reuse and integration. On many types of assembly and provisioning projects large chunks of these activity types are by-passed altogether, thus saving the high levels of effort typical of traditional development projects.

Work is often subdivided into several increments, with e-business improvement planning, software requirements and component architecture only needed in the first increment, and delivery only performed in the last as shown in Figure 7.2. The types of activity are shown in sequence for convenience of representation. However, remember from Chapter 4 that the CBD process works in iterative fashion as component models evolve in line with the business needs. Activities also typically overlap in order to compress project duration, and due to rework identified in subsequent phases.

> **A keynote of *integration* projects, as opposed to previous generation *development* projects, is that the type and number of activities varies according to project type**

7.2.3   Applying gap analysis

Gap analysis helps decide provisioning strategy at increasing levels of detail through the stages of a project at decreasing levels of abstraction, not just once at the specification stage as is sometimes mistakenly thought. CBD affects software's entire lifecycle.

In particular, it is important to apply gap analysis at the e-business improvement planning stage. That way, we can identify commodity processes that can

Figure 7.2
Parallel incremental
activity types

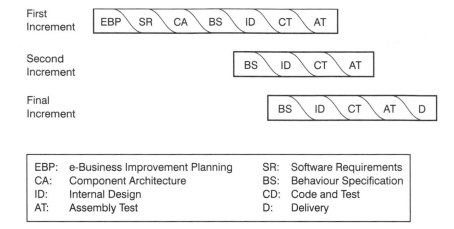

First Increment: EBP \ SR \ CA \ BS \ ID \ CT \ AT

Second Increment: BS \ ID \ CT \ AT

Final Increment: BS \ ID \ CT \ AT \ D

EBP:	e-Business Improvement Planning	SR:	Software Requirements
CA:	Component Architecture	BS:	Behaviour Specification
ID:	Internal Design	CD:	Code and Test
AT:	Assembly Test	D:	Delivery

be effectively outsourced and allow the business to concentrate on its core competencies, an important aspect of e-business. We reuse at the process level, not only at the software level.

> **A component framework that supplies 80% of business functionality in a quarter the time it would take to build from scratch is hugely attractive. But how critical is the missing 20%? Is the business prepared to wait for the required extensions?**

Good business knowledge is an absolute necessity in making trade-offs as we move through the lifecycle.

At software requirements level, it may happen that someone remembers that some part of the current problem had already been solved for an earlier project. If this partial solution has the form of a separate component, it can be reused in the new project, thus saving time and cost.

At architectural level, gap analysis is applied in broad-brush fashion to compare planned components, shown in the architecture, with available software. The available software may come in many forms. For example, there may be existing components that provide a good fit. This includes components previously built by the organization, externally supplied components or frameworks, services available on subscription or package software with component interfaces. On the other hand, there may be non-component software in the form of existing software or databases that looks like a good candidate for adapting or wrapping.

Similarly, at specification level interfaces are assessed against already available interfaces to see if these can either be reused 'as is' or perhaps extended or specialized. Sometimes it is necessary to compromise the original requirement or ideal interface in order to save time and money by buying in a component that comes close to requirements and that is extended later.

The point at which component provisioning is triggered depends on when the gap analysis is completed. It may be that the gap analysis 'completes' in stages, in which case it could be that provisioning projects are triggered in graduated fashion after business improvement, requirements definition, architecture design or behaviour specification phases. In the example shown in Figure 7.3, we assume for simplicity, that component provisioning is triggered in its

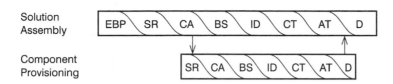

Figure 7.3
Parallel solution
assembly and
component
provision[1]

entirety, following component architecture. The assembly test phase of solution assembly cannot be completed until the new component has been delivered and incorporated into the assembly.

Component provisioning projects may themselves spawn further component provisioning projects, so we can get 'nested' component provisioning projects, with the lowest level component not requiring an assembly test, as shown in Figure 7.4.

Again it is important to realize that component provisioning often involves only a sub-set of activity types. For example, component implementation may be outsourced, suitable components may already exist for purchase or virtual services may be available on a subscription basis. Better still, the component is already available in-house, and can be reused. These cases are depicted in Figure 7.5.

True solution assembly occurs only where a solution can be developed entirely from pre-existing components. This corresponds to the upper-most provisioning route in Figure 7.5. The solution logic is limited to just assembly logic (the 'glue') and the user interface design. We have already seen, in Chapters 5 and 6, that component modeling techniques can be used to pinpoint service requests on interfaces.

If existing services can be pinpointed early in the process, this can represent dramatic savings in development time, as well as a better quality solution based on established components

Requirements can be expressed as extensions to established prototypes linked to interface services as indicated in Figure 7.6. This is a much more rigorous specification than a purely textual specification, if the prototypes are linked to properly documented and catalogued interfaces.

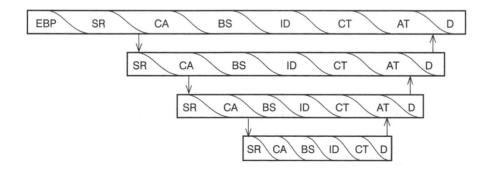

Figure 7.4
Nested component
provision

1. Figures 7.3 to 7.6 are based on original graphics by John Dodd, working on Sterling Software's *Advisor* method.

Figure 7.5
Hybrid component
provision

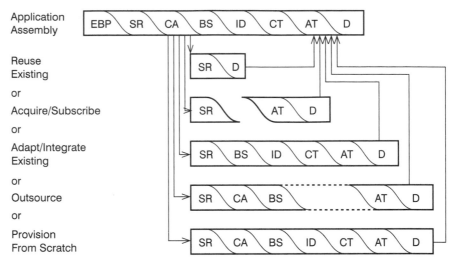

Figure 7.6
Rapid solution
assembly using
components via
prototypes

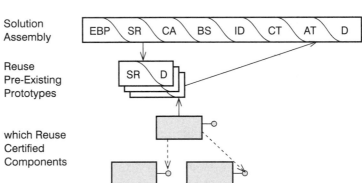

A repository of certified components and an effective tool for browsing and cataloguing the components takes us out of the constricting realm of traditional development: it is no longer necessary to extract every last requirement for a 'new' system. Instead, having understood overall business needs, the relevant reusable components are assembled into prototypes. To the extent that prototypes reflect already implemented requirements, they avoid the time and effort involved in gathering them again. The prototypes speak to the business people: 'We can do this very cheaply – what adjustments do you need?'

7.3 Component provisioning keynotes

In this section, we consider three particular keynotes that influence provisioning strategy:

1 The importance of business specification standards.

2 The effect of component architecture.

3 Granularity of business components.

7.3.1   The Importance of business specification standards

One of the biggest challenges to a healthy component market at the business level, as opposed to the technical level of widgets and scroll bars, is the need for effective business specification standards. Such standards need to address the need for clear specification of business services and data, aside from the technical standardization (for example, EJB, CCM and COM+; see Appendix 1, Section A1.1.2-5). XML perhaps provides the best bet on the data front as industry groups work toward common semantics (see Appendix 1, Section A1.1.6).

Standardization of business logic has been much more challenging. In a sense, this book is actually a rallying call for better standardization in this area. We have used the component forms (Cheesman and Daniels, 2000) as a meta model, based interface specifications upon the use of interface type models, used UML (OMG, 1999) where possible and followed design by contract (Meyer, 1997) for the specification of services using pre- and post-conditions. However, it has to be said that the industry as whole is still a long way off the mark when it comes to specification of business logic.

In assessing the suitability of components on the open market, it is important to bear specification models in mind and select only those vendors that at least approximate to a standard

7.3.2   Visualizing provisioning strategy

Component architecture diagrams can often be used to express and communicate provisioning strategy at project level or for the enterprise as a whole as shown in Figure 7.7. For example, components that sit in the lower levels of the business layer are often well catered for by purchasing software packages or component frameworks. The functionality at this level is usually stable and often non-strategic, provided by commodity components as opposed to value-

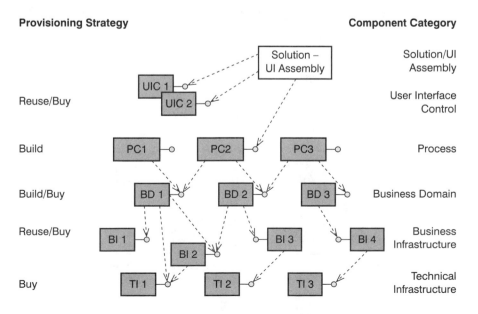

Provisioning Strategy   **Component Category**

Reuse/Buy

Build

Build/Buy

Reuse/Buy

Buy

Figure 7.7
Component architecture and provisioning strategy

add components. Similarly, most user interface functionality is based around purchased libraries of small grained user components such as widgets and icons, and also on reusing internally developed user interface components that help ensure standardization 'on the glass'. In contrast, components that sit at the upper levels of the business layer are often good candidates for building in-house. This is because they often provide value-added business functionality that may give the company competitive advantage. In between these extremes are domain components, like Customer and Product, that require careful analysis to see if it is really worth building in-house, or whether existing components can be extended.

7.3.3   Component granularity

In deciding provisioning strategy, it is important to consider the granularity of the proposed business component as depicted in Figure 7.8.

Fine grain business components are readily available both on a purchase and subscription basis. Coarse grain packages and legacy systems are pervasive in many organizations today and, as we saw in Chapter 6, EAI software often provides an effective way of utilizing the established functionality they provide within an e-business setting.

It is at the middle levels of business component that more interesting possibilities are starting to emerge. Wrapping and adapting are techniques for developing these kinds of business component based upon existing systems and databases. Indeed, again coupled with the use of EAI tools, this is often the most viable short-term way of exploiting information contained within existing databases and of maintaining a consistent service to existing customers and suppliers.

The increasing availability of large-scale component frameworks that provide sets of interfaces for extension in different business domains and the emergence of larger scale virtual services also provides an increasingly strategic route to component provision.

Figure 7.8
Component
granularity

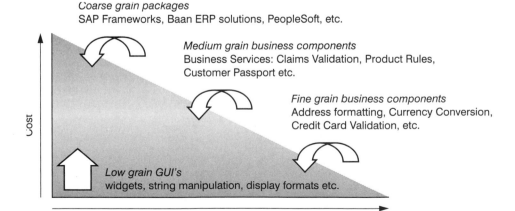

Coarse grain packages
SAP Frameworks, Baan ERP solutions, PeopleSoft, etc.

Medium grain business components
Business Services: Claims Validation, Product Rules,
Customer Passport etc.

Fine grain business components
Address formatting, Currency Conversion,
Credit Card Validation, etc.

Low grain GUI's
widgets, string manipulation, display formats etc.

Cost

Volume

7.4   Routes to component provision

In this section, we discuss some of the different options for component provision:

- Purchasing components.
- Outsourcing component design and implementation.
- Wrapping.
- Adapting.
- Extending interfaces.
- Subscribing to virtual services.
- Outsourcing using ASPs.

7.4.1   Purchasing components

Component vendors can be divided into developers and brokers (Harmon, 1999). Developers are companies that have developed components themselves. Brokers are retail component vendors who sell on components developed by other companies. Note that there are many other companies that deal in technical components, such as libraries of GUI and utility components that are not within our scope. The focus here is on business components.

Most developers focus on niche business domains, such as telecommunications or finance. Often, the components are available in the form of frameworks, the interfaces of which can be extended in various ways (see Section 7.4.5). Table 7.1 provides a few examples of component vendors, drawn

Table 7.1   Component vendors

Vendor	Framework/component	Technology	Website
BEA[2]	Frameworks	EJB	www.beasys.com/theorycenter/
Castek	Frameworks	CBD96	www.castek.com
CASE Masters	Frameworks	CBD96	www.casemasters.com
EC Cubed	Frameworks	Open API, Java	www.eccubed.com
EDS	Components	COM	Via www.componentsource.com
IBM	Frameworks	EJB	www.ibm.com/sanfrancisco/
Mim Software GMbh	Components	Java	www.mimsoftware.de
Raft	Frameworks	COM	www.raftinternational.com

2. BEA acquired Theory Center in 1998.

from information provided by the CBDi Forum (CBDi Forum, 2000a,b). The list shown is in fact just the tip of an iceberg of emerging vendors; *see* www.componentsoftware.net for an online directory.

A product that comes with a component specification written to standard can be readily assessed against the buyer's behaviour specifications using gap analysis

For example, Sterling Software (now Computer Associates) supports the CBD96 (Sterling Software, 1996) standard, the foundations of which are the component forms we discussed in Chapter 3. Companies such as Casetek and CASE Masters create specific business components based upon CBD96. They can then generate the actual component implementations in any one of several specific commercial specifications, including COM, EJB or Sterling's COOL:Gen (Arellano and McGlaun, 1999).

Component brokers act as retailers of components developed by others. For example ComponentSource (www. componentsource.com) trades financial components developed by EDS. As well as trading in a diverse set of components, Flashline (www.flashline.com) act as an outsourcer of component implementations (see Section 7.3.2).

In selling on components developed by others, the main challenge for brokers is achieving consistency of specification, to enable prospective purchasers to make effective gap analyses

Clear and precise component models, as described in this book, are critical as they help to communicate the business capabilities of components to prospective customers.

7.4.2   Outsourcing component design and implementation

Once an interface is specified, a developer in the same team, down the hall, somewhere else in the country or anywhere in the world can design and code the actual implementation.

Component outsourcing is a natural progression of the general trend toward outsourcing in software development. IT outsourcing offers many advantages to organizations that have become frustrated at what they see as the shortcomings of internal IT departments. These advantages include:

● Decreased cost and time to market.

● Access to a greater pool of resources.

● Focus on core competencies.

● Freedom from burdensome overheads.

While continuing to offer these traditional strengths, component outsourcing offers two important additional ones. First, by outsourcing interfaces, or sets of interfaces, risk is reduced by outsourcing at a lower, much more manageable level of granularity, than provided by complete solutions. Second, interfaces by their very nature offer a much more rigorous specification than traditionally found in applications. Precise interface definitions provide a contract between the consumer of the services provided through the interface and suppliers of those services. The quality of outsourcing work, that is so difficult to measure traditionally, becomes much easier to verify against rigorously specified contracts.

For example, Flashline.com provide a 'Beans by Design' service that allows companies to post requests for specified JavaBeans that are then bid on by developers.

The main challenge here is in controlling the relationship with the service provider. Assessment of work to contract is a notoriously difficult area; how do you prove that the delivered component does the job it is supposed to do? Clear component models are again a critical success factor in resolving this issue.

The internet is opening up exciting possibilities for realizing component outsourcing through an online component marketplace

7.4.3 Wrapping

A wrapper is a component that provides services implemented by legacy software. Wrapping is a technique that takes legacy assets and encapsulates them inside components. Wrappers provide three key advantages:

1 Insulating new component-based software from legacy code, in particular from the effects of changes.

2 Reusing that code in a component-based setting.

3 Migration to component technology while protecting investments in existing code and at the same time providing new innovative solutions to business problems.

The component offers standard interfaces, for example, EJB or COM+ interfaces. Methods residing inside the component are written in code which interfaces with the legacy product, for example SQL procedures defined in the database schema.

A wrapper can be used to bury existing system dependencies and provide legacy functionality for new component-based solutions in much shorter time than it would take to build a replacement from scratch and recreate those dependencies – often a major headache.

Transaction wrapping involves encapsulating a legacy transaction (for example, a COBOL transaction using CICS) as a component (for example, using COM+ to invoke the CICS transaction through SNA). Encapsulating at the transaction level ensures that the integrity of all related systems is preserved. In practice, a higher level of granularity is desirable, so several related transactions may be wrapped together and offered through a single component interface. The difficulty here is to isolate the legacy transaction from its traditional context so that it can be employed in a new context, for example, over the internet. Often it is difficult to mimic the previous preconditions for successful execution of the transaction in its new context as well as the post-conditions that can cause other transactions or routines to be triggered.

Data wrapping operates at a lower level of abstraction, exposing database CRUD routines as services. Legacy data access is a good low-risk starting point. A popular strategy is to provide customer searching, based upon existing database access routines, as part of a new component-based solution. Legacy data update is much more difficult as there are the inevitable integration issues and change knock-on effects to consider.

In a nutshell, although wrapping is often tempting, it needs careful analysis if pitfalls are to be avoided

The essence of the difficulty with wrapping is that it is very much an 'all or nothing' affair. For example, it becomes impossible to wrap one transaction without including another, without including another and so on. Knock on effects of change also require careful consideration. Existing systems may need re-engineering before they are in a fit state for wrapping. Before we know it, we are trying to wrap the world! This is why adapting is often a better, if less ambitious strategy.

7.4.4   Adapting

An adapter is a component that uses services implemented by legacy software as a basis upon which to offer new services. Adapting is a technique that uses legacy assets in combination with newly developed component code. Unlike a wrapper, an adapter does not guarantee the integrity of the legacy code that it employs. Though it is generally a less ambitious undertaking than wrapping, the advantages of adapting are broadly the same though the risks are usually lower.

Figure 7.9 illustrates how a wrapper effectively envelops legacy code. The only code is code to call the legacy routines and to make the necessary conversion to components. In contrast, an adapter contains new component code that may contain new business logic or rules and usually does more than simple conversion.

7.4.5   Extending interfaces

A component's interfaces may be extended through inheritance or delegation. Business-oriented component frameworks provide families of related component interfaces that are designed to provide common functionality in such a way that it can be readily extended for the particular needs of an organization.

The SanFranscisco™ Component Framework (Monday *et al.*, 2000) is perhaps

Figure 7.9
Adapter versus wrapper

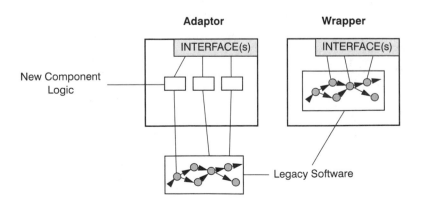

the most well established of the large business-oriented component frameworks. Such business-oriented frameworks are typically available in different implementations; for example SanFranscisco™ (and its subsequent descendents) are available as EJB components.

If we consider a component to be a black box that we can only address through its interface, then the framework is a white box – we can tinker inside it until it is just right. In the context of a component (as opposed to an object) this means we can tinker with the interface, not the internals of the component, which remain hidden. The framework may well be based on patterns,[3] which have been used to guide its creation.

Business-oriented component frameworks are particularly useful for well-understood and stable business domains that are subject to differentiation and change in value-added areas. For example, in the life insurance domain a great deal of functionality is common across organizations. All life organizations have to make standard underwriting calculations to establish basic risks. At the same time, an individual organization might want to differentiate its processes, for example by introducing a special policy for higher risks (such as smokers), requiring further special calculations. A life insurance component framework allows its users to take full advantage of standardized features provided by an underwriting interface while allowing extension as shown in Figure 7.10.

A gap analysis helps reveal the extent to which the component framework matches requirements. Where innovation is not required, for example payroll, then there is little point in using a component framework, as you will be paying for extendibility that is not required. In a case like this, a software package is likely to be appropriate. On the other hand, if lots of innovation is required in a

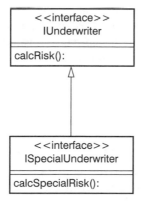

Figure 7.10
Extension of interface by inheritance

3. Patterns are reuseable analysis or design knowledge that describes a problem and its recommended solution. Do not make the common mistake of equating patterns with complete solutions or methods: you need to understand the problem you are trying to solve first and then use the right pattern for the job! A good pattern is concise: small but packing a heavy punch. This helps an experienced practitioner recognise a pattern, including its core concepts, so that its benefits can be exploited.

new business area, for example an e-business marketing system, it may well be the case that the core functionality is itself subject to change. In a case like this a bespoke design is likely to be appropriate.

Component frameworks are particularly relevant to e-business with its emphasis on leveraging core competencies in niche markets, while saving costs by outsourcing commodity processes

One of the difficulties with component frameworks is the issue of granularity that we described in Section 7.3.3. It is important to realize that the concept of component framework should operate at different levels of granularity. A life insurance framework represents a high level of granularity; a life insurance claims framework at a mid level; a life insurance underwriting calculation might be low level. Suppliers of component frameworks tend toward the very high grain granularity frameworks, whereas from a client viewpoint, migration from small to large grain sets of interfaces is often desirable. Risk can be mitigated by starting small, with a low-level granularity piece of a component framework, and moving incrementally to higher levels of granularity in the light of experience.

A second challenge with component frameworks is the need for better documentation, especially at the business level. Again many of the modeling techniques described in this book are aimed at clear communication of business capabilities of components.

7.4.6 Subscribing to virtual services

The internet has created the opportunity for 'virtual services' to be externally supplied on a subscription basis, as we saw with the credit checking and payment services in the Harry's scenario.

For fixed types of low granularity logic such as address formatting, purchasing the component is usually a good option. However, for components that need regular updating, subscription to an external provider's service can make more sense. For example, currency conversion is likely to be better handled by a finance broker rather than the user having to update conversion tables every time there is a currency change.

Recently, higher grained business services have started to emerge. Microsoft has coined the term 'Megaservices' to describe these business services and cite the example of their Passport service, which provides customer identification and authentication. (CBDi Forum, 1999). Customers register their details once with www.passport.com and receive a user id. The user id, when used with a Passport compatible e-commerce site, enables the vendor to retrieve all the shipment, billing and other details from Passport without further customer interaction or the need to consult internal databases.

A traditionally based process would be for the e-tailer to store the customer information in their database and check it each time it is needed. The megaservice concept cuts through the attendant problems associated with ensuring consistent customer data by storing the customer's user id and passing that to the necessary business partners, who can retrieve the required information themselves as required. Providing the customer is committed to keeping their

Passport details up to date, then correct information is ensured across the supply chain.

Obviously the success of this process is dependent on the customer keeping their details up to date. However, megaservices provide an important 'tool in the bag' providing they are used within the business process context (in this case e-tail) for which they are designed.

They open up the vision of accessing timely and accurate business information, using the internet, from a centralized owner without having to worry about duplication and fragmentation of that information across a company's internal systems. Common business data, such as customer data, would be provided along the lines of the Passport service. Domain specific information such as product might be handled by a group of like-minded organizations in that domain. Again, supply chain information might be owned by a group of related parties across the supply chain.

Megaservices have far reaching consequences for the issue of data integration that has plagued organizations for many years

7.4.7   Outsourcing using ASPs

The growth of ASPs (Cherry Tree and Co., 1999) deserves a special mention. The outsourcing of IT services, as opposed to design and coding of specific components, is being driven by a number of factors:

- Increased predictability of costs as an aid to the planning and budgeting of software projects.

- Management of the long-term total cost of ownership of a solution by assigning responsibility for maintenance to a third party at a known fixed cost.

- Improved flexibility by reducing internal information technology assets and allowing new skills and resources to be acquired from external vendors and consultants as needed.

- Apparent simplicity and economy of commercial arrangement: a single contract and service level, through which all aspects of a solution are delivered.

ASP providers have emerged in response to the need for customized solutions. Typically, they specialize either within a particular application domain, such as the financial services industry, or in a specific technology, such as IBM-based solutions using technologies such as MQSeries and WebSphere.

A number of these companies now offer hosted web-enabled services, running customers' applications over the internet with high performance and security, but without complicated middleware software to be installed and managed at the customer's site. The latest advances in distributed technologies are combined to offer customers 24x7 application availability, fast access to database services, robust virtual private networking (VPN), firewall security and high bandwidth availability. Additionally, the pricing model is a simple, usage-based program that enables customers to achieve enterprise-scale with vendor-managed upgrades and no software maintenance (Brown, 2000).

The apparent benefits of ASP need to be weighed against risks. Many of the ASP organizations are small in size, and work on tight profit margins in a competitive market. This can often lead to economic volatility that causes occasional quality problems in the solutions, lack of capacity for support and post-installation services and a possibility that the solution provider may go out of business all together.

Integrating an ASP-based solution with a company's existing systems can also present serious challenges, especially where those systems are working on different technical foundations.

More significantly, while application service provision may work well for treadmill functionality that delivers little strategic advantage, an organization needs to think much more seriously about whether this is good approach for value-added solutions. The question assumes a particular poignancy in the case of e-business systems. As we have emphasized throughout this book, software is no longer a supporting piece in the business jigsaw, but an integral piece.

It is important to determine the dividing line between those business services that can be viably delegated to an ASP and those that have a strategic significance that warrants more internal control

Again a component architecture can help put these issues into context, helping in managing the provision, integration and evolution of e-business solutions.

7.5   Summary

In this chapter, we considered the importance of effective planning in deciding how to provision components. In particular, we looked at two important factors that are often neglected, with disastrous consequences, in the rush to innovate using the internet: the roles of gap analysis and component architecture in shaping the provisioning strategy. No longer are 'clean white sheet' approaches assuming bespoke design appropriate; we live in a world of increasing diversity and choice. A range of different options for provisioning components are considered including framework extension, wrapping, adapting, outsourcing, purchasing and virtual services. Each approach to provisioning has its overall pros and cons that must be weighed up in specific circumstances. Gap analysis and component architecture help in making these decisions.

7.6   References

Arellano, M., and McGlaun, J., 'Eating elephants: EWA flies high with component-based development', *Distributed Computing*, November 1999.

Brown, A., *Enterprise Scale Application Development in the Internet Age*, Prentice Hall, 2000.

CBDi Forum (www.cbdiforum.com), *Interact*, December 1999.

CBDi Forum a (www.cbdiforum.com), *Interact*, February 2000.

CBDi Forum b (www.cbdiforum.com), *Interact*, March 2000.

Cheesman, J., and Daniels, J., *Component Modeling With UML*, Addison Wesley, 2000.

Cherry Tree and Co., 'Application service providers', *Spotlight Report*, available at www.cherrytreeco.com, October 1999.

Dodd, J., Cheesman, J., and Jones, M., Sterling Software, *CBD96 Standards V2.1*, 1996

Harmon, P., 'The component market', *Component Development Strategies*, Cutter Info Corp., vol. IX, no. 12, December 1999.

Meyer, B., *Object-Oriented Software Construction*, Prentice Hall, Englewood Cliffs, New Jersey, 2nd edn, 1997.

Monday, P., Carey, J., and Dangler, M., *SanFranscisco™ Component Framework*, Addison Wesley, 2000.

OMG, *OMG Unified Modeling Language Specification*, V1.3, June 1999.

CBD funding strategies[1]

8.1   Introduction

Return on investment (ROI) is traditionally calculated on a project-by-project basis, in which the project owner pays for the development with common infrastructure centrally charged. We will see in this chapter that funding for CBD is considerably more challenging and presents a major cultural challenge for most companies, especially those that remain unaware of the problem!

We will look at some tactical measures for dealing with these problems, starting with some broad funding models and how these can be applied on different types of CBD projects. We move on to provide metrics and costing criteria before considering how to identify benefits of CBD relating these to business objectives in the context of e-business.

8.2   Funding challenges

Traditional funding models charge use of infrastructure proportionately to application owners on the basis of measured usage. Funding for CBD is considerably more challenging. For example, issues arise over ownership of shared

---

1. This chapter was inspired by work that the author did as chair of the DSDM and Component-Based Development technical task group in producing a White Paper (DSDM Corporation, 2000). The author is indebted to the members of that task group, particularly Paul Turner, Christine Robertson, Howard Lewis, Kevin Trembath and Steve Ash.

components. Investment costs are often difficult to spread across the organization. Diverse consumer needs must be balanced. Political problems such as 'Why should I pay for her functionality?' need to be addressed with diplomacy. The size and scope of a CBD project, and whether other CBD projects have already been completed also dramatically affect its benefits.

The type and sophistication of the organization have an important bearing. At one extreme a software supplier, producing generic financial frameworks for the insurance sector might justifiably invest considerable up-front resources to ensure adaptability and robustness of its offering. In contrast, an end-user organization needing a just good enough order capture system may prefer to cut corners under the pressure of tight deadlines.

The underlying cause of the difficulties is that software is commonly shown as a cost (not an asset) on the corporate balance sheet. As components are intrinsically predicated on the concept of software as an asset that can be reused and extended in different contexts, this presents a set of major cultural challenges for most companies.

Although these cultural challenges are a subject for a book in their own right, it is important that we at least itemize the challenges and suggest some measures for dealing with them. We will then move on to consider a set of more tactical measures in the form of funding models, metrics, costs and benefits.

8.2.1   Cultural challenges

Organizations that adopt CBD techniques do not magically gain the benefits of reuse. In fact, reuse can be achieved using traditional techniques. The underlying critical success factors are less technical than organizational and cultural. The management challenges of reuse are well documented (Griss, 1995; Goldberg and Rubin, 1995). To fully exploit the reuse potential of components requires instituting the right cultural conditions, for example:

Software reuse does not happen in a vacuum

- Provision of easy access to reusable components in the form of catalogues, browsers and other tools.

- Procedures that encourage and support reuse. Effective team structures are so important that Chapter 9 is devoted to this subject.

- Instituting the right communication mechanisms between IT and business people to promote collaboration and synergy of ideas and ensure that technical innovation is not pursued as an end in itself.

- Training and education in the theory and practice of reuse.

Such conditions do not 'happen overnight' and require a fundamental shift in an organization's culture. This takes time; for example, many organizations find they have to iterate through several versions of a repository before they have one that is solid.

8.3 Funding models

There are two major types of funding model: corporate and project. In reality a combination of the two is often sensible.

8.3.1 Project funding

The project funding model assumes a basket of money provided by a group of projects with like-minded interest to reduce costs through common components. Motivation is often provided in these cases by a need to leverage existing systems or databases. For example, there may be several projects that use different product databases that contain duplicated or fragmented information. This results in an attendant drain on resources to maintain consistency across the different databases. A basket of money is set aside to unify and rationalize the databases. Designing a set of components to provide unified data services on top of the existing databases might be a good logical first step toward unification. This also allows the organization to cut its teeth on component technology and provides a good justification in terms of the effort that is saved in integration activities. The component services produced can be published using a developers' gallery as an early step toward promotion of reuse of components. There must also be sufficient funds to cover up-front investments in component infrastructure, education, planning, architecture and enterprise analysis, though to a much lesser degree than with corporate funding. Such costs should be factored into ROI calculations.

The advantage of project funding is that ROI can often be demonstrated reasonably quickly. The disadvantage is that there are risks in overlooking wider requirements and that project owners may still balk and argue about their own interests. If one owner is paying most of the money then he or she may influence requirements to the detriment of the common interest

The project group might well seek return on their investment, not only through improved quality, reduced time to market and increased business benefit, but also by selling or licensing the components they have developed. In fact, this may well be an initial step toward evolving the project group to the role of a corporate clearing house that assesses common needs and supports projects

8.3.2 Corporate funding

The corporate funding model assumes an enterprise wide investment that is used to provide a jump-start to projects seeking to reduce costs through reuse of components. A corporate clearing house or architecture team acts as a component custodian that assesses common needs and supports projects. Ideally this team will focus on the most important common business processes, identify the required business components with respect to the overall software architecture, and specify the interfaces of business components with very high reuse potential.

The architecture team may work in different ways to achieve these goals. At one extreme a top-down approach necessitates large up-front investment in architecture, component planning, detailed design and quality engineering. On the other hand, the corporate budget may be smaller with the architecture team acting more in the role of high-level planners, delegating work to projects subsidized from the corporate fund. Either way, the corporate fund must be sufficient to cover up-front investments in component infrastructure, education, planning, architecture and enterprise analysis. There is also the investment in component management tools and techniques to help sow suitable components. We can expect a significant up-front rise in IT costs to cover the up-front expenditure. It may not be possible to directly recoup these costs and some organizations may simply write them off, although they can be factored into ROI calculations.

> **The advantage of the corporate funding model is that because projects do not pay for component reuse, they are more likely to do it! The disadvantage is that it may be a long time before any ROI is realized**

The corporate clearing house might well seek early return on their investment, not only through improved quality, reduced time to market and increased business benefit, but also by selling or licensing the components on the open market. After the initial period of 'free components' (often of around two years), components are sold or licensed internally to projects.

8.3.3   Charging for components

CBD involves a change in the traditional manpower estimation approach to charging. It would be unfair to pass the full component development costs on to the first client. A way of addressing this problem is to employ a form of licensing model: either licensing of interfaces or service usage.

In an interface licensing model, a consumer effectively pays to use an interface or set of interfaces (component specification) in development. The consumer is free to enhance the interface as appropriate, often through specialization or extension.

In a service usage model, a consumer effectively pays to execute a service or set of services provided at run time.

8.4   Choosing the right funding model

Choosing the right funding model depends on the organization's approach to CBD. We will consider three different approaches:

1 Components in advance.
2 Components as you go.
3 Components by opportunity.

A common theme is to employ reuse checkpoints to encourage adaptability and generality to be built into the component interface specifications

It is important to understand that the approaches are paradigms. Often, a combination of approaches may be appropriate and different areas of the organization may follow different paradigms.

In all cases, it is important to articulate benefits against the costs. This must include business benefits, not only software benefits.

8.4.1   'Components in advance'

'Components in advance' (CAV) is a top-down, architecture-centric approach that aims to significantly improve adaptability of software to match changing business processes, ensuring that business data and behaviour likely to be required by multiple applications is specified (and subsequently developed) only once. The focus is on the most important business processes that exhibit significant commonality and reuse potential and provide scoping criteria for architecture planning. The component architecture drives component provisioning and integration, which work in parallel with respect to the track-based pattern. Figure 8.1 illustrates the process with major flows highlighted.

This approach implies a corporate funding model. The ultimate promise of long-term reusability necessitates more up-front investments in component infrastructure, education, planning, architecture and enterprise analysis. There are also investments in component management tools and techniques that help to sow suitable components.

By removing the overheads of component analysis and design from the project teams, the approach gives the project teams free rein to focus on immediate business needs. In essence, it helps to reduce the conflict of priorities between project teams and the architecture team. However, although it removes the burden of up-front costs from the project teams, it may well delay projects

Figure 8.1
Components in advance within the track-based pattern

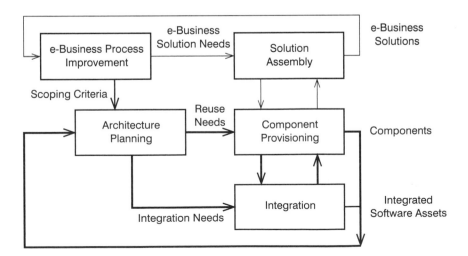

especially in the early days. This is because of time taken to ensure that a component is in fact 'right for the project', as well as greater time taken over activities such as integration and assembly testing.

A good ploy is to concentrate on a significant sub-set of business processes with good reuse potential and high value-add.

It is a mistake is to expect projects to start paying for components on Day 1. Project managers under pressure of deadlines and tight budgets will usually trust their developers to produce the goods before outsiders. Worse still they will be very resistant to paying for the privilege!

CAV perhaps works best as a 'jump-start' strategy, in which a few key components are provided free of charge for an initial period as a corporate booster injection to get a reuse culture rolling. Later, once trust has been established with the project teams, charging can be gradually introduced.

Metrics will not be available, so some rough rules of thumb for costing are required (see Section 8.5).

It is a mistake to bite off too much too soon with this approach. Attempting to 'model the enterprise' will often result in failure as witnessed by many of the corporate data modeling initiatives of the late 1980s

8.4.2 'Components as you go'

'Components as you go' (CYG) sets out to incrementally deliver business solutions and components in parallel. Each increment must deliver business benefit and at the same time contributes to the evolution of the component architecture, as illustrated in Figure 8.2. Although the approach does not mandate detailed up-front domain analysis and architectural modeling, it does nevertheless rely on a good understanding of both the business domain and an established CEE (see Appendix 1, Section A1.1). With CYG, the level of detail should generally be much less than with a CAV project.

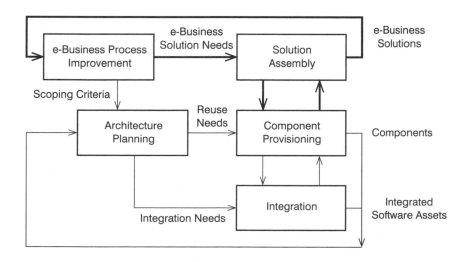

Figure 8.2
Components as you go within the track-based pattern

The approach relies on evolutionary incremental development to evolve components to fit the business need. The approach should work both horizontally and vertically through an evolving architecture. Horizontal work addresses overall business needs and involves a shallow pass across families of interdependent services that require high user interaction. Vertical work addresses integration of new technologies where components are to be implemented using different technologies that have not been used in combination before.

CYG implies a project funding model, supported by some corporate funding. The essence of the approach is to 'start small', focus on early delivery of business benefit and build toward larger grained components, with the advantage that metrics can be gathered and evolved as part of the program. Use of a developers' gallery works well as part of the approach.

Again, reuse checkpoints (see Chapter 4, Table 4.1) encourage adaptability and generality to be built into the component interface designs. This enables a solution initially targeted at one business group to be later evolved for more general use. However, even with the best will in the world, such honourable intentions can soon evaporate in the heat of a late software project. Therefore a certain degree of corporate help is expedient. This can take the form of subsidies to projects to focus on reuse and secondment of component designers or architects from the architecture team[2] to help build in sufficient software flexibility and encourage the sowing of reuse.

8.4.3 'Components by opportunity'

'Components by opportunity' (CBO) involves assembling business solutions by reuse of pre-existing components as the overriding strategy, as illustrated in Figure 8.3. With CBO the level of detail should generally be less than with a

Figure 8.3
Components by opportunity within the track-based pattern

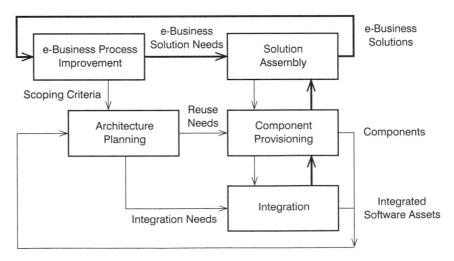

2. The component assessor role, described in Chapter 9, is particularly relevant here in promoting the right kind of culture.

CYG project. Gap analysis is again used to conduct component provisioning on a 'reuse before you buy before you build' basis using the techniques described in Chapter 7. However, there is perhaps more of an emphasis on deciding whether business requirements might be adapted in order to exploit components for business advantage, rather than the traditional approach to gap analysis of measuring available software against an ideal requirements set.

The key benefits of the approach are shorter time to market, and avoidance of 'analysis paralysis'. The approach is rooted in the need to solve business issues by **opportunity**. For example, it may happen that right at the start of the project someone remembers that some part of the current problem had already been solved for an earlier project. If this partial solution has the form of a separate component it can be reused in the new project, thus saving time and cost.

This approach may appear to be 'the cheap option'. However, if it is not to be a free for all in which components are bolted together in a frenetic rush to meet project deadlines, a degree of planning and architectural coordination is required

If the approach is to be taken seriously, it needs up-front investment in education, tools and techniques that help to harvest suitable components. Architectural work is needed up-front to establish the CEE. Suitability of components and architectural impact must be assessed. This is particularly important for low-level business infrastructure components (such as Currency or Address) that are often the subject of CBO. Overall, we should expect roughly a 50:50 split between corporate and project funding.

There are some particular risks with the approach:

- It must be possible to identify and acquire appropriate components from multiple sources, both internal and external to the organization over the internet. Component management and repository technology is therefore a key enabler of the approach.

- While time spent on most activities, especially coding, is reduced by assembling from components, there is a greater emphasis on assembly and integration testing.

- There is unlikely to be time to go through a full certification process with purchased components. This may have to follow as a separate exercise if they are to be used regularly on subsequent projects.

Metrics will not be available, so some rough rules of thumb for costing are required (see Section 8.5).

It is interesting to note that as the CAV and CYG approaches begin to reap benefits in terms of component architecture and availability of components, so the CBO approach gains momentum. Eventually, it will become the standard scenario for CBD.

8.4.4   Examples of funding and charging

Example 1   Subscribing to virtual services through project funding

A group of projects in purchasing and procurement have a common requirement for a supplier interface. The project group decides to subscribe to a set of common party services, provided over the internet, by an external service provider using project funding. The project group build their own adapter based on usage of the core party services, such as locate party address and verify party history. The adapter provides services such as find best supplier and find cheapest supplier. This is reflected in the dependency shown in Figure 8.4. This scenario corresponds to the CBO approach described earlier.

Figure 8.4
Subscribing to a set
of virtual services

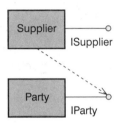

Example 2   Specializing an interface through project funding

Again a group of projects in purchasing and procurement have a common requirement for a supplier interface. The project group license a party interface from a component framework provider, using project funding. A supplier interface is specialized from the Party interface and funded by the application project. In this case, the project group owns the supplier interface. This scenario corresponds to the CBO approach described earlier. Figure 8.5 shows the inheritance of IParty by ISupplier; note that Party and Supplier remain separate components as in the previous example.

Figure 8.5
Specializing an
interface

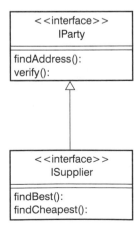

An alternative would be to fund provision of the IParty interface and specialization of the Supplier interface at corporate level and charge to the project group for that interface on a licensing or usage basis. In this case, a consolidated Party component provides both IParty and ISupplier interfaces as illustrated in Figure 8.6.

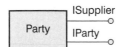

Figure 8.6
Providing dual interfaces through a common component

Example 3   Generalizing modules to form a component through corporate funding

Different software modules in an automobile dealership are providing overlapping functionality for car and van sales. There is a need to generalize this functionality, both to remove redundancy and duplication and also to provide a common set of services for other types of vehicle. Other benefits are marketability, flexibility, integration and maintainability.

There is therefore a good case for corporate funding. The corporate clearing house harvests results from application projects to form a generalized Vehicle component. The Van Sales and Car Sales are charged to projects on a licensing or usage basis. This scenario, illustrated in Figure 8.7, corresponds to the CYG approach described earlier.

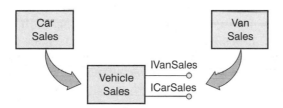

Figure 8.7
Forming a new component using CYG

Example 4   Provisioning a new component through corporate funding

There is enterprise-wide need for a common Party component. The corporate clearing house develops the Party component, the interface of which is initially provided free to provide 'jump-start' for application projects; later it is charged to projects on a licensing or usage basis. This scenario, illustrated in Figure 8.8, corresponds to the CAV approach described earlier.

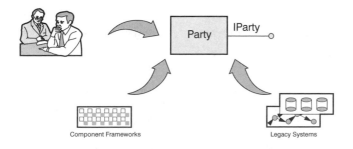

Figure 8.8
Forming a new component using CAV

8.5 Metrics

ROI for IT poses a set of questions that have always been thorny and difficult. Although there is a wealth of literature on software metrics and estimation models, most organizations continue to struggle here. Here are some reasons why:

- The difficulty of collecting meaningful software metrics and using these to make accurate predictions of development time and cost.
- Software is a moving playing field: five years worth of history in software is equivalent to fifty years in most industries, so even when metrics are established they tend to lose their validity as the technology changes.
- 'Metrics' are not perceived as a priority by management. In fact, metrics are often seen as 'getting in the way' of tight deadlines and 'real project work'.

The upshot is that meaningful cost–benefit analysis for the introduction of new techniques is, despite what the research papers might say, actually quite rare in mainstream software. Realizing e-business with components lends a new urgency to cost–benefit analysis – no longer is it the poor relation – migration to CBD involves grasping this nettle!

The good news is that though it is early days for components, metrics information for reusable software is starting to mature (Jacobson *et al.*, 1997; McClure, 1997; Poulin, 1997). In the next section, we look at some rough rules of thumb for CBD metrics. The figures provided can be used as a starter for weighting according to specific organizational circumstances and for evolving in the light of experience, as part of a metrics change management program (DeMarco, 1982).

8.5.1 Some rules of thumb

The literature (Poulin, 1997; Tracz, 1995, McClure, 1997; Jacobson *et al.*, 1997) suggests that as a rule of thumb:

> "**It costs between 150% and 250% more to develop reusable software than developing it without reuse**"

> "**It saves 80% to develop software by reusing software over developing software from scratch**"

We will use these figures to make high-level estimates of ROI.

ROI is calculated in terms of payback (the number of times the software is used, before ROI > 0). Rogers' Rule of Thumb states:

> "**A component must be reused 3 times to get payback**"
>
> Rogers, 1995

More formally Henderson-Sellers (1996) provides the following formula:

$$\text{ROI} = \frac{\text{Cost of IT efforts without reuse} - \text{Cost of IT efforts with reuse}}{\text{Cost to develop reuse}}$$

Applying our rules of thumb, in the context of the formula gives:

$$\text{ROI} = \frac{(n \times \text{saving}) - \text{investment}}{\text{Investment}} = \frac{(n \times 0.8) - 2}{2}$$

$$n = 3$$

Interestingly, this tallies with Rogers' Rule of Thumb. Rules of thumb are not precise scientific formulas, but they are at least a start. They can be used as baselines from which organizations can cultivate their own metrics.

We also note that these are rules of thumb for reusable software, not components. Clearly, the costs of components will be slightly higher due to increased quality standards of rigour implied by components in terms of activities such as certification[3] and integration testing. However, much will depend on the level of certification required, which may vary from organization to organization. We therefore can weight the overall rule of thumb appropriately according to the level of certification.

8.6   Component cost–benefit factors

Though a complete analysis of IT costs is outside the scope of this book, we need to be aware of the particular cost factors that make CBD different.

In this section, we will provide some pointers on the costs of CBD both in terms of component provision and solution assembly. We will also take a look at the likely reduction in costs as a result of using CBD, first within IT and then in overall business terms.

8.6.1   CBD cost factors

The cost to develop a component embraces a possible range of factors, over and above those considered for traditional software. These factors include the following:

---

3. Levels of certification can start at the very informal, in which case the component is probably published as no more than 'a good idea' via a developers' gallery. At the other end of the spectrum, a component might be fully integration tested and tested in a wide variety of different contexts as well as being specified to rigorous standards using a standard such as OCL for specification of services and invariants. In that case, the component would be formally published through component management software. A well-known bank operated five levels of certification, gradually promoting components through the different levels as part of an evolutionary and incremental migration strategy.

- Cost to analyze generic need (for example using viewpoint analysis).
- Cost to determine reuse potential.
- Cost to find a component (greatly reduced by effective component management software).
- Cost to buy or license a component.
- Cost to engineer a component; or cost to produce a component adapter or wrapper.
- Cost to generalize the component for reuse.
- Cost to context test (by unknown clients) and integration test (with known clients and servers).
- Cost to specify interfaces.
- Cost to certify component.
- Cost to document.

The cost to reuse a component also includes factors not applicable to traditional software. However, these factors should be more than offset by savings in other activities. Cost to reuse a component includes the following:

- Cost to find the component (greatly reduced by effective component management software).
- Cost to buy or license the component.
- Cost to modify/adapt/specialize the component.
- Cost to understand the component.
- Cost to assembly test the component.
- Cost to integrate the component into the component architecture.

8.6.2   Identifying IT benefit factors

IT benefits can be divided into benefits through cost reduction and benefits through increased value. Cost reduction is usually expressed in terms of increased software productivity, increased value in terms of software quality. The astute reader will note that productivity and quality are intimately related. However, to keep things as simple as possible within our scope, it is useful to consider them separately.

The arguments for increased software productivity through software reuse are well covered elsewhere. These are usually based on effort to complete various development tasks with and without software reuse. Here are some estimates of the effect of CBD from Jacobson *et al*. (1997):

" **Maintenance cost: reductions of 5 to 10 times. Time to market: reductions of 3 to 5 times**"

There are some key factors that need to be measured in identifying the costs and response times that are most typically reduced by CBD. We need to measure the numbers and rates of new and changed requirements, and software defects[4] and how long it takes IT to respond.

CBD should help to reduce requirements overload with software that adapts to business needs, and localize the effects of changes resulting in decreased time to repair, and a reduction in the ripple effects of changes. For example, spending on major technology changes, such as conversion and upgrade costs, decreases as a result of de-coupling interfaces from implementations.

Increased value in terms of software quality can only be determined by measuring quality. We have stressed the importance of capturing non-functional requirements, of which quality attributes are an important element, within component specifications (see Appendix 2, Section A2.7).

Quality attributes are statements about *how well* the system is expected to function; examples include reusability, maintainability, accuracy, clarity, replaceability, interoperability and scalability, performance, flexibility and adaptability. A full discussion of quality attributes is outside our current scope; the reader is referred to Fenton (1991) for a useful discussion on quality models and to Gilb (1988) for a discussion of quality templates as a means of measuring quality attributes.

8.6.3 Identifying business benefit factors

Most organizations, while addressing IT productivity adequately, continue to either treat the business issues as somehow separate, or simply ignore them altogether. Justification for the new approach is, from the very outset, one step removed from real business needs such as an increased ability to take advantage of new markets. This helps fuel the unhelpful but pervasive view of IT as a cost to be reduced and controlled rather than an asset to be nurtured and exploited.

The continued rise of e-business means that most organizations will go out of business if they continue to treat it as a mere support function

We therefore address business benefits in direct relation to software benefits. Again, we will divide these benefits according to cost reduction and increased value.

The most obvious savings in business cost are often a result of the application of IT for previously manually implemented processes, for example, a reduction in front office staff as a result of a data capture system. While a valuable part of the business case for IT, of more interest here are the costs incurred by the business as a result of **not** changing to CBD. We need to assess the impact of IT cost reductions that we expect to achieve with CBD on the business itself.

Most basically, we can measure the amount of over-spend incurred by the business resulting from late or over-budget IT development and maintenance. For example, a project that was two months late might not only have resulted in inflated project cost, it might also have caused a temporary clerical labour force to be employed for manual data entry over the two months. What was the cost? How much would have been saved by getting the system in on time?

---

4. Jacobson *et al.* (1997) estimates defect density reductions of 5 to 10 times using CBD.

In the case of an e-business system, the consequence of such a two-month delay might cause the company to rapidly lose market share. The e-business window of opportunity closes through the two-month period, as competitors get their own e-business systems to market ahead of the game.

It is important to identify the number, type, significance and cost of factors such as:

- Current business opportunities that are either lost or delayed because of IT constraints, or perhaps not discussed with IT until it is too late.

- Situations where business has altered to reflect inadequacies of previous IT solutions.

- Situations where the business has been unable to exploit new technologies because of IT solutions with 'built-in obsolescence'.

We can quantify the advantages of CBD by measuring the consequences of previous failure, and explaining that CBD addresses the underlying causes. Resulting figures should be factored in to the ROI rules of thumb (based solely on software productivity) provided earlier to render a solid business case. If the business suffered this much, last time IT got it wrong, what are the consequences of failure using e-business?

We also need to look at increased value as a result of CBD. Typical examples include better customer service as a result of process integration using components, or an increase in high-value business as result of purchasing, or outsourcing commodity components and releasing development effort to focus on value-added functionality. However, although useful and important, it is often difficult to measure increased service and the results become relegated to the status of 'intangibles' on the spreadsheet.

We need to relate software quality attributes (see section 8.6.2) which must be *measured*, with concrete business benefits. Table 8.1, drawn from experiences with different organizations, shows quality attributes commonly associated with components in terms of both the IT and business benefits that they might realize. Feel free to adapt it to develop arguments for CBD that are aligned with your own organization's business goals.

Table 8.1   Relating quality to business benefits

Quality attribute	CBD feature	Business goal
Reusability	IT productivity is enabled though reuse, not only of code, but also interfaces. Reuse of legacy code through integration.	Time to market; reduced costs. Protect and capitalize investment in legacy assets, including costs of Y2K work.
Maintainability	Software problems are localized, ensuring robust design.	Reduce maintenance costs releasing energy to focus on business need.
Accuracy	Comprehension of specifications assisting efficacy of software process. Outsourcing of design and programming work to clearly agreed contracts.	'Fitness for business purpose' through clear interface specifications. Saving cost by utilizing externally provided services.
Clarity	Rigorous interface specification allows certification and authentication techniques to ensure that the correct interface is being used.	Corporate consistency and development of intellectual capital.
Replaceability	Component can be easily replaced with another having different implementation code.	Reduce costs in migration path to future technology.
Interoperability	Removal of dependence on specific technology, increase agility to exploit new technologies.	Exploit business benefits of new technologies.
Scalability	Management of scale and complexity; different components can be allocated to separate teams or projects, for example, isolation and management of quality measurement and testing.	Ability of business to scale-up smoothly to exploit new business opportunities; increasingly it is key niche areas, rather than traditional treadmill business processes, that are adding most value.
Performance	Components can be deployed using technology appropriate to varying run-time constraints.	Ability to respond to business needs efficiently at busy 'crunch times' with peak transaction volumes.
Flexibility	Liberation from binary build or buy 'one-track' development; enables hybrid solutions.	Leverage software market opportunities for business advantage.
Adaptability	Components can be reused and extended in 'plug and play' fashion in different business contexts.	Response to fundamental business change, including mergers and takeovers, virtual enterprises.

Your company might simply go out of business as a result of a poorly conceived or badly designed e-business solution

As IT people our business case for moving toward CBD naturally focuses primarily on software productivity. Witness the number of efforts to justify new approaches on the reuse argument alone: reuse rules ok! Other software features, such as better performance or scalability also figure, but normally in a poor second place. But much worse still, we neglect to understand the business benefits that we should be seeking to achieve. It is important to identify the business benefits, relate these to software features and factor these into our ROI calculations if we are to start to treat software as an asset to be nurtured and exploited.

8.7   Summary

Financing of CBD is significantly more challenging than traditional development. Different CBD routes require different funding and charging strategies. Baseline metrics are available to help organizations make initial quantification of the costs. More accurate metrics can be evolved from the initial figures through metrics change management programs.

Equally we must consider benefits. e-Business greatly increases the stakes in the application of software for business advantage. Although the prizes, for example, in the form of dramatically increased market share, are much bigger, the consequences of failure are equally staggering.

8.8   References

DeMarco, T., *Controlling Software Projects*, Prentice Hall (Yourdon Press), 1982.

DSDM Corporation, *DSDM and Component-Based Development*, DSDM White Paper, 2000.

Fenton, N. E., *Software Metrics*, Chapman and Hall, 1991.

Gilb, T., *Principles of Software Engineering Management*, Addison-Wesley, 1988.

Goldberg, A., and Rubin, K., *Succeeding With Objects: Decision Frameworks for Project Management*, Addison-Wesley, 1995.

Griss, M., 'Software reuse: objects and frameworks are not enough', pp. 77–9, 87,*Object Magazine*, February 1995.

Henderson-Sellers, B., *Object Oriented Metrics: Measures of Complexity*, Prentice Hall, 1996.

Jacobson, I., Griss, M., and Jonsson, P., *Software Reuse*, Addison Wesley, 1997.

McClure, C., *Software Reuse Techniques*, Prentice Hall, 1997.

Poulin, J. S., *Measuring Software Reuse*, Addison Wesley, 1997.

Rogers, D., 'Reusing objects: avoiding the object legacy', *Software Development*, November 1995.

Tracz, W., *Confessions of a Used Program Salesman*, Addison Wesley, Reading, MA, 1995.

e-Business team organization   9

9.1   Introduction

An increased diversity of specialist skills both technical and business, is needed
to realize successful e-business systems. Business people are taking a much more
central role in software development, and IT people are having to apply a much
greater level of business understanding. New breeds of individual are emerging
as the dividing lines between business and software grow blurred.

Increasingly, we are seeing the emergence of teams whose members are not
only geographically separated but also work for different employers (including
self-employed contractors) with different cultures. This presents new and interesting management challenges. The e-business solutions that such 'virtual
teams' work toward, span easily across organization boundaries, different geo-
graphical locations and different hardware and software technologies
(Mittleman and Briggs, 1998).

These factors add new dimensions of scale and complexity to the organization and management of teams. Above all they bring an attendant risk of low
team spirit. In this chapter we will define a set of team roles that help address
these challenges. We provide organizational guidance on how to use the roles to
structure teams tasked with realizing effective e-business systems, using the
process framework described in Chapter 4.

9.2 Team roles in context

Let us start with some basic definitions and consider the significance of team roles.

9.2.1 Basic definitions

Project A set of activities that organizes and employs resources to create or maintain a product (or part of a product).

Team A number of individuals working together in a coordinated fashion to meet a defined set of objectives.

Team Role A related set of responsibilities and skills.

9.2.2 The significance of team roles

Team roles bring objectivity to the process in that one person may fulfil more than one role and one role can be supplied by many individuals. Different roles, played by various individuals at appropriate times, are applied through the stages of a project.

Good professionals know their roles. Ask an airline pilot or air steward, and there is no question about what they have to do in flying the aircraft or keeping the passengers happy. In most industries the situation is pretty much the same. On a film-set, you will find a director, a gaffer, a make-up artist and the various actors and actresses with clearly defined parts to play. In software the situation is not so clear-cut: many of us have become generalists, epitomized in titles like analyst/designer that disguise a multitude of different roles. The more virtual the project and the more that the lines between business and software start to blur, the more lack of role definition starts to hamper the project.

> A major reason that many of today's teams are ineffective is that they overlook the implications of the obvious. People do not make accommodations for how different reality is when they and their colleagues no longer work face-to-face. Teams fail when they do not adjust to this new reality. Lipnack and Stamps (1997)

9.2.3 Traditional teams versus e-business teams

Traditionally, software project team members worked in close proximity for the same employer within a common corporate culture that separates IT and business worlds.

This traditional team of the 1970s and 1980s was the team in which I grew up. Corporate loyalty and careers for life were the order of the day. Skills such as project management, systems analysis and programming were neatly pigeon holed.

Fixed hierarchical management structures reinforced an environment of ordered stability that could border on the bureaucratic. A personal focus also dominated the software landscape as one's weaknesses were addressed through training or through the support of colleagues. Team spirit was not a major risk. Deadlines were met through informal agreement and a willingness to burn the midnight oil in the interest of the common cause. Business and IT people inhabited different worlds.

In traditional teams roles were not an issue, because they actually corresponded with job titles!

Sometime in the mid-1980s this world started to change irrevocably. As businesses started to downsize and streamline their operations, so IT too started to downsize. Software team members either lost their jobs or moved out of their corporate silos into much leaner and meaner 'empowered' teams with a focus on meeting defined business objectives, in whatever fashion got the job done. By the mid-1990s, team membership had grown increasingly diverse, both organizationally and geographically. Virtual teams were born. The focus switches away from the team and toward the individual. The risk of low team spirit becomes critical. Increasingly specialist skills become necessary to utilize rapidly emerging technologies. Accurate contracts are required that stipulate deliverables to be produced by stated deadlines (Thomsett, 1998). At the same time, business people start to take a much more central role in software development, and IT people are having to apply a much greater level of business knowledge. There is a major need for clear team roles to bring a sense of understanding of each other's strengths and weaknesses, to gel the team and renew business focus.

9.2.4 Leadership

e-Business team members operate with a high degree of independence. Commitment is very much 'arms length'. Leadership tends to be more informal and *ad hoc* than with traditional models of leadership (Belbin, 1981). How can we achieve coordination and collaboration in the context of this new autonomy?

First, it is essential that all members of an e-business team understand the e-business process improvement plan. As new members join they must be given an opportunity to familiarize themselves with this plan. More than that, they should be given the opportunity to influence the plan to reflect their own skills and experience. Such collaborative sharing of project vision breaks the mould of traditional teams in which individuals are pigeon holed by job function into narrow sub-sets of the project.

Leadership of e-business teams involves sharing the project vision

Second, contractual details assume a greater significance. It is essential that team members understand exactly what they are being tasked with and the constraints (deadline and budget) and codes of conduct within which they will have to work. Leadership of e-business teams is correspondingly focused on ensuring compliance of deliverables to agreed objectives and to time and budget constraints.

Both shared vision and working to contract rely heavily on effective modeling to communicate plans and document deliverables. The component modeling techniques described in this book are ideally placed to help here

9.2.5   Shedding IT's anorak

The sheer diversity of technical skills required to realize effective e-business systems range from web-wizardry, graphic design ability and HTML/XML/Java programming to knowledge of component standards. The increasingly hybrid nature of the software process, based on an integration as opposed to a development model, presents diverse component provisioning routes that need to be managed and controlled. Clear definition of team roles is imperative.

At the same time, realizing e-business using CBD raises the bar in terms planning and business analysis skills. For example, objectives for e-business systems are generally more challenging and diverse than those of traditional systems, often including things like better corporate image, advertising, STP, IT cost savings, better customer and supplier relationships and gathering customer information. Highly skilled people are needed to clarify and prioritize these objectives and to resolve the tensions between them. Business folks are starting to get much more IT savvy. However, the push in the other direction is often less obvious. Our role set therefore needs to supply some innovation in getting IT to 'think business' using internet technologies based on CBD.

9.2.6   Further team attributes

The general subject of team working has been covered extensively in the literature and we do not wish to re-tread that ground here. However, three particular attributes of healthy teams deserve some mention:

1 **The right size**
   Consider that if there are X number of staff in a team, then the number of possible communications on a person to person basis is $X(X-1)/2$. Thus if the team is 6 then the number of paths is 15; if the team is 10 then the number of paths is 45. A number of studies (Martin, 1991) have measured the relative productivity between large and small teams showing a differential of up to an order of magnitude. Teams should be limited to around 6 full-time individuals at any one time. At the same time, remember that a number of individuals will typically jump on and off the project at various stages of a project, and also that the project may call on a number of part-time individuals through its course.

2 **The right environment**
   Despite the move to virtual working, good working environments remain critical to project success. Cramped, open plan office environments predicated on short-term cost savings are not conducive to success. A number of studies have demonstrated the effect of environment on productivity (DeMarco and Lister, 1987). The team also need education in and easy access to the right technologies, for example, up-to-date 'groupware' (Duarte and Synder, 1999).

3 **The right communication mechanisms**
   While traditional methods of communication, such as interviewing and reports, conference calls and video conferencing, have their place in the

world of CBD for e-business, dynamic environments assume greater significance. Interactive workshop environments that follow the principles of JAD are an important team tool for fostering good communication and accelerating the development process (August, 1991). JAD can be applied in traditional or electronic contexts.

9.2.7   Types of e-business teams

It is useful to distinguish different types of e-business teams. In migrating to e-business using CBD three families of team emerge:

1 e-Business solution-oriented teams work toward providing specific results that have immediate business impact. This type of team is essentially transient and works to short timescales (weeks or months rather than years). Membership is frequently diverse and fluid, with individuals coming into and out of the team as their skills are needed. Individuals working within the network may not even be aware of certain others within the team.

2 Component-oriented teams work toward providing functionality that is typically shared by solution teams. These teams may carry out proactive architectural work or work over specified timescales toward provisioning of components. The team is again essentially transient, but is likely to stay together much longer than a solution-oriented team. It is also less likely that individuals working within the network are unaware of certain others within the team.

3 Business-IT alignment teams are management teams that work toward ensuring that all software projects serve business needs. The work involved is ongoing and proactive. Membership is frequently of long duration and individuals working within the network are very much aware of each other. They collaborate on a regular basis on the use of e-business in the achievement of corporate objectives. Team members have top-level authority to direct solution-oriented teams in achieving these objectives and to ensure sufficient resources and funds are available.

9.3   e-Business solution-oriented roles

Many of the roles described in this section emphasize the business-driven development culture that is fast becoming characteristic of successful solutions development. These roles (see Sections 9.3.1–9.3.7) draw on work that the author has carried out applying the principles of Dynamic Systems Development Method (DSDM). Descriptions are kept deliberately brief as details are supplied elsewhere (DSDM Consortium, 1997; Stapleton, 1997), though e-business keynotes are added. The remaining roles are described in more detail.

9.3.1   Executive sponsor

The executive sponsor owns the solution as this person is ultimately responsible for it. The role must hold a sufficiently high executive position to resolve business issues and make sure funding is available.

9.3.2   Visionary

The visionary acts as the driving force behind the project and is responsible for ensuring the project delivers a solution that meets original business objectives defined in the e-business process improvement plan. The role is normally from the senior business community which may include organizations with whom the organisation is partnering in e-business. The role contributes to key design decisions and resolves any conflicts arising from different business areas.

9.3.3   Ambassador user

The ambassador user drives the business requirements and provides a key focus for bringing in input from the business community in general. The role is normally from the business community, and understands and communicates the business context of the project.

9.3.4   Adviser user

The adviser user brings practical knowledge of relevant business practices to the project. The role is often fulfilled by someone who will eventually use the solution to be developed and plays an important part in prototyping and usability testing. In e-business solutions, involving large communities of 'anonymous' customers, the adviser user may act as a surrogate of an internet customer.

9.3.5   Solution designer

The solution designer is responsible for designing and assembling software that meets needs for e-business process improvement and is of direct value to business users. The role is very much an all-rounder ranging from analysis of business needs through to implementation of a solution. Skills are required in user communication, software requirements modeling, user interface design, high-level coding and scripting languages and testing.

9.3.6   Project manager

The project manager coordinates projects involving several teams, ensuring good team motivation and reports to senior management. The role plans, estimates and performs risk management. The responsibility is to ensure that the solution as a whole is delivered as agreed. The role may be staffed from either the business or IT communities.

9.3.7   Team leader

The team leader runs the team on a day-to-day basis and ensures the solution for which the team is responsible is delivered as agreed. The role is responsible for promoting team well-being and motivation, and is likely to be staffed from the IT community.

9.3.8   e-Challenger

e-Business systems can be adapted and extended very rapidly to cover new business requirements. Such systems can also be configured over very short timescales. It is important to have dynamic skills for rapidly prototyping these systems not only at a technical level, but also at a business level. It is here that the role of e-challenger employs techniques such as storyboarding and scenario playing to ensure that the correct requirements are addressed.

Yet more significantly, the e-challenger not only ensures the correct requirements are met, but also that the software can adapt to possible changes in the business. Future scenario playing – the work-shopping of things that could impact the business – is immensely useful here.

The e-challenger must be able to coordinate wide groups of remote users to ensure they provide effective feedback to scenarios and prototypes. The e-challenger must be able to act as 'surrogate' for the group. Good inter-personal skills and political awareness are therefore essential. This role has a working knowledge of how to use the internet coupled with good business knowledge, including understanding of relations with business partners. The essence of the role is to challenge existing business practices through innovative application of new technologies. The role must therefore not be afraid to challenge the status quo!

9.3.9   Web master

The web master is responsible for ensuring the design of web pages meets the needs and objectives of the e-business process improvement plan. The role advises on design and ergonomics of the web user interface, and provides specific expertise, such as graphic design skills for web pages. Equally, the role helps ensure that web designs are consistent with the company's marketing strategy and takes a central responsibility for key web aspects, such as portal design. The role requires a combination of up-to-date knowledge of the very latest techniques for designing good web user interfaces plus excellent marketing skills and partner awareness.

9.3.10   e-Business integrator

As we have continually stressed, e-business systems work within the context of a business process. It is imperative to clarify how the business process as a whole will operate with the new e-business piece. For example, in an electronic store the process might have links to other internal processes (Invoicing), external processes

(Inventory and Shipping), internal components (Customer Relationship) and external components (Credit Check). Exceptions must be identified; for example, what happens if the item is out of stock or the Customer Relationship component is down?

The e-business integrator must have a good overall knowledge of the business, business modeling skills and proficiency in techniques such as storyboarding and scenario playing to enable identification and resolution of business integration issues.

Also, objectives for e-business systems are generally more challenging and diverse than with traditional systems. Another function of the e-business integrator role is to clarify and prioritize these objectives as well as resolve the tensions between them.

9.4   Component-oriented roles

9.4.1   Component sponsor

The component sponsor authorizes resources for component projects and ensures that component provisioning or integration projects are not just technical fads; that is, they address real business needs as identified in the e-business process improvement plan.

The role should be of sufficiently high managerial level to gain organizational commitment and funding for component provisioning or integration projects. This is particularly important, as such projects will initially be of higher cost, but often not realize any immediate business value. Without this commitment, the cost effectiveness of using CBD would be compromised.

9.4.2   Business component architect

The business component architect is responsible for architecture planning of business components. The role is responsible for the business layers of the enterprise component architecture, and helps and advises with project component architectures. This includes identifying and acquiring business components, ensuring consistency of business component usage across projects and promoting the value of reuse via the component sponsor and e-vangelist. The role has similar skills to a very experienced senior business component designer, with further political awareness skills. There is a need for overall vision, good awareness of strategic business needs, technical awareness of patterns and frameworks, and keeping good contacts with industry bodies. Note: this role typically works in tandem with the technical component architect. Although classified as a component-oriented role, it is important for the role to participate proactively in e-business solution assembly. This encourages a collaborative climate and ensures that the business component architect is very much aware of the practical consequences of his or her decisions.

9.4.3 Technical component architect

The technical component architect is responsible for architecture planning of technical infrastructure components covering areas such as user interface, communications, device handling and data storage management. The role is responsible for the enterprise component implementation architecture. This includes identifying and acquiring technical components, ensuring consistency of technical component usage across projects and advising on component and middleware standards. The role has similar skills to a very experienced senior technical component designer, with further political awareness skills. There is a need for overall vision, good knowledge of component infrastructure technologies and EAI products, and keeping good contacts with industry bodies. Note: this role typically works in tandem with the business component architect.

9.4.4 Component assessor

The component assessor identifies areas for reuse improvement and pollinates reuse across solution projects. The role acts as a centre of excellence for provisioning strategy knowledge, for example, keeping up to date with the latest developments in component frameworks, virtual services and EAI capabilities. In particular, the role is responsible for monitoring CBD industry trends and initiatives and the use of IT by competitors. The role has good awareness of existing systems, packages, databases and available components. This knowledge is used to assess reuse opportunities and to evaluate reuse requirements. This is a very proactive role, calling for good inter-personal skills, in that it must help solution designers to grow reuse into their solutions where appropriate as well as alert them of opportunities to reuse existing services. In a recent article, Alan O'Callaghan (2000) talks of a 'Keeper of the Flame' pattern, a role for ensuring conceptual integrity of architecture through facilitation. The component assessor is indeed very much a keeper of the flame.

9.4.5 Reuse manager

The reuse manager plans and controls the overall activities of component projects and makes policy decisions concerning reuse. The role assesses and reports on the impact of software reuse on business needs, often in liaison with the metrics expert role. The role works closely with the component assessor role (from a technical viewpoint) and the provisioning strategy manager role (from a business viewpoint).

9.4.6 Business component analyst

The business component analyst models generic business requirements and develops business component specifications for these requirements. As it is free from concerns about how the specification might be implemented, the role has a renewed focus on the business requirements. The role requires excellent business awareness of the business areas covered by the business component specifications and has a good working knowledge of CBD techniques and, where appropriate, of CBD tools.

9.4.7   Business component designer

The business component designer develops and integrates implementation models for business component specifications and codes, tests and implements the resulting business components. The role typically applies container technology to implement components. The business component designer requires an excellent knowledge of internal component design techniques, component implementation technologies and tools. A good appreciation of the business contexts in which those technologies are put to work is important.

9.4.8   Technical component designer

The technical component designer models generic technical requirements, develops component specifications for these requirements and ensures technical integration. The role designs implementation models for these specifications and codes, tests and implements the components. An important aspect of the role is the ability to design components that integrate different technologies, for example, by applying EAI tools. The technical component designer requires an excellent knowledge of internal component design techniques and component implementation technologies.

9.4.9   Legacy expert

The legacy expert advises on the suitability of legacy assets (applications, databases or software packages) for wrapping or adapting and conversely on the impact of proposed new components on legacy assets. The role should be expert in renovation and mining tools and techniques to get legacy assets in a fit state for wrapping, as well as maintaining the legacy asset to align with any changes to wrapper design and code. In a large organization, the role may split into separate roles for legacy system code, legacy databases and software packages. Clearly, the role must have excellent legacy application knowledge as well as a good appreciation of CBD.

9.4.10   Component librarian

The component librarian is responsible for managing the component library, ensuring that all documentation is up to date and easily accessible to designers. The role publicizes capabilities of components, checks components in and out of the library and controls configuration management of components. The role will also often be responsible for component configuration management tools, though increasingly this aspect constitutes a separate role. An excellent knowledge of component management software and good administrative and classification skills are mandatory.

9.4.11 Component certifier

The component certifier is responsible for setting component specification standards, communicating them to the development teams and ensuring full compliance to these standards before any component is allowed to be stored in the component library. Certification should be continuous in the sense that quality must run right through the process and is not 'bolted on' as an afterthought. The role is expert in component specification standards and should have a thorough knowledge of quality requirements.

9.4.12 Component tester

The component tester provides independent advice and assistance on testing strategy, planning and practice. CBD presents the tester with the added challenge of whether the component's interfaces can be extended or specialized to support the kinds of contexts for which it was designed. With the incremental approach, the role must encompass regression testing to ensure that previous increments, as well as the current increment, are up to scratch.

9.5   Business–IT alignment roles

9.5.1 E-vangelist

The e-vangelist promotes organizational enthusiasm for e-business using CBD and helps set CBD in business context. The e-vangelist is responsible for presenting the business case for CBD and influencing the component sponsor role. The role is most appropriate when an organization is making its first foray into CBD. In contrast to the 'Visionary' role, the e-vangelist does not monitor CBD projects – this is performed by the reuse manager role. The skills required for this role are similar to the visionary, but also include an excellent knowledge of e-business and its strategic impact on the organization as well as good appreciation of CBD and how it is used at reference organizations.

9.5.1 Provisioning strategy manager

The provisioning strategy manager is responsible for sourcing and controlling use of external component provisioning (see Chapter 7 for details on provisioning strategy). The role acts as a central service broker and manages the relationships with partners, outsourcers, virtual service providers and ASPs. The provisioning strategy manager must be able to negotiate contracts, understand financing and ensure that the provisioning strategy meets business needs. The purpose of the role is to ensure that the provider understands the business needs and that the business understands the technology decisions. The role is likely to be staffed by a senior executive with excellent IT industry knowledge, a working knowledge of the business and good business management skills. The role works closely with the reuse manager and component assessor roles.

9.5.3   Business process coordinator

The business process coordinator is responsible for ensuring that services provided by business components match the business capabilities required by business processes. The role stands at the intersection of business process improvement planning and CBD software projects. The purpose of the role is to supply the glue that is often missing to ensure that the disciplines work together effectively by coordinating business models and software models. The business process coordinator is expert in business process modeling and understands the relevance of the components to business needs. The role understands the effects of new, changed or acquired components across different business processes and must therefore have broad business knowledge.

9.5.4   Component funding manager

In Chapter 8, we saw that funding for CBD is considerably more challenging than with traditional projects. Dealing with these challenges presents a major cultural challenge for most companies, that demands a component funding manager role.

The component funding manager has responsibility for establishing CBD funding and adapting funding models in line with business needs. The role plans and controls overall funding and charging of components across projects, assesses and reports on the economic impact of component reuse on business needs, and develops metrics often in liaison with a metrics expert role.[1] Unlike the metrics expert role, which is very much tactical and support oriented, the component funding manager is very much a strategic role.

The component funding manager assesses the strengths and weaknesses of the different funding models and helps articulate benefits against the costs (see Section 8.6).

9.6   Organizational models

In this section, we consider how to apply the roles using organization models. We will look briefly at the significant shifts in organizational models over recent years, a shift so rapid that it is occurring as I write this book! We will then move on to explain how the roles can be adapted to suit specific organizational needs, before considering an example organizational model, based upon the process described in this book, that looks set to be pervasive over the coming years.

---

1. A metrics expert is responsible for both project metrics (time and cost data) and quality metrics (for example, fitness for business purpose, component performance or usability data). The role works at a tactical level to provide projects with guidance with estimation, collects project and quality metrics and maintains a metrics database.

9.6.1   Brief historical observations

One approach to CBD, quite pervasive in the mid-1990s but still alive today, is continually to remind ourselves that reuse is a long-term investment. This involves fighting the 'Not Invented Here' syndrome, providing artificial incentives and constantly preaching the gospel of reuse. A separate reuse group is housed in an ivory tower with the mission of issuing reuse by edict to the developers in the jungle below.

At the other extreme are organizational models that are a reaction to the failure of such IT-driven approaches. These models advocate distribution of value-added IT to the business units, with wholesale outsourcing of the IT infrastructure functions to ASPs (see Chapter 7).

The internet has accelerated this trend, often by entering businesses not through the IT department but through the 'back door' marketing department, keen to use the new technology as a commercial window to the world. Business unit managers were thus the first to develop relationships with the new technology providers. IT simply did not have the expertise needed for internet issues. The upshot has been a shift in strategic decision making away from IT departments, to the business units. Indeed, at the time of writing, articles abound on the demise of traditional IT and the growth of ASPs, for example Whittle (2000).

9.6.2   Customization

Effective e-business using CBD does not 'happen over night', it requires a migration plan, an important element of which is the question of team-working. Roles should be introduced to fit business needs in graduated fashion. For example, an organization can choose to implement some roles, but leave others until it has moved further through the internet spectrum of sophistication. Again, there are some roles that may be combined especially in smaller organizations, or perhaps split into further roles in very large organizations.

The roles presented are an abstract set that can be mixed and matched according to the needs of your own organization and projects. Different organizational structures are possible. In the next section we will consider one alternative.

9.6.3   Using the track-based pattern

Back in Chapter 4 we introduced the track-based pattern as one way of structuring the CBD process. Broadly, the team types and their roles map particularly well to the track-based process pattern as shown in Figure 9.1.

In this model, business-IT alignment work is carried out at executive level by the most senior people in the organization often with the help of external consultants who are experts in the field. This team operates across all tiers of the track-based framework ensuring that solution- and component-oriented work is in line with the business goals.

Figure 9.1

Team types and the
track-based pattern

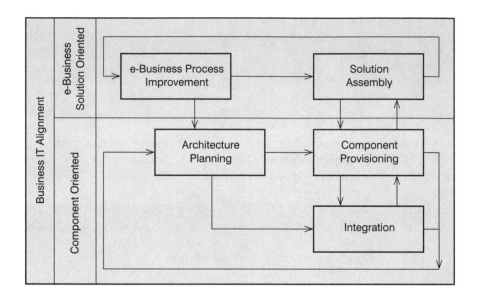

e-Business solution-oriented work is typically carried out by the business units. The focus is on assembly of e-business solutions using services provided by the component provisioning teams. Development work is only peformed where it can add business value.

Component-oriented work is performed either by central IT groups or out-sourced to component providers or ASPs. A typical scenario is for a central IT group to perform architecture planning and component specification work, but for an increasing proportion of component provisioning to be sourced through a diversity of routes, discussed in Chapter 7, such as virtual services and framework extension. Integration forms a significant amount of the work of component oriented teams, both integration of existing systems, for example using EAI tools, and integration of external component frameworks and virtual services.

9.7   Summary

Teams are growing increasingly virtual, resulting in greater individual autonomy and with great potential for communication problems. There is a parallel increase in specialization. At the same time, e-business makes technology a central business enabler and means that IT is no longer merely a support function. Coupling the two, realizing e-business with CBD involves some fundamental shifts and an increased blurring of the border between business and IT. Clear focus is required if corporate software anarchy is to be avoided.

The team roles presented in this chapter are intended to help remedy this situation. We looked at how they can be used to catalogue and communicate responsibilities and to help organize resources within the context of the process framework described in Chapter 4.

Team roles are only one element of a much larger cultural equation. In particular, we briefly looked at how the nature of leadership is changing and at how organizations are changing to exploit the world of e-business. More broadly, organizational cultures must change toward collaboration and away from departmental self-interest to be successful in e-business.

9.8   References

August, J. H., *Joint Application Design*, Prentice Hall, 1991.

Belbin, M., *Management Teams*, Heinemann, 1981.

DeMarco, T., and Lister, T., *Peopleware*, Dorset House,1987.

DSDM Consortium, *DSDM Version 3*, Tesseract Publishing, 1997.

Duarte, D., and Synder, N., *Mastering Virtual Teams: Strategies, Tools and Techniques That Succeed*, Jossey-Bass, 1999.

Lipnack, J., and Stamps, S., *Virtual Teams*, Wiley, 1997.

Martin, J., *Rapid Application Development*, Macmillan, 1991.

Mittleman, D., and Briggs, B., 'Communication technology for teams: electronic collaboration', in E. Sunderstrom and Associates, *Supporting Work Team Effectiveness: Best Practices for Fostering High-Performance*, Jossey-Bass, 1998.

O'Callaghan, A., 'Architects and superheroes', *Application Development Advisor, SIGS/101* Communications, vol. 3, no. 4, March 2000.

Stapleton, J., *DSDM – The Method in Practice*, Addison Wesley Longman, 1997.

Thomsett, R., 'The team is dead – long live the virtual team', *Proceedings of Cutter IT Summit*, Cutter Information Corp., Boston, 1998.

Whittle, S., 'Surviving the new economy', *Computing*, VNU Business Publications, 17 February 2000.

A1 Appendix 1[1] Component-oriented technologies

A1.1   Component and internet standards

A1.1.1   Component execution environments

A component execution environment (CEE) is required to provide run-time technical infrastructure services and to hide low-level technology issues from the business solution developer. The CEE offers its infrastructure services through sockets, software written to well-defined and well-known standards, into which components can plug.

There are many kinds of services that may be offered, for example, packaging, distribution, security, transaction management and asynchronous communication.

The CEE complies with a component specification, a set of standards, including a component meta-model. A number of competing component infrastructures exist based principally on one of three technologies: Microsoft's Component Object Model (COM+), Sun's Enterprise JavaBeans (EJB) and the OMG's CORBA. The latter two in large part converge as evidenced by the CORBA 3.0 specification. In providing an overview of these technologies, we should be mindful of what is meant by 'component standard' as eloquently noted by Paul Harmon:

> Although there is a tendency to compare COM+ and EJB, you must be very careful when you do this. EJB is a specification published by Sun. It assumes class libraries and other specific code utilities incorporated into the Java platform. However, in

---

1. This appendix draws on work by Alan Brown in his book (Brown, 2000) and is provided here with permission of the author.

addition to the code provided by Sun, the EJB specification defines products that only exist when others implement them. In contrast COM+ can only loosely be termed a standard. There is no Microsoft document that completely defines all the elements of COM+ ... in fact it is code that's available in Windows 2000.

Harmon, 2000

A1.1.2   Microsoft's COM+

To enable sharing of functionality across desktop applications, Microsoft developed the Component Object Model (COM) as the basis for interapplication communication (Box, 1997). Realizing the value of COM as a generic approach to component interoperation, Microsoft defined its strategy of component-based applications to consist of two parts. The first is its packaging and distribution services, Distributed COM (DCOM), providing intercomponent communication. The second is currently referred to as Microsoft's Distributed interNet Applications (DNA) architecture, providing the additional categories of component infrastructure services making use of DCOM. Collectively, these ideas are referred to as Microsoft COM+ (Platt, 1999).

The packaging and distribution services implemented in DCOM consist of three major aspects:

1 The Microsoft Interface Definition Language (MIDL), which describes how business functionality is packaged for external access through interfaces.

2 The COM component model describing how components can make requests of each other's services.

3 The DCOM additions to COM providing support for location transparency of component access across a network.

Additional component infrastructure services are provided by Microsoft via two products, both making extensive use of the underlying packaging and distribution services:

1 The Microsoft Transaction Server (MTS), which provides security and transaction management services.

2 The Microsoft Message Queue (MSMQ), which provides support for asynchronous communication between components via message queues.

The Microsoft component infrastructure services offer significant functionality to builders of component-based applications for Windows platforms. For anyone building a distributed WindowsNT or Windows2000 solution, these services provide essential capabilities to greatly reduce the cost of assembling and maintaining component-based applications.

A wide range of Microsoft-focused components are available from third-party software vendors (for example, there are well in excess of 100 COM components listed at ComponentSource – see www.componentsource.com for details).

A1.1.3   CORBA

The Common Object Request Broker Architecture (CORBA) (Siegel, 1998) provided by OMG defines the basic distribution architecture for component-oriented applications. There are three major aspects of CORBA:

1 The OMG's Interface Definition Language (IDL), which describes how business functionality is packaged for external access through interfaces.

2 The CORBA component model describing how components can make requests of each other's services.

3 The Internet Inter-ORB Protocol (IIOP), which allows different CORBA implementations to interoperate.

Together with the CORBA standard, a set of additional capabilities is defined in the CORBAServices standards (OMG, 1999). A wide range of services has been defined, or is currently under investigation. However, the following services are those that are most often found in currently available implementations:

● Lifecycle services, which control the creation and release of component instances.

● Naming services, which allow identification and sharing of component instances.

● Security services, which provide privacy of connection between a client and provider of services.

● Transaction services, which allow a user to control the start and completion of distributed transactions across components.

A1.1.4   EJB

There are a number of Java technologies providing packaging and distribution services. These include (Austin and Powlan, 1999):

● JavaBeans, which is the client-side component model for Java. It is a set of standards for packaging Java-implemented services as components. By following this standard, tools can be built to inspect and control various properties of the component.

● Remote Method Invocation (RMI), which allows Java classes on one machine to access the services of classes on another machine.

● Java Naming and Directory Interface (JNDI), which manages the unique identification of Java classes in a distributed environment.

An additional set of technologies support the remaining component infrastructure services. These are necessary to allow Java to be used for the development of enterprise-scale distributed systems. These technologies are defined within the Enterprise JavaBeans (EJB) standard for server-side portability of Java applications (Sun Microsystems, 1999). EJB provides the definition of a minimum set of services that must be available on any server conforming to the specification.

The services include process and thread dispatching, and scheduling, resource management, naming and directory services, network transport services, security services and transaction management services.

The goal of the Enterprise JavaBeans specification is to define a standard model for a Java application server that supports complete portability. Very briefly, a user develops an Enterprise JavaBean implementing the business logic required. The user also defines a Home interface for the bean defining how the EJB objects (i.e. instances of the EJB) are created and destroyed, and a remote interface for clients to access the bean's behaviour. An EJB executes within an EJB container. Many EJB containers can operate within a given EJB server. The EJB server provides many of the basic services such as naming, transaction management, and security.

Toward the end of 1999, Sun Microsystems announced a new initiative to provide a standard platform on which to build distributed applications in Java. This initiative, known as the Java 2 Enterprise Edition (J2EE) standard, builds on the Java 2 standard, and adds most of the important programming interfaces in an application server (Roman, 1999). To fulfil the promise of making the development of component-based systems in Java easier, the J2EE augments this collection of standards and interfaces with (Flurry, 1999):

- A programming model for developing applications targeting the J2EE platform, including a number of key design heuristics for creating efficient, scaleable solutions in Java.

- A compatibility test suite verifying J2EE platform implementations conform to the J2EE platform as defined by the collection of standards and APIs.

- A reference implementation that offers an operational definition of the J2EE platform. This demonstrates the capabilities of the J2EE platform, and supplies a base implementation for rapid prototyping of applications.

By collecting these elements together under a single umbrella, Sun aims to simplify the creation of distributed systems development for Java.

A1.1.5   EJB and the CORBA component model

A primary element of the EJB specification is the definition of the interface to an EJB container. In essence, this is an abstraction of the lower-level Java services, but because it is abstract, it can be implemented in a technology other than the Java services themselves. For example, many of the early EJB-based application servers layer this interface above an implementation of the Common Object Request Architecture (CORBA) services. This has allowed them to rapidly support the EJB standard on top of a mature existing product. OMG has now moved ahead with the creation of a component standard. In essence, it differs from the EJB specification in four main ways (Frankel, 1999):

1 It provides a simplified abstraction of the CORBA services. By building on the EJB specification, the CORBA component model provides a language-neutral API for building and assembling components with common infrastructure

services. One of the benefits of this is that it promotes interoperability among server vendors by specifying a standard way in which to use CORBA services to implement the EJB container API.

2 It supports an extended concept of a component. A rich set of component concepts is supported in the CORBA component model based on the notion of ports and channels. A component defines the events it emits and consumes, together with the interfaces it provides and those it uses. Each source or destination for interfaces and events are modeled by the generic concept of a port. Connections between ports establish a channel with specific semantics (e.g. a channel may be defined to be exclusive to those ports).

3 It distinguishes between four types of components with different semantics based on the kind of lifecycle and persistence required for the component. *Entity components* are expected to have long-term persistence and will typically be involved in transactional behaviour. Management of the persistence is delegated to the container. *Process components* also are persistent, but have no client-accessible primary key. *Session components* have no container-managed persistence and have a transient state that the component must manage. *Service components* are stateless.

4 It allows packaging and deployment elements to be defined as part of the definition of components. XML descriptors are used to describe the packaging and deployment of the components. Additionally, an assembly descriptor describes component dependencies as port connections from one component to another.

The EJB and CORBA standards define the basic structure and vocabulary for an architectural style of building distributed systems. This style, involving containers, ports, channels and assemblies, will undoubtedly become the common language for designing, documenting and discussing distributed systems architectures.

A1.1.6   XML

The Extensible Markup Language (XML) is a relatively simple tag-based language that can be used to describe and communicate information between senders and receivers (Harold, 1999; Deadman, 1999). The XML document format embeds the information within tags that express the information's structure. XML also provides the ability to express rules governing the structure of the information. These two features allow automatic separation of data and metadata, and allow generic tools to validate an XML document against its grammar. XML is an open technology standard of the World Wide Web Consortium (W3C).

One of the reasons that XML has gained so much popularity so quickly is that it provides a simple solution to a range of different problems. Most notably, XML can be used in three different situations (Goulde, 1999):

1 In building and maintaining web-based information systems, XML provides a markup language similar to Hypertext Markup Language (HTML), but with the ability explicitly to define the structure of the data being displayed.

2 In the exchange of structured documents between systems, a standardized approach based on the Standard Generalized Markup Language (SGML) is popular. However, SGML is complex and difficult to implement and support. XML offers a simpler approach in which only a core set of concepts is defined.

3 Many distributed applications require interchange of data to provide integration and coordination between the various pieces. XML offers a standardized approach for defining these integration schemes. Its simplicity, and the ease with which it can be extended, allow it to be used in a wide range of integration scenarios in many domains.

Due to its simplicity, XML can encode a wide variety of information structures. The rules that specify how the tags are structured are called a Document Type Definition (DTD). An XML DTD defines the different kinds of elements that can appear in a valid document and the patterns of element nesting that are allowed.

The big issue occurs in agreeing on the definition of the tags. For example, if multiple partners in an e-business are to take advantage of XML they need to agree on the semantics of business terms such as 'vehicle' and 'reservation date'. Otherwise the syntactical advantages of XML are lost. Not only do organizations need to standardize internally on business terms, but they need cross-organizational agreement.

Many standardization groups are therefore working in different business domains attempting to create standard DTDs to allow greater sharing among solutions within that domain:

- Microsoft is working hard to facilitate rapid adoption of XML through its BizTalk initiative, collaborating with several industry groups to create a set of standard XML tags. Its BizTalk server is an XML server aimed at encouraging rapid use of XML (Harmon, 2000). In addition, www.biztalk.org currently publishes about 350 XML schemas ready for use.

- The Open Applications Group (OAG) was formed in 1995 to address the need for interoperability across software packages. Its integration domain model (OAGIS) provides common definitions of business objects and business interfaces, that now offer a full set of XML DTDs (www.openapplications.org).

- RosettaNet is an XML-based initiative formed by a group of IT industry players to establish an e-business framework for IT supply chain integration.

- XML.ORG is an independent resource for news, education, and information about the application of XML in industrial and commercial settings. Hosted by OASIS, the Organization for the Advancement of Structured Information Standards, it is a non-profit, international consortium dedicated to accelerating the adoption of product-independent formats based on public standards.

The limitation of XML is that it is data-centric. However, the strong industry initiatives that centre on XML reveal a deeper significance: a rapid dawning that the interfaces of business systems are important.

A1.2   Physical architecture

In this section, we provide an overview of server-based architecture and consider the main features of EAI tools.

A1.2.1   Server-based architecture

Early successes with client–server architectures were quickly followed with a recognition that such an approach suffers from severe limitations. Recently, these limitations have become all too apparent with support required for large numbers of browser-based clients, the need to target different web-based infrastructure technologies and the struggle to integrate with a wide variety of back-end servers and application systems.

In response to these concerns, a server-based architecture continues to evolve supported by a growing number of products from vendors specializing in various aspects of these solutions.

Different servers are distinguished, where the term 'server' refers to a set of services that may be implemented in hardware, software or a combination of both.

- **Web browser** The web browser supports the internet user interface and should provide a common look and feel for all applications. Web browser infrastructure typically consists of Java applets. The user interacts with the web browser by selecting links or by entering information into fields on a web-based form. This information is transmitted across the internet to the web server which recognizes requests for external data and passes the request to an application proxy whose task is to map data requests to the application server.

- **Web server** To enable a variety of web-based clients requires web servers capable of delivering the content using standards such as HTML and XML. Navigation between pages and initial data validation is typically performed on the web server to reduce communications traffic and limit requests to the other servers. A specific kind of web server called a 'portal server' has assumed significance. The whatis online dictionary (www.whatis.com) defines a portal as a 'World Wide Web site that is or proposes to be a major starting site for users when they connect to the Web or that users tend to visit as an anchor site'. Portal servers allow users the capability to customize portals for individual client requirements.

- **Application server** The application server provides a core set of technical services, including ability to handle transactions and deal with asynchronous communication across distributed systems. It achieves this with application server-specific technologies, or via integration with existing transaction processing or message-oriented middleware solutions. Business components are typically deployed within the application server. To allow this, an application server provides a description of its available services, defines the interfaces to those services, provides deployment capabilities for installing the software on the application server and provides the necessary CEE. Different kinds of application server technology are now available from a variety of vendors (Garone, 1999).

- **EAI server** The EAI server provides EAI tools for creating EAI software units that manage consistency between existing systems, databases and packages. It provides a focal point for all integration code, reducing the complexity of complex system integration scenarios. Many EAI products have recently become available. Initially, these were based on proprietary standards, but lately many have converted to use XML as a standard interchange mechanism.

- **Asset server** The asset server supports existing systems, databases and package, packages, databases and screen designs. A range of techniques has been developed to achieve reuse of existing core functionality, including approaches such as wrapping and mining. Many products are available to assist with these techniques. Indeed, many of the existing middleware and transaction monitor products now offer wider capabilities to support these approaches.

A1.2.2   EAI tools

The concept of EAI is a mixture of existing technologies and new perspectives, wrapped up with a large dose of marketing hype. It is important to look at a number of broad aspects of the EAI approach and their impact on enterprise-scale solutions as a whole. Most large systems and packages provide APIs to expose their services and data to third-party access. Typically, new applications make calls through these APIs to access and retrieve data from the existing systems.

The additional challenge facing EAI is that many different APIs exist for a variety of existing systems and packages. In the past, organizations building integrated systems were required to develop and maintain that integration infrastructure themselves. They faced the challenge of keeping the infrastructure up to date as each of the constituent systems and packages evolved. This is a costly and error-prone task.

What is required is a consistent way to connect a variety of existing systems and packages. To assist with this, a number of EAI connector solutions have been developed. Initially, these connectors provided an intermediate proprietary representation, a set of translators into this intermediate representation from many of the common packages (e.g. SAP, Baan and PeopleSoft), and a toolkit for developing custom translators for other packages and systems. Use of these connectors helps to greatly reduce the effort required to integrate a collection of systems.

Proprietary connector-based solutions are now available from a number of vendors, and are used quite extensively in assembling new systems making use of existing services. However, the proprietary nature of the solutions does introduce a significant limitation to their use. To address this, many of the EAI connector vendors are moving towards a standard connector approach based on the XML. In addition, package vendors themselves are currently moving toward the use of XML as the standard technology for import and export of data from their packages. This should reduce the effort and improve the consistency of EAI solutions using a connector approach.

A1.4　References

Austin, C., and Powlan, M., 'Writing advanced applications for the Java platform', Sun Microsystems, available at http://java.sun.com, December 1999.

Box, D., *Essential COM*, Addison-Wesley, 1997.

Brown, A., *Enterprise Scale Application Development in the Internet Age*, Prentice Hall, 2000.

Deadman, R., 'XML as a distributed application protocol', *Java Report*, October 1999.

Flurry, G., 'The Java 2 enterprise edition', *Java Developers Journal*, December 1999.

Frankel, D. S., 'CORBA components – alive and well', *Java Report*, October 1999.

Garone, S., 'IDC's definition and segmentation of the application server market', *IDC Bulletin*, International Data Corporation, 1999.

Goulde, M., 'Is XML the answer? Depends on the question', *Application Development Trends*, October 1999.

Harmon, P., 'Windows 2000, DNA 2000, and COM+', *Component Development Strategies*, vol. X, no. 2, February 2000.

Harold, E. R., *XML Bible*, IDG Books Worldwide, 1999.

OMG, 'The object management architecture (OMA) guide', available from www.omg.org, 1998.

OMG, 'CORBA services', available from www.omg.org, 1999.

Platt, D. S., *Understanding COM+*, Microsoft Press, 1999.

Roman, E., *Mastering Enterprise JavaBeans and the Java 2 Platform, Enterprise Edition*, John Wiley Press, 1999.

Siegel, J., *CORBA Fundamentals and Programming*, John Wiley Press, 1998.

Sun Microsystems, 'Enterprise JavaBeans Standard', Version 1.1, available at http://java.sun.com, 1999.

Appendix 2
Techniques at a glance

A2.1   Introduction

This appendix presents a set of core modeling concepts for applying CBD for
effective e-business systems. The purpose of this appendix is not to describe a
complete definitive methodology, but to establish 'just enough' semantics and
notation using practical techniques that lend themselves to a component-
oriented approach. Hints and tips have been included to guide the reader. The
following techniques are presented in catalogue form for ease of use:

- Business modeling.
- Business type modeling.
- Use case modeling.
- Interaction modeling.
- Architecture modeling.
- Specification modeling.

The techniques have evolved from numerous sources, including Sterling
Software's Advisor method (Dodd *et al.*, 1999), which was itself inspired by the
ideas of Catalysis™ (D'Souza and Wills, 1999), as well as the author's experiences
in developing and applying the SELECT Perspective™ (Allen and Frost, 1998)
approach.

The Unified Modeling Language (OMG, 1999) has become the generally
accepted standard for object-oriented analysis and design modeling notation
and semantics. The notations for most of the techniques use UML as a base,
only extending notation where it is not explicitly provided. We also employ

some business modeling extensions to UML (Penker and Eriksson, 2000). Additionally we use a couple of techniques (use case refinement maps and interface responsibility maps) which, though they make use of UML, are used as thinking tools rather than formal UML diagrams. We refer to these as 'maps' (rather than 'diagrams') to make this clear.

It is important to understand that we do not cover specifically OO techniques in this book. Our focus is on business analysis, architecture and specification. There are many books on applying UML on OO analysis and design projects (Fowler and Kendall, 1997; Penker and Eriksson; 1998; Oestereich, 1997; Page-Jones, 2000) though fewer on applying UML to CBD (Allen and Frost, 1998; D'Souza and Wills, 1999). If you wish to design your components using OO implementations specifically for e-business systems the choice is more limited though books are now available (Conallen, 2000).

A2.2   Business modeling

There are many different modeling techniques that can be used for business modeling and the reader should feel free to use their favourites. However, cosmetics are irrelevant here: it is correct application and understanding of concepts that is critical for effective e-business using business components as we emphasize throughout this book.

A.2.2.1   Business modeling concepts

> A **business concept** represents a key information category.

> A **business proposition** can be a rule that defines or constrains aspects of the business, a goal that directs or a problem that inhibits an aspect of the business. Business propositions are assertions that are essentially binary; that is they can be verified as true or false.

Business rules may be expressed as textual constraints (for example, 'payment ok = order ok + money ok') or invariants (see Section A2.7.1). It is also possible to use hierarchy diagrams (see Section A2.2.2).

Business goals (for example, 'must achieve 70% increase in orders by January 1st 2001'), and problems (for example, 'sales are currently 70% down on forecast') may be global or associated to business processes and shown on process flow diagrams (see Section A2.2.2).

> A **business process** is a group of related business capabilities that add value to a customer. The capabilities are realized by families of tasks, that may collaborate in different event-driven groups to fulfil the business process.

A business capability is provided by one or more services thus providing the connection point to software requirements.

Business processes work (at a higher level) in business process groups and are analyzed (at a lower level) in terms of atomic business processes (see below). There are three types of business process:

A **customer process** provides value-added deliverables to the external customer, for example, Market Vehicle or Service Vehicle.

A **sustaining process** adds value to the external customer, however it does not exchange information or material directly with the customer, for example, Price Vehicle or Administer Warranty.

An **enabling process** has internal customers. It provides the services necessary to support the core processes and manage the business; for example Legal Management or Financial Management.

A business process may also be distinguished as an atomic process to assist with achieving a good level of granularity and prevent over-analyzing to unhelpful levels of detail.

An **atomic process** is a task that is the responsibility of one role acting in one place at one time, in response to a business event, which adds measurable business value and leaves the data in a consistent state, for example, Approve Credit or Price Part.

A **role** is a set of responsibilities that may correspond with a job title (purchasing agent) or organizational unit name (Purchasing), but may also be abstract (Purchaser).

A2.2.2   Business modeling notation

Business concept diagram

Key business concepts are sketched out on a business concept diagram as illustrated in Figure A2.1. The diagram is very much a thinking tool used to help understand the business domain. Business concepts are declared as boxes; lines between boxes represent associations between business concepts. Note that the diagram is a form of UML class diagram; multiplicity and association names are optional.

Figure A2.1
Business concept
diagram

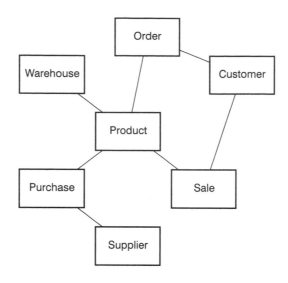

Organization flow diagram

An example organization flow diagram[1] is shown in Figure A2.2. Roles are shown as boxes and arrowed lines represent information dependencies. The roles shown on an organization flow diagram are usually physical things: organization units, external agents (including customers and suppliers) or computer systems. Both 'as is' and 'to be' diagrams are possible.

An organization flow diagram illustrates all external and internal organization interactions that significantly influence performance. This diagram provides 'the big picture' and helps determine the business context, as well as helping uncover possible end-to-end processes and suggesting channels to market and third-party involvement.

Process flow diagram

The process flow diagram notation is indicated in Figure A2.3. Note that we use a 'lite' version of UML activity diagrams, in which business processes or business process fragments are modeled as UML activities. As a general rule we would not use the diagram at a sub-atomic process level. Sometimes the diagram is known as a swim-lane diagram as roles are diagrammed as parallel bands (Rummler and Brache, 1995). A process may be shared between roles, but is positioned in the swim-lane depicting the role that has prime responsibility for the process. Goals and problems may be attached to processes as indicated (Penker and Eriksson, 2000). Unfortunately the activity diagram notation does not provide an explicit representation of business events that occur following constraints imposed by the business environment. This is an important requirement for BPM. We

---

1. Note that UML does not supply a diagram for this purpose.

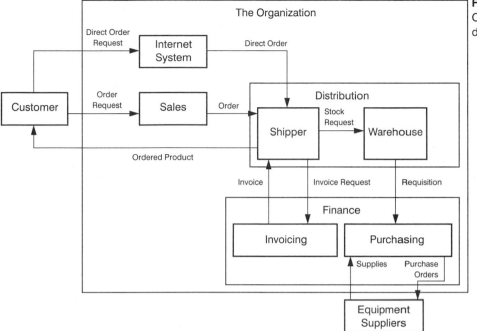

Figure A2.2
Organization flow
diagram

therefore extend the notation with pseudo-activities that simply wait for business events to occur. A pseudo-activity name appears in brackets.

In one sense the process flow diagram is a lower level version of the organization flow diagram, with roles shown as swim-lanes instead of boxes. However, process flow diagrams are essentially prototypical and best employed to model scenarios, whereas the organization flow diagram provides an overview of the business.

Rule and goal hierarchy diagrams

Hierarchy diagrams, such as rule hierarchies and goal hierarchies, can be created, as shown in Figure A2.4, following the Eriksson–Penker business extensions to UML (Penker and Eriksson, 2000).

A2.2.3   Business modeling quick guide

Here is a quick guide to business modeling, based around the activities of business process planning itemized in Section 2.2.2:

● **Envision** Sketch out 'to be' business concept and organization flow diagrams for the overall strategy and use these to scope the e-business improvement plan. Set out the overall business goals and problems.

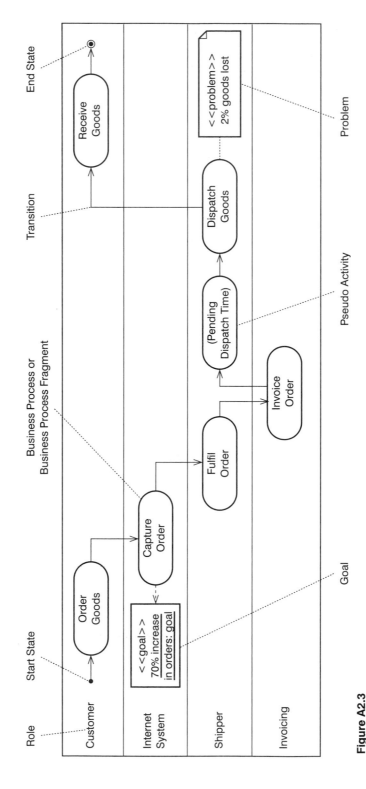

Figure A2.3
Process flow diagram notation

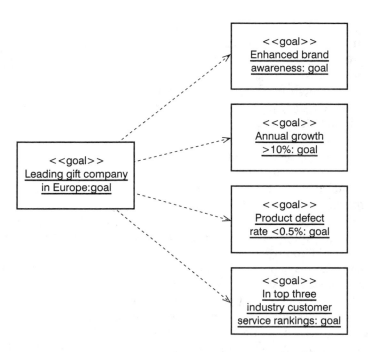

Figure A2.4
Goals hierarchy
diagram

- **Reflection** If appropriate,[2] build an 'as is' organization flow diagram for the chosen scope. On subsequent iterations build process flow diagrams. Refine business goals and problems.

- **Conception** Refine the 'to be' business concept and organization flow diagrams for the chosen scope. On subsequent iterations build process flow diagrams. Refine business goals and problems.

- **Organizing** Use the 'to be' models to scope areas for improvement, identifyng e-business solution needs for software projects (typically in terms of sets of customer processes) and scoping criteria for architecture planning (typically in terms of enabling or sustaining processes). Use the 'as is' models to help define migration paths.

- **Iterate!**

A2.2.4   Business modeling tips and hints

In process flow analysis it is important not to over-analyze (or under-analyze) the threads and achieve a useful level of atomic granularity. 'Time-slice' groups

2. If starting up a new .com business this does not apply. In other cases, it is often appropriate to build at least an 'as is' organization flow diagram if only to have an understanding of your starting point for improvement. However, it is sometimes better to leave this until the 'to be' model has been built in order to avoid prejudicing your thinking about where the business is going with preconceptions based on where it currently is.

of activities by events that denote ~~essential constraints imposed by the business, not by technology.~~ That way, you stand a greater chance of finding atomic processes.

Business processes that are strategically important need to be understood and commonality identified across those business processes. ~~Use sustaining processes and enabling processes to help identify areas of commonality.~~

Process flow diagrams are helpful for gaining business insight. However, e-business processes seldom support information flow in regulated chains. ~~The effective e-business provides business capabilities that are configured in adaptable fashion to meet customer needs.~~ Therefore do not worry too much about the detail and rigor of the flow. Concentrate rather on achieving a good set of atomic processes and the roles involved.

~~Use process flow diagrams selectively to model the interesting, problematic or strategically important scenarios.~~ Do not try and use these diagrams to 'define the world' in huge detail – such a path leads to guaranteed failure.

Business rules may appear in various guises and at various places through the different models, ~~for example, as business goals on a process flow diagram~~ or ~~textual constraints attached to a business concept or business process.~~ Where there are lots of potential rules consider modeling rules separately, for example, using techniques such as rule hierarchies (Veryard, 1999).

In a book of this size and scope we have not been able to cover all possible business modeling techniques. For example, business simulation tools are useful in providing dynamic visualization of the models. Also, there is significant work in the area of business patterns and extending UML for business modeling (Penker and Erikkson, 2000).

A2.3   Business type modeling

Business type modeling is a technique for modeling business concepts and their inter-relationships with a sharper focus than found in business concept modeling. Information needs of a domain are established independently of any implementation. The business type model is used to drive the component architecture.

A2.3.1   Business type modeling concepts

> A **type** is a technically neutral pure specification construct that does not define how its instances are implemented. A type is a classifier[3] whose instances have identity. A type defines data structure (attributes) and operations, but not the methods of operations. Types may be related through association, inheritance or dependency. Type is a UML stereotype of class.

---

3. A classifier is a general UML construct for defining data structure and behaviour.

Types are very similar to classes. However, whereas classes assume a particular implementation (say C++ or Java), types are technically neutral. In contrast to the operations of a type those defined for a class have methods. This feature of types is very important in an interface-based approach that is focused on business capabilities.

Types will often be realized as classes if an object-oriented language is used to implement them. Equally they may map closely to tables if a relational database language is used.

The term 'business type' is used to emphasize a type that is a formal reflection of business policy (for example, Invoice or Supplier) as opposed to a type that is used to abstract a technology feature (for example, Database Server or Protocol). However the term is not used in any formal sense.

A2.3.2   Business type modeling notation

A stereotyped class is used to represent a type. The notation for a type is indicated in Figure A2.5. Note that attributes and operations are both optional. It is also possible to suppress attributes and operations on type diagrams.

A summary of main type modeling notations is shown in Figure A2.6; the reader is referred to UML (OMG, 1999) for full definitions.

Business type diagram

A business type diagram models business types and the associations between them. In Figure A2.7 attributes and operations are suppressed.

A2.3.3   Business type modeling quick guide

Here is a quick guide to business type modeling:

- **Identify and map key business concepts** Think about the main subjects of interest in the business domain using a business concept diagram (*see* Section A2.2.2).

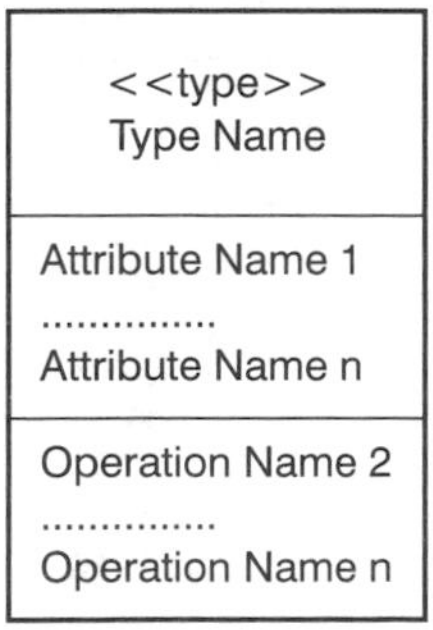

```
   <<type>>
   Type Name

 Attribute Name 1
 ...............
 Attribute Name n

 Operation Name 2
 ...............
 Operation Name n
```

Figure A2.5
Type notation

Figure A2.6
Type diagram
notations

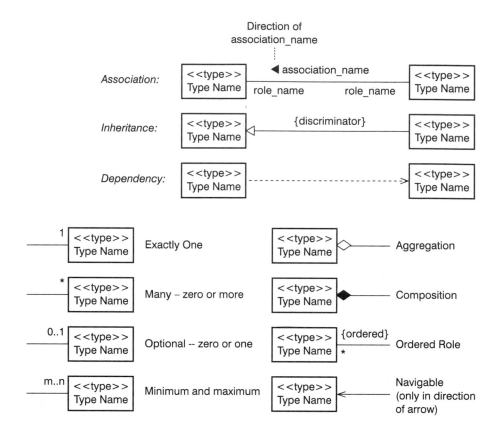

Figure A2.7
Business type
diagram

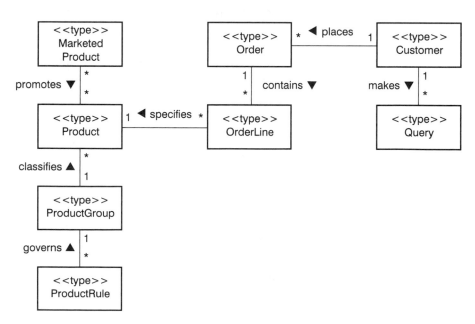

- **Discover and scope candidate business types** Search use cases and requirements documents, consider information needs. Add key attributes and responsibilities (as operations) but do not define details yet.

- **Abstract further types** Look for roles and apply type model patterns (Fowler, 1997).

- **Refine in the light of the component architecture** Consider changing the type model[4] to reflect common business capabilities or help with closure and reuse.

- **Define type details** Gradually add and define attributes, relationships and invariants as they are discovered, only providing detailed definitions once the type model has stabilized.

- **Iterate!**

A2.3.4   Business type modeling tips and hints

Generally, discovery of types occurs earlier than invention or abstraction of types; 'Key abstractions reflect the vocabulary of the problem domain and may either be discovered from the problem domain, or invented as part of the design' (Booch, 1994). This is sometimes referred to as the 'discovery before abstraction' principle.

Knowledge of system requirements and use case descriptions is used to refine the 'concept map', in particular by adding attributes, developing types and associations, noting responsibilities as operations and removing redundancy. Requirement prototypes may be used to help verify the use cases.

In applying use cases to help with the type model focus on responsibilities, on key business capabilities, that relate to the business process in the BPM. The responsibilities will later be assigned to specific interfaces as services and factored into constituent operations as appropriate.

Types must be clearly and concisely defined. It is often useful to use the form: 'a <generalization> that <qualifies> noun'; for example, Customer: 'A person who buys goods from our company'.

Patterns are reusable analysis or design knowledge. A pattern describes a problem and its recommended solution. A good pattern is concise: small but packing a heavy punch. An example type diagram associated with the composite pattern (Gamma *et al.*, 1995) is shown in Figure A2.8.

> **Analyst's Health Warning:** Patterns are not complete solutions; you must understand the problem you are trying to solve first, then use the right pattern for the job!

---

4. Changing the type model may involve combining or splitting, removing or introducing model items. Model items are types, responsibilities or attributes.

Figure A2.8
Type diagram for
composite pattern

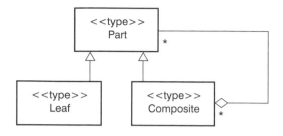

A2.4   Use case modeling

Use case modeling is applied to help verify business requirements, involve business people and understand software scope. Use cases also provide a natural mechanism for identification of software increments in project planning and test cases in the testing phase. Use case modeling is primarily a software requirement capture activity.

A2.4.1   Use case modeling concepts

Use case 'A behaviorally related sequence of interactions performed by an actor in a dialogue with the system to provide some measurable value to the actor' (Jacobson, 1994). A use case represents a collection of scenarios. A use case is formed from the subset of actor – system interactions from an atomic process.

Actor A role (or set of roles) that is played in relation to a software system; it could be a person, a group of persons, an organization unit, another software system or a piece of equipment. An actor can be external or internal to the business, for example, Customer or Credit Controller.

A2.4.2   Use case modeling notation

Use case diagrams

Use case diagrams are used to depict the main actors and use cases within the software scope as shown in Figure A2.9. Lines between actors and use cases are associations which are assumed to be bi-directional unless specifically arrowed (as in the case of a system report, for example).

Includes and extends relationships, which are stereotyped usage dependencies,[5] may also be shown on the use case diagram in Figure A2.10. The includes relationship is used to abstract out commonly occurring use cases, that often

---

5. A separate generalization relationship is also available in UML.

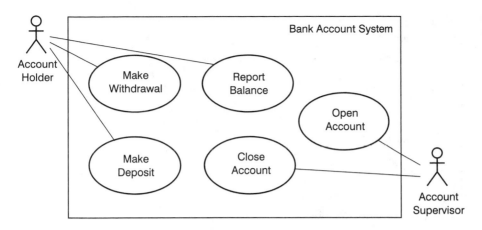

Figure A2.9
Use case diagram

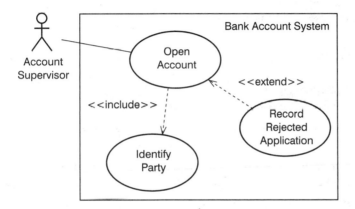

Figure A2.10
Use case diagram
showing 'include'
and 'extend'
relationships

correspond to business services. The extends relationship is used to separate out exception processing in order to avoid cluttering the main use case with unnecessary detail.

Use case descriptions

A use case description effectively talks us through the normal sequence of actor-system interactions. It is vitally important to describe the use case in business language, from the initiating actor's point of view.

Use case descriptions should be formatted. A simple example is as shown in Table A2.1. The intent of the use case is a concise description of its business purpose. The description itself should be partitioned into steps. Variations from the normal sequence (which may be modeled as extensions) are usefully appended at the foot of the description.

Other information may also be included in the format including:

● **Pre-conditions and post-conditions** The states of the system before and after successful execution of the use case.

Table A2.1   Use case description

Use Case Name	Make Withdrawal
Use Case Intent	To provide an account holder with timely and secure means of withdrawing verified monies.
Use Case Description	

1. Enter bank card

2. Enter security number

   If invalid security number, try again until valid.

3. Enter required amount

   If sufficient account balance wait for cash.

4. Take cash

Variations
Systems eats card on third invalid security number.
System rejects card if insufficient account balance.

- **Non-functional requirements** Implementation constraints, such as platform, as well as quality attributes such as response time and mean time to repair.
- **Business rules** Business conditions specific to the use case.

A2.4.3   Use case modeling quick guide

Here is a quick guide to use case modeling:

- **Identify business need** Ideally, start with atomic processes and roles from your BPM. Focus on operational customer facing processes, not information management processes.
- **Discover use cases and actors** Map atomic processes and roles to use cases and actors respectively. Draw use case diagrams.
- **Storyboard the use cases** Use JAD sessions to storyboard the use cases with your business people. Break the use cases into simple steps.
- **Factor out 'includes' and 'extends' use cases** Look for commonality of use cases or parts of use cases and model using the 'includes' dependency. Similarly look for variations and exception conditions and model using the 'extends' dependency.

- **Describe each use case** Use JAD sessions to detail the use cases with your business people, refining to include business rules and non-functional requirements. Use prototyping techniques to help understand the use cases and include sample screens and web pages with the documentation.

- **Iterate!**

A2.4.4 Use case modeling tips and hints

A common problem with use cases is lack of clear definition. If you asked ten analysts to define the term 'class' then you would probably get very similar definitions. If you asked the same ten to define 'use case' chances are the replies would vary significantly. So clear definition is a basic worry. Use the basic definition above, but also apply guidelines on abstraction (coming up next).

Aim for useful levels of abstraction. A very high-level abstraction is a major function like Sales. A very low level would be specific routines like Find Customer Address. We can apply some guidelines to help. A use case must:

- Be a *self contained* unit with no intervening time delays imposed by the business.

- Be initiated by a *single actor in a single place*, although it might result in output flows which are sent to other passive actors.

- Have measurable business related *intent*.

- Leave the software in a *stable state*; it cannot be left half done.

Apply the 80:20 principle (Koch, 1997). It is important to stick to the normal paths through a use case that constitute 80% of the functionality; an example might be 'Schedule instructor to teach course'. Focusing unnecessarily on low-level detail may result in over-long and complicated use case descriptions; an example might be 'Requested date is out of range'.

At the same time there is another side to the 80:20 principle. Often 80% of the value of a solution may result from its ability to innovate in the more unusual cases. It is important therefore to also think of key business problems that could occur and how your solution will respond.

Use cases can lead to a functional decomposition analysis, if not applied carefully, resulting in function components, which are little more than main routines, controlling dumb data components – in other words, components that are not responsible. Avoiding this trap means using use cases in their true spirit – focusing externally, on what the system is *for*, before getting into internal system mechanics. This is actually very critical with CBD, as the goal is specification of interfaces (separate from internal implementations).

Use cases are ideally suited to a particular sub-set of functional requirements: operational or event driven functionality. It is important not to forget other types of functional requirements that are less suited to use cases: for example, information, maintenance, reporting and business policy requirements.

Obsession with use cases can lead projects totally astray as in the case of a major telecommunications company who had reached 400 use cases, and still rising, on one of their projects. On closer investigation, it was revealed that this was a management information system involving flexible inquiries over a range of varied telephone network information. Thinking of the possible inquiries for such a system was like an open-ended shopping list! And yet the team had not even started building a class diagram, which would have provided useful insights into the required information structure.

In medicine, we often read of latest miracle cures, usually in the form of a pill, for example, a pill to cure obesity. The truth is that correct weight is a function of many things. Obviously pills can help, but we also need to consider metabolism, diet, exercise, environment, stress levels and so on. The same is true of good software practices – balance is needed. The point is that use cases have acquired something of silver-bullet status. Used selectively and correctly, like any tool, they will produce results but they are not a miracle cure for the problems of software development.

A2.5   Component architecture modeling

Component architecture modeling explores and defines the scope of components and their interfaces, the   dependencies between components and interfaces, and also dependencies concerning non-component *software units*.[6]

A2.5.1   Component architecture modeling concepts

> An **interface** is the definition of a set of behaviours that can be offered by a component object.

Interfaces may be related through association (in the direction of the interface), inheritance or dependency. An interface may not have attributes. However, a type model is used to specify the information that the interface provides access to and that is required to help define its services. Interface is a UML stereotype of class.

Interfaces may be 'manager interfaces' or 'instance interfaces'. A manager interface is responsible for multiple instances of one or more types, whereas an instance interface handles single instances of types.

> A **component specification** is the specification of a unit of software that describes the behaviour of a set of component objects, and defines a unit of implementation. Behaviour is defined as a set of interfaces. A component specification is realized as a component implementation.

---

6. Software units include software packages, legacy systems, special subroutines and software assemblies that are not themselves formal components.

A **component implementation**[7] is a realization of a component specification, which is independently deployable. This means it can be installed and replaced independently of other components. It does *not* mean that it is independent of other components – it may have many dependencies.

A **component object** is an instance of an installed component. A run-time concept. An object with its own data and unique identity.

The above four definitions follow (Cheesman and Daniels, 2000) and are described in more detail in Chapter 3 (3.4.4). A dependency between software units means that a change to one software unit (the independent software unit) will affect the other software unit (the dependent software unit). Where the dependent software unit (the consumer) is a component specification, then the dependency expresses a specification rule, which all implementations of that component specification must adhere to. Where the dependent component (the consumer) is a component implementation, then the dependency expresses an implementation design choice. There are different types of dependency.

Realization A component implementation realizes a component specification.

Offers A component specification offers an interface.

Uses A software unit requires the presence of another software unit to function successfully.

Invokes A software unit calls an operation of another software unit.

Instantiates A software unit instantiates another software unit.

In deployment architecture (see below) there are two further concepts to note:

Nodes are the processors of the technical infrastructure, for example, PCs, servers or mainframes.

Connections are communication paths between nodes. These can be labelled with the nature of the communication path. For example, the protocol used for communication.

7. Note: The UML (OMG, 1999) definition of component is very general encompassing both implementation and executable level concepts, including executable programs, static and dynamic libraries, database tables, and source code files or documents. The UML definition is 'an executable software module with identity and a well-defined interface'. The above definition of component can be thought of as a specific kind of UML component.

A2.5.2   Component architecture modeling notation

Interface naming conventions

It is useful to adopt the convention that interface names are prefixed 'I'. Manager interface names are the plural of the type that they primarily manage, whereas instance interface names are the singular of their corresponding type.

Interface responsibility map

Interface responsibility maps are primarily a thinking tool for identifying interfaces and planning specification architecture. They are simply type diagrams with candidate interfaces overlaid over corresponding types. Optionally, as shown in Figure A2.11, dependencies between interfaces may be shown with the reasons for the dependencies noted where helpful. The interfaces sketched on the interface responsibility map are generally 'manager interfaces' as opposed to 'instance interfaces' though there are no hard and fast rules.

   An alternative notation, where overlays are not practical or where overlays overlap, is simply to draw interfaces separately with 'uses' dependencies drawn to their managed types.

   There are various guidelines for identification of interfaces (see below). These include maximizing reuse cohesion, centralizing responsibilities and minimizing dependencies and static associations between types that are accessed by different interfaces. The interface responsibility map helps with visualization of alternative interface choices but is not a formal diagram. Any responsibilities allocated to types will be migrated out of the types and on to interfaces once we have thought through the architecture sufficiently.

Interface dependency diagrams

Dependencies between interfaces are usefully shown separately on an interface dependency diagram as shown in Figure A2.12. Note how responsibilities have now been allocated to the interfaces.

Component architecture diagrams

A component architecture diagram is a plan of software units and their dependencies. Architecture diagrams are used in different ways at specification, implementation and deployment levels. Hybrid diagrams showing elements from different architectures are also possible. All types of architecture diagram are used to explore dependencies. The overall set of notations is shown in Figure A2.13. Stereotypes may be used to describe other component forms (such as <<installed component>>) and dependency relationships (such as <<instantiates>>). Note that we extend UML by allowing class to be stereotyped as <<component specification>>. By convention, the stereotypes of component specification and usage dependency are suppressed.

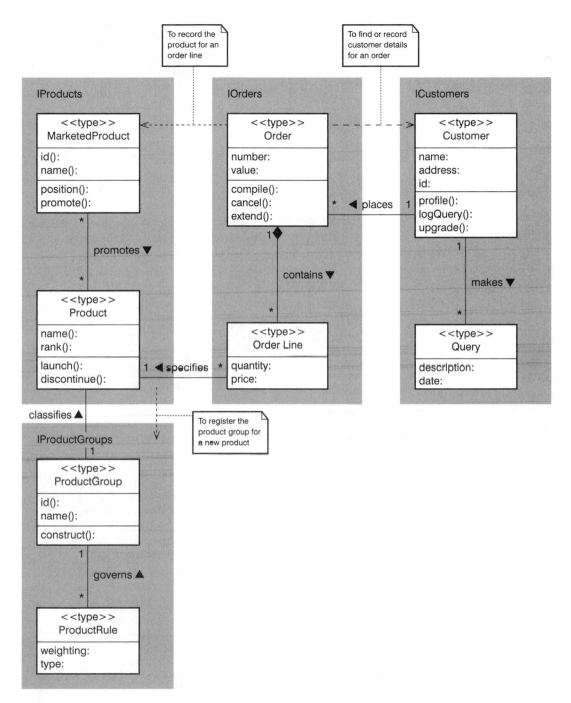

Figure A2.11
Interface responsibility map

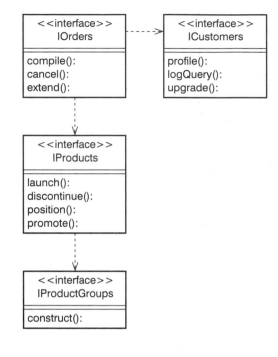

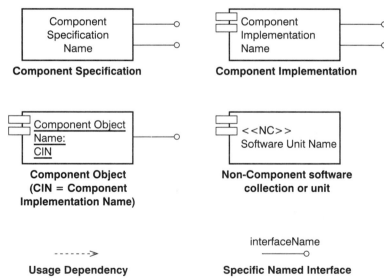

A component specification architecture diagram is used to model component specifications, interfaces and their inter-dependencies as shown in Figure A2.14. As a first step each interface identified in the interface responsibility map has been allocated to a single component specification. Each specification dependency captures a specification rule requiring *all* implementations of the

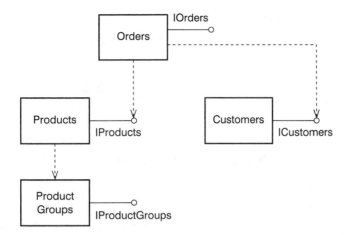

Figure A2.14
Component
specification
architecture diagram

dependent component to use the independent component. It acts as a constraint on implementation and deployment architectures.

Implementation architecture diagrams depict component implementations, and interfaces, plus their dependencies. Sometimes we wish to illustrate dependencies involving both component specifications and component implementations: in that case we use the term 'component architecture diagram'.

In the example shown in Figure A2.15, we have decided that the Orders component implementation uses a specific interface of the Products component implementation. But in the case of Products, we decide it uses the Product Groups component specification without being specific about which interfaces, or even which implementation is to be consumed.

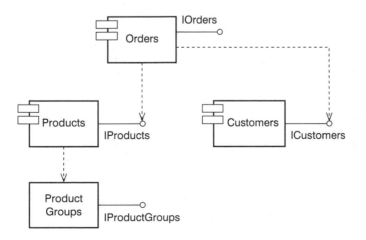

Figure A2.15
Component
architecture diagram

Deployment Architecture Diagrams

Deployment architecture diagrams are used to show allocation of software units to nodes, the connections between nodes and the dependencies between software units, as illustrated in Figure A2.16. Note that, as well as run-time component objects, installed components, installed modules, non-component modules, the databases or files managed by a particular node may also be shown. This architecture is only used selectively, to explore distribution issues.

A2.5.3   Component architecture modeling quick guide

Here is a quick guide to component architecture modeling:

- Identify and scope interfaces using the business type model, the use cases and the interface responsibility maps. Apply interface identification guidelines below.
- Adjust the initial set of interfaces in the light of the enterprise component architecture for consistency. Seek to reuse existing interfaces where appropriate.
- Use interface dependency modeling to understand usage dependencies between interfaces, providing a basis for a first-cut component architecture, by initially assuming one component specification will be implemented for each interface.
- Refine interfaces using interaction modeling.
- Apply interface sizing and partitioning guidelines below.
- Examine possible component implementations and implementation dependencies to help ensure our choice of interfaces is pragmatic and achievable.

Figure A2.16
Component
deployment
architecture diagram

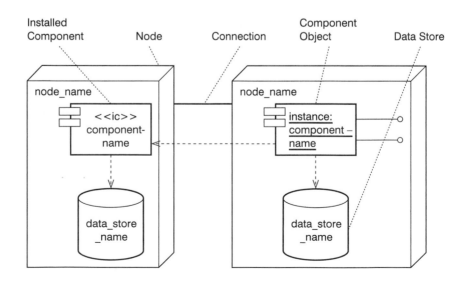

- Review grouping of interfaces to component specifications.
- Check out cross-component associations making sure it is possible to maintain the integrity of the associations.[8]
- Additionally, if the implementation is highly distributed it may also be useful to model deployment architecture.
- Iterate.

A2.5.4   Component architecture modeling hints and tips

Interface identification guidelines

- Use cases and interaction models are used alongside the business type model to expose roles and help identify responsibilities. They are also used to help identify associated existing systems and interfaces.
- The interface responsibility map is used to identify core types, which are independent in the sense that they do not have any mandatory associations to other types (for example, Customer and ProductGroup in Figure A2.11). Manager interfaces are created that correspond to the core types. Other types that depend on a core type will be managed by the manager interface. The family of types that are managed by an interface should form a cohesive group likely to be reused together (for example, Product and Marketed Product in Figure A2.11).
- Responsibilities that relate specifically to the needs of an actor initiating a use case or interaction often map to interfaces that offer local business capabilities using local business rules.
- Responsibilities that are common to several use cases or interactions (for example, 'includes' use cases) often map to interfaces that offer common business capabilities using generic business rules.
- Further interfaces may be factored out or combined from initial interfaces to minimize dependencies.

Interface 'size' guidelines

Aim for around 5–15 types per manager interface as a rough rule of thumb.

Interface partitioning guidelines

Appraise associations between types managed by different interfaces:

- Minimize associations between types managed by different interfaces. More than two indicates strong coupling and suggests it may be beneficial to merge the two interfaces or allocate the two interfaces to the same component specification.

---

8. Some mechanisms for implementing cross-component associations, such as relationship management components or the call-back mechanisms may involve changes to the initial architecture, such as adding new components or dependencies.

- Group together types that have multiple associations and assign to the same interface.

- Ensure that mandatory associations only apply 'downward' from user to used component specifications; that is, associations between types assigned to different interfaces that have been allocated to different component specifications.

Appraise usage dependencies between types managed by different interfaces:

- Adjust usage dependencies according to the position of the component in the architectural layers or 'main sequence' (see Chapter 3).

- Avoid circular dependencies.

- Aim for cohesive interfaces, more by types commonly reused together, rather than simply functionally cohesive.

- Aim for 'closure': try to group together types that are changed together. Minimize the ripple effects of change; see guideline on change below.

Keep pattern aware, to take advantage of the best work of others. There are several important industry initiatives in this area, including OMG work through the business object task force (BOTF) as well as useful work on architectural patterns (Buschmann, 1996) and business-related patterns (Fowler, 1997), not only design patterns which are now well-covered in the literature (Gamma *et al.*, 1995).

Two architectural patterns commonly crop up, as also described in Section A2.6.4. A hierarchical architecture pattern is reflected in the use of 'application interfaces' which assume responsibility for flow of control within an interaction. A network architecture pattern is reflected in a set of interfaces each of which has responsibility for carrying out part of an interaction. However, the question that often comes up is 'which pattern is better'?

The most important criterion is to place responsibility at the point of natural ownership. Where several interfaces are involved in a use case and results need to be compared from several sources, there is often no natural point of ownership. Generally, a hierarchy pattern works best for such situations. However, suppose we want to know whether a product qualifies for a discount according to the rules of its product group. One approach might be to centralize invocation of all required interfaces from a product application interface, which also makes the decision on whether a discount applies. A second approach would be to delegate responsibility for making the decision on whether a discount is due to a product group interface. In this example, the application interface treats the other interfaces as pure data handlers; the network pattern is preferred because responsibility for making the decision is at the point of natural ownership with the product group interface working out whether a product qualifies for a discount.

Having constructed an initial component architecture, think of the things that could typically change as the organization migrates through the internet spectrum. Play the changes through the architecture, testing that the interfaces 'hold water'. Look for the ripple effects of change. Try grouping together components that change together, or splitting a component that handles diverse types of change. Aim to localize the effects of change and for increasing reusability 'downward' through the layers of the architecture.

A2.6   Interaction modeling

Interaction modeling helps understand behaviour and the roles that types play in that behaviour, through decreasing levels of abstraction. For the purposes of this book, we will be focusing mainly on the use of interactions, at specification level, to examine messaging between interfaces and assign responsibilities to interfaces. A good distribution of responsibilities across interfaces is a keynote of CBD.

A2.6.1   Interaction modeling concepts

> A **collaboration** is an abstraction of a set of related actions between typed objects playing defined roles, typically within an operation or use case. Another way of stating this is to say that 'a collaboration defines a set of participants and relationships that are meaningful for a given set of purposes' (OMG, 1999).

> An **interaction** represents the messaging between objects that is required to realize required behaviour within the context of a collaboration.

A2.6.2   Interaction modeling notation

Use case refinement maps

A use case refinement map is a thinking tool that is useful in breaking a use case into its use case steps and associating those steps with types as shown in Figure A2.17 for a Take Order use case. Though not a formal interaction diagram the use case refinement map can be useful as a preparatory step in assigning responsibility for use case steps to types, and thence to interfaces.

Collaboration diagrams

Collaboration diagrams help to assign responsibilities to interfaces. A collaboration diagram is shown in Figure A2.18. In this example, the Establish Customer use case step has been factored into two operation calls (findCustomer and checkCustomerCredit) on the ICustomer interface. The operation checkCustomerCredit in turn calls the operation findAccount on the IAccounts interface. The objects are anonymous in this example.

Figure A2.17
Use case refinement
map

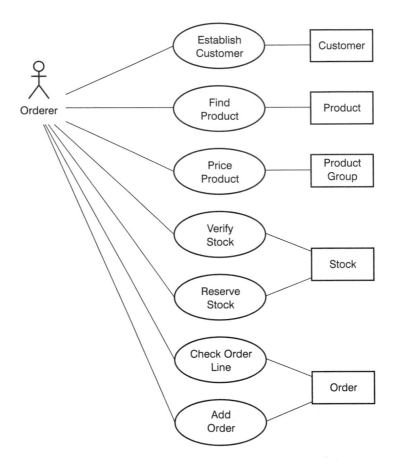

Message descriptions are structured as described in OMG (1999) using nested sequence numbering of messages. The message notation is, of necessity, more complex if you wish to specify the choice and repetition involved in a complete description of a collaboration. Incidentally, if this level of detail is really needed then it is likely that a sequence diagram is a much more appropriate tool for tackling the problem, as described below.

Figure A2.18
Collaboration
diagram

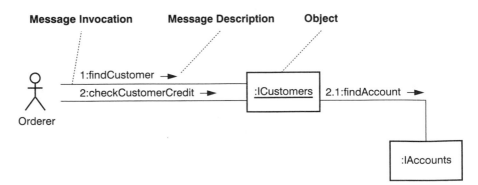

Sequence diagrams

Sequence diagrams help to explore the detailed mechanics of interaction between typed objects and are commonly used in object-oriented design. However, they may also be used to assist in architecture and specification modeling. Time runs downward through the diagram. A structured language description is usefully appended to the left margin of the diagram to describe sequence, choice and repetition. This helps to avoid cluttering the diagram itself. The notation is shown in Figure A2.19.

In the sequence diagram shown in Figure A2.20 the interaction described previously has been refined to show the message invocations occurring 'behind' the interfaces so to speak. To avoid clutter, return of information from operation calls is assumed to be implicit, although this can be shown if it adds value.

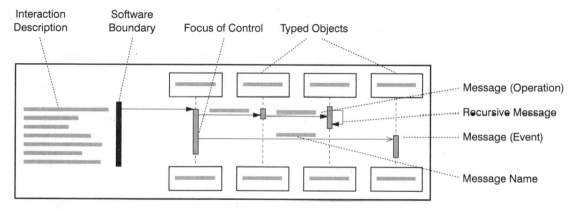

Figure A2.19
Sequence diagram notation

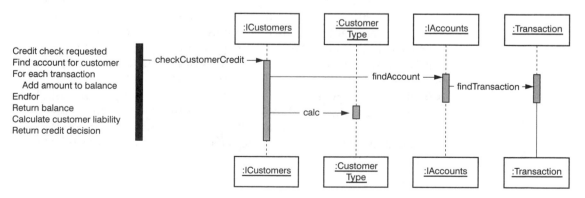

Figure A2.20
Sequence diagram

A2.6.3   Interaction modeling quick guide

Here is a quick guide to collaboration modeling:

- Break use cases into use case steps.
- Map the use case steps to their responsible types or interfaces.
- Look for existing interfaces that can supply the required behaviour.
- Use collaboration diagrams to help to further factor responsibilities to interfaces.
- Apply viewpoint analysis (see below) to the interfaces, depending on level of desired reusability.
- Use sequence diagrams[9] to help to explore the detailed mechanics of interaction between interfaces.
- Iterate!

A2.6.4   Interaction modeling hints and tips

Interaction modeling is usefully applied in helping to evaluate the reusability of an interface and to engineer generic interfaces. The idea is to examine the interface from as many viewpoints as reasonable, given the amount of reusability that is being sought, hence the term 'viewpoint analysis'. If an interface plays a specific role in relation to that other types, it is always worth asking the question, 'Might this interface also be used in other contexts'? For example, we might have identified an interface to provide tickets for theatre- goers using the internet. Could the interface be used similar contexts, for example sports events, TV or cinema, with the minimum of extension or additions?

Collaboration diagrams are most appropriate for modeling specific threads or scenarios. It is generally best to avoid cluttering with the extra notation that needed for modeling complete operations or use cases. If timing, sequencing and conditionality are important then use sequence diagrams, which are often more useful for modeling complete operations or use cases.

A key principle with interaction modeling is to preserve implementation independence of the resulting interfaces. Coupling between implementation components and business components must be minimized. It is vital to keep this principle in mind in working out the required messaging between interfaces.

It is useful to distinguish different sorts of interaction patterns, which are closely related to the architectural patterns discussed in Section A2.5.4. For example, a fork structure (see Figure A2.21) corresponds to a hierarchical architecture pattern and is exhibited by the formally defined 'observer' and 'mediator' patterns (Gamma *et al.*, 1995). A stair structure corresponds to a network architecture pattern and is reflected in the 'chain of responsibility' pattern (Gamma *et al.*, 1995).

---

9. If appropriate also use these diagrams to model collaboration between typed objects as part of an internal object-oriented design for the component.

(a) Fork
structure

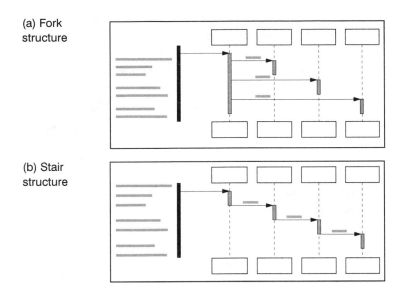

Figure A2.21
Fork versus stair
structures

(b) Stair
structure

These patterns become immensely useful for furnishing designs that are both optimized and consistent with the component architecture.

A2.7   Specification modeling

Specification modeling is used to rigorously define interfaces and component specifications. The relevance of specification modeling is twofold:

- To provide consumers of interfaces with an 'information and services' catalogue.
- To act as a compliance document for suppliers seeking to provide implementations for component specifications.

A2.7.1   Specification modeling concepts

A **component specification** describes a set of interfaces, any constraints that apply between interface type models and non-functional requirements that apply to any component implementation that realizes the component specification.

An **interface specification** consists of an interface type model (see below), a list of operations that the interface offers and a list of invariants that constrain its behaviour. Each operation is defined in terms of its signature and the contracts it conforms to.

An **interface type model** defines the information accessible to the interface[10] in terms of types, attributes and associations depicted on an interface type diagram. Types appearing in an interface type model have attributes but are excluded from having operations. Pre and post-conditions (below) reference the interface type model.

In a simple case, as in the case of an instance interface, the interface type model may be a single type with a list of attributes. More commonly, as in the case of manager interfaces, the interface type model consists of a collection of types, attributes and associations.

Precise operation specification to contract (Meyer, 1997) is achieved by writing a set of pre- and post-conditions for each operation.

A **pre-condition** is an assertion that must be true prior to execution of an operation. A pre-condition can be empty, which means it is always true.

A **post-condition** is an assertion that must be true following an execution of an operation given that the precondition is true. A post-condition always has a corresponding pre-condition.

Pre-conditions and post-conditions are conditional expressions, whose value is either true or false, and which make reference to the types, attributes and associations in the interface type model. They may contain any number of sub-conditions connected by Boolean operators. An operation may have one or more pre- and post-condition pairs. If at execution no precondition is true, the effect of the operation is undefined. It is up to the initiator to ensure that at least one precondition holds true on invoking an action. The action only guarantees effects if a pre-condition holds. This is the detail of the 'contract' between the consumer and service provider.

An **invariant** is a condition concerning the elements of a type model, which must always hold true while no operation is in progress.

A2.7.2   Specification modeling notation

Interface type diagrams

- An interface type diagram is akin to an information catalogue of the interface. The notation is illustrated in Figure A2.22.

10. In implementation terms we say that this information is retained by a component object between operation calls.

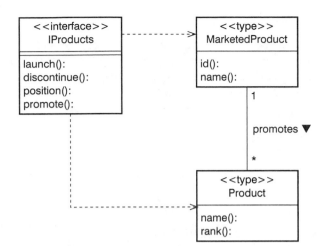

The interface type diagram is composed of:

- The interface itself, showing its list of operations.

- The types and associations that provide information required by the interface.

- Usage dependencies from the interface to the 'entry point' types; more accurately these are types whose objects must be accessed initially by operations of the interface in order to navigate all objects successfully. For example, the specification of the launch operation of IProduct must start by creating a valid occurrence of Product, hence the dependency to Product.

- References to types, whose attributes are the responsibility of other interfaces, but which must be identifiable, often (but not necessarily) as a result of required mandatory associations; Figure A2.23 shows two referenced types Customer and Product. These are required because of mandatory associations to Order and OrderLine respectively.

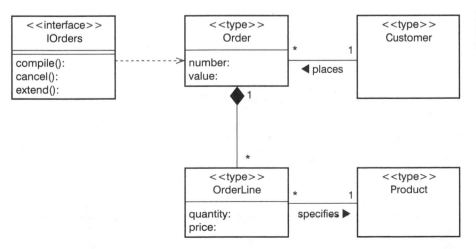

Figure A2.23
Interface type
diagram for IOrders

Pre-conditions and post-conditions

Each operation is specified using pre- and post-conditions as illustrated in Figure A2.24. Note that a formal notation such as Object Constraint Language (OCL) (Warmer, 1999) can be used to define pre- and post-conditions, although informal narrative can be used. In fact, even if using a formal language like OCL, it may also be necessary to add informal narrative to assist readers of the specification.[11]

Invariants

Invariants can apply to types, interfaces or component specifications. Some examples follow:

- Type invariants.
  - OrderItem quantity must be in range 0 to 20.
- Interface invariants of IOrders:
  - The sum of (order item price × order item quantity) holds true for the order's total value across all operations.
  - The sum of all order items for an order < 10,000.

Component specification invariants

These are used to ensure integrity between interfaces allocated to the same component specification. For example, if we decided to group IProducts and IOrders to a single Product Orders specification, an invariant might specify that an object of the Product type occurring in the interface type model of each interface was always one and the same object for any occurrence of the Product Orders

Figure A2.24
Pre-conditions and post-conditions

```
productNew(in n:string, in busID:number, return r:Result)

pre  NO Product q EXISTS IN products WITH q.businessID = busID
post Product p is CREATED IN products WITH
     p.instanceID = some unique value
     p.businessID = busID
     p.name = n

pre  Product p EXISTS IN products WITH p.businessID=busID
post r.errorcode=12
```

11. There is an argument that approaches based on pre- and post-conditions and invariants cannot furnish complete specifications or deal with re-entrancy. However, there is no widely accepted alternative at this time. Be aware therefore that informal language may be needed to clarify the specification. The reader is referred to Szyperski (1998) for more details.

component object. Note that OCL may be used to specify invariants. Some invariants may be specified graphically in the interface type model (e.g. multiplicity).

A2.7.3   Specification modeling quick guide

Here is a quick guide to specification modeling:

- Use the interface responsibility map (see Section A2.5) to help identify types, that provide information required by each interface.
- Declare these types on an interface type diagram.
- Declare interface responsibilities in the form of a first-cut list of operations with objectives.
- Migrate responsibilities from types on the interface responsibility map to their appropriate interfaces.
- Appraise interface ensuring coherent set of responsibilities.
- Evaluate interfaces for reusability (see below).
- Assess and record the mechanism to be used for implementing cross-component associations in the interface definition.
- Specify invariants on types and interfaces.
- Specify responsibilities (operations) as services using pre- and post-conditions.
- Group interfaces to component specifications.
- Specify non-functional requirements, invariants and suggested implementation mechanism (outsource, internal design, etc.) of component specification.
- Consider different presentation styles before publishing the component specification (for implementers) and interfaces (for clients).

A2.7.4   Specification modeling hints and tips

The reusability of the interface should be evaluated, for example, using viewpoint analysis (see Section A2.6.4), before specifying operations and invariants. Here are some questions to ask in checking out reusability of interfaces:

- Is the interface applicable in other related business contexts?
- Would significant changes be required?
- What is likely to change in the business?
- How could this interface be changed to accommodate likely changes?
- Would significant rework be required?

Do not try to specify inquiry operations in the interface type model. These operations are implicitly available on all types declared in the interface type model. Inquiries involving multiple types are implicitly supported by navigating associations declared in the interface type model. This greatly assists in streamlining the specification.

In specifying pre- and post-conditions, it is advisable to focus on 'normal, successful' processing first, so as not to be overwhelmed with too much detail. Often this will correspond to the basic courses of use cases. As with the use cases, we can work on various alternative outcomes once we have understood the normal cases.

Non-functional requirements such as security, performance and reliability are an important element of interface specifications and component specifications (see Table 8.1). Although much of this is beyond the state of the art in terms of formal languages, it is nevertheless important to capture this information albeit informally; for example, in the form of quality templates. The reader is referred to Szyperski (1998) for a discussion of the issues involved and to Gilb (1988) for information on quality templates.

Invariants should be used to simplify the pre- and post-conditions. It is important to check that each variable to which the pre- and post-condition pairs refers is either a parameter of the operation, or an element of the interface type model.

Although there are similarities between the interface type model and data model, *the interface type model is not a logical database design*. For example, an interface type model differs from a data model in that repeating attributes, repeating structures of attributes and conditional groups of attributes are not allocated to additional types. Each type in the model should be some type of thing from the business perspective. It should not be structured or normalized to suit an envisaged database design.

A2.8   References

Allen, P., and Frost, S., *Component-Based Development for Enterprise Systems: Applying The SELECT Perspective*, Cambridge University Press-SIGS Publications, 1998.

Booch, G., *Object-Oriented Analysis and Design with Applications*, 2nd Edn., Benjamin Cummins, 1994.

Buschmann, F., Meunier, R., Rohnert, H., Sommerlad, P., and Stal, M., *Pattern-Oriented Software Architecture*, Wiley, 1996

Cheesman J., and Daniels, J., VML Components, Addison-Wesley, 2000.

Conallen, J., *Building Web Applications With UML*, Addison-Wesley, 2000.

Dodd, J., *et al.*, *Advisor 2.4*, Sterling Software, 1999.

D'Souza, D., and Wills, A., *Objects, Components and Frameworks With UML: The Catalysis Approach*, Addison-Wesley, 1999.

Fowler, M., *Analysis Patterns: Reusable Object Models*, Addison-Wesley, 1997.

Fowler, M., and Kendall, S., *UML Distilled*, Addison-Wesley, 1997.

Gamma, E., Helm, R., Johnson, R., and Vlissides, J., *Design Patterns: Elements of Reusable Object-Oriented Software*, Addison-Wesley, 1995.

Gilb, T., *Principles of Software Engineering Management*, Addison-Wesley, 1988.

Jacobson, I., Ericcson, M. Jacobson, A., *The Object Advantage – Business Process Re-engineeting with Object Technology*, Addison Wesley, 1994.

Koch, R., *The 80:20 Principle*, Nicholas Brealey, 1997.

Meyer, B., *Object-Oriented Software Construction*, Prentice Hall, Englewood Cliffs, New Jersey, 2nd edn, 1997.

Oestereich, B., *Developing Software With UML*, Addison-Wesley, 1997.

OMG, *OMG Unified Modeling Language Specification*, V1.3, June, 1999.

Page-Jones, M., *Fundamentals of Object Oriented Design in UML*, Addison-Wesley, 2000.

Penker, M., and Eriksson, H., *UML Toolkit*, Wiley, 1998.

Penker, M., and Eriksson, H., *Business Modeling with UML: Business Patterns at Work*, Wiley, 2000.

Rummler, G. A., and Brache, A.P., *Improving Performance*, Jossey-Bass, 1995.

Szyperski, C., *Component Software*, Addison-Wesley Longman, 1998.

Veryard, R., *Notes on Business Rules*, www.users.globalnet.co.uk/~rxv/kmoi/rulemodelling.htm, 1999.

Warmer, J., and Kleppe, A., *The Object Constraint Language*, Addison-Wesley, 1999.

Abbreviations

API	application programming interface
ASP	application service provider
BOTF	Business Object Task Force
BPR	business process re-engineering
BPI	business process improvement
BPM	business process modeling
CBD	component-based development
CEE	component execution environment
CIA	component implementation architecture
CGI	common gateway interface
COM	Component Object Model
COM+	an extension of COM
CORBA	Common Object Request Broker Architecture
CRM	customer relationship management
CSA	component specification architecture
DCOM	Distributed COM
DNA	Distributed interNet Applications
DTD	Document Type Definition
DSDM	Dynamic Systems Development Method
EAI	enterprise application integration
EDI	electronic data interchange
EJB	Enterprise JavaBeans
GUI	graphical user interface

HTML	Hypertext Markup Language
IDL	Interface Definition Language
IIOP	Internet Inter-ORB Protocol
IT	information technology
J2EE	Java 2 Enterprise Edition
JAD	Joint Application Development
JNDI	Java Naming and Directory Interface
KPI	key performance indicator
MIDL	Microsoft Interface Definition Language
MSMQ	Microsoft Message Queue
MTS	Microsoft Transaction Server
OCL	Object Constraint Language
OMG	Object Management Group
OOPL	object oriented programming language
RAD	rapid application development
ROI	return on investment
RMI	Remote Method Invocation
SGML	Standard Generalized Markup Language
STP	straight through processing
UML	Unified Modeling Language
VPN	virtual private networking
W3C	World Wide Web Consortium
XML	Extensible Markup Language

Index

abstraction 9, 31, 39, 60, 119, 129, 199
  'discovery before abstraction' principle
   195
  enterprise and system levels 39
accuracy 157, *159*
actors *def* 196, 198–9, 207
adaptability 2, 5, *11*, 57, 68, 98–101, 118,
   119–21, 122, 124–5, 128, 130, 134,
   142, 148, 157, *159*, 167, 170
adapters 37, 70, *81*, 138, *138*, *def* 138, 152,
   156
adviser user, role of 166
Allen, P., and Frost, S. 70, 86, 186
ambassador user, role of 166
Amor, D. 118
APIs (Application Programming Interfaces)
   40, 82, 179, 183
applications and application servers 35–6,
   38–9, 83, 153, 170, 176–84, *def* 182,
   208
  and integration 32–3, 40, *41*
architecture 1, 4, 10, 12, 24–6
  changing 37, 40, 57, 62, 68, 89, 107, 150
  component-based *see* CBD
  layering 44–6
architecture team 148, 150
ASPs (Application Service Providers) 36,
   128, 141–2, 171, 173–4
associations 40, 208, 214–15
  multiplicity associations 91, 208

atomic processes 35, 108, *def* 187, 187–8,
   198
attributes 214–15, 218
Austin, C., and Powlan, M. 178

Baan 66
Bass, L. *et al.* 38
Belbin, M. 163
BizTalk server 181
Booch, G. 195
BOTF (Business Object Task Force) 208
BPI (Business Process Improvement)
   15–28, *21*, 32, 53–4, *55–56*, *59*, 68–9,
   69, 70, 99–100, 130, *148–150*, 158,
   163, *174*
  conception stage *17*, 17–18, 19, 191
  envisioning stage 17, *17*, 189
  measuring and monitoring 18–19, *19*
  organizing stage *17*, 17–18, 191
  planning 10, 16–19, 32, *51*, *58*, 100–1,
   167, 172
  reflection stage *17*, 17–19, 191
  see also process frameworks ...
BPM (Business Process Modeling) 16, *def*
   19, 19–22, *20–1*, 34–8, *41*, 186–92,
   198
BPR (Business Process Re-Engineering) 16
Brown, A. 10, 68, 141, 176
business capability *def* 32, 34
business component analyst 169–70
business component architect 168–9

223